Books by Janice Hardy

Foundations of Fiction Series

Planning Your Novel: Ideas and Structure

Planning Your Novel: Ideas and Structure Workbook

Revising Your Novel: First Draft to Finished Draft

Polishing Your Novel: Adding the Shine (forthcoming 2017)

Skill Builder Series

Understanding Show, Don't Tell (And Really Getting It)

Novels

The Healing Wars Trilogy:

The Shifter

Blue Fire

Darkfall

Revising Your Novel: First Draft to Finished Draft
Copyright © 2016
Janice Hardy

Published by Janice Hardy
Printed in the United States of America.

This book is also available in e-book format.

ISBN 978-0-9915364-5-0

REVISING
Your Novel
First Draft to Finished Draft
A step-by-step guide to a better novel

Janice Hardy

Fiction University's Foundations of Fiction

Contents

51 Workshop Two: Character Work

92 Workshop Three: Plot and Structure Work

203 Workshop Four: Point of View Work

219 Workshop Five: Description Work

252 Workshop Six: Setting and World-Building Work

266 Workshop Seven: Dialogue and Voice Work

281 Workshop Eight: Pacing Work

308 Workshop Nine: Word Count Work

317 Workshop Ten: A Final Look

325 Bonus Workshop: Salvaging Half-Finished Manuscripts

336 It's Over!!

340 Appendix

356 Glossary

359 Thanks!

361 Acknowledgments

Welcome to Revising Your Novel: First Draft to Finished Draft

There's something both exhilarating and terrifying about finishing a first draft. The story is finally written down, and you've seen how your characters have grown and developed, but you also see all the plot holes, weak areas, and parts you know for sure don't work.

Most of the time, turning that first draft into the novel in your head takes work. A lot of work.

Just as there is no right way to write, there's no right way to revise. It's a process every writer must work out for themselves, and can even vary from book to book. You never know what extra effort a manuscript will need until you see how that first draft shakes out.

For first-time revisers, this can be overwhelming. There's so much to consider, keep track of, and remember. They often don't know how to start or what to work on first.

For seasoned writers, it can be just as intimidating, especially if revision isn't something they enjoy doing.

For those of us who love revisions and do our best writing after we know how the story unfolds, it's still a lot of work. Fun work, but there's still a long way to go from "the end" to "It's done!"

My goal with this book is to help writers of all skill levels revise a first draft, and help you develop your rough manuscript into a finished draft. This book will provide guidance if you're new to revisions, and work as a stand-in critique partner if you're not yet ready to show the manuscript to another person. It will help you determine which revision techniques and processes work best for you, how to think about the revision process, and how to put those skills into practice.

Get ready to roll up your sleeves and get to work.

What You'll Get From This Book

Revising Your Novel: First Draft to Finished Draft is a mix of book doctor and personal editor. The goal of the analysis sections is to help you develop your book doctor skills and teach you what you need to objectively review your manuscript. The revision steps and options will guide you to the best way to fix any issues you'll find during your analysis.

You'll review the manuscript from the top down, looking at the larger macro issues of structure and plot, all the way to the micro issues of how an individual scene works. You'll focus on the pieces and how they fit within the larger framework of the novel.

There's a *lot* of information in these pages. Take it session by session and work at a pace that's comfortable for you. No one expects you to revise an entire novel over a weekend, so don't worry if it takes you more time. Revising a novel is often hard work, but well worth it in the end.

This information is here to guide you, encourage you, give you goals to strive for, and most of all—help you.

By the end of the workshops, you'll have a clean, well-developed story that's ready to move on to the next step. For most writers, that will be polishing the finished draft. Others will send the manuscript to beta readers and critique partners for a final read. Some writers (and manuscripts) will be ready for submission to agents and editors, and others will be ready to be self published.

Whatever your goal for your novel, this book will help you get there.

What You'll Encounter in This Book

Revising Your Novel: First Draft to Finished Draft is a series of self-guided workshops designed to lead writers through the revision process. Each workshop covers one step of that process, with smaller sessions that focus on individual topics within that step. At the end of this book, you'll have a cleaner manuscript and a novel that fits your vision.

Workshops: The workshops go step by step through revising a novel. Each workshop offers topics with questions, directions, tips and tricks, plus common problem areas within each topic and suggestions on how to fix them.

Analysis: Each workshop starts with an analysis that examines an aspect of the manuscript and helps you determine where any weak spots might be.

Revision Tasks: These go step by step with tasks to do, or further questions to ask to fix the problems found in the analysis.

Revision Options: Most workshops offer multiple options on how to revise that aspect of the manuscript, focusing on the most common problems in that area.

Revision Red Flags: These prompts draw attention to common problems found in early drafts of a novel.

Problems Found? These prompts suggest where to go to solve problems found during the workshop analysis.

How to Get the Most From the Sessions

I've structured *Revising Your Novel: First Draft to Finished Draft* in a way I find the most helpful when revising, but feel free to adjust the order of the workshops to best suit your own writing process.

For example, when I write a first draft, I focus on the plot first, then flesh out the characters once I see the story unfold. So when I revise, I flip it and focus on the *characters* first, and adjust the plot as needed. I find this gives me the best balance to ensure both sides get enough attention.

If you know what areas you want to work on already, feel free to jump ahead to the workshops that fit your needs. Use this book to guide you, but don't feel you must follow every last suggestion and do every single option. This is why I'll frequently say, "probably" "likely," and "often" throughout this book, and suggest things to "try," "consider," and "think about." Just because advice or a technique typically works a certain way, every novel *is* different and what you're trying to achieve with it must be taken into consideration when applying my advice and tips.

Different manuscripts have different issues, so focus on what *your* novel needs. If something suggested here doesn't apply, it's okay to ignore it; just be objective and honest about what the manuscript needs. If you feel you're strong in an area and skip a section, but still can't fix a particular problem, try looking at those sections anyway. You might find the answer you need *is* there after all, for example, writers with strong goal—>conflict—>resolution skills might *over* plot and run into pacing problems.

There's a lot of overlap in writing, so in some cases, you might need to jump ahead (or back) to specific sessions in a different workshop. For example, dealing with infodumps is covered in depth in Workshop Five: Description Work, but it's also a common problem found in a slow beginning, so it's also mentioned in Workshop Three: Plot and Structure Work. The story structure session will send you to Workshop Five to do those exercises if you discover infodumping issues in your beginning.

Revising a novel is just as much about studying the story as it is tweaking the text, and the analysis sessions were designed to help you examine your manuscript objectively. Some questions will be easy to answer, focusing on general reminders and clarification aspects of the novel, while others will be tougher and require hard looks at the manuscript. There will likely be times when answering these questions feels too hard or not necessary, but this is where the real work lies—it's difficult to revise a novel when you don't know where it's weak.

The more effort you put into figuring out what your manuscript needs, the better prepared you'll be to meet those needs.

Getting Ready to Revise

Sometimes, you *think* you're ready to revise, but there's often a period between finishing a first draft and starting the first revision when you're "done" with the manuscript, even though you still have a few tasks left to do. You're tired of drafting; you want to move on to revising and get the novel out the door.

This can be a dangerous time, because if you jump in before the manuscript is truly finished, you'll create more work for yourself. The rougher that first draft is, the more prep work you might need to do. However, if you tend to write clean first drafts, you might indeed be ready to move forward and start your revisions.

Be objective and honest. The more truthful you are regarding the state of your draft, the better prepared you'll be to revise it.

Take a little time and finish a not-quite-done-yet-draft (if needed), run it through your beta readers, get organized, and mentally prepare for all the work you're about to do.

First, Fill the Holes

Look at your manuscript objectively—is it *really* ready or do you still have a few holes to fill? (Be honest.) It's not unusual to have a manuscript with a few holes that you promise you'll "fix in revision." Sometimes you *can* fix these holes while you revise, but other times they need filling before you move forward.

In this session, the goal is to finish the first draft before you begin your revision.

Step One: Finish (or Write) Any Scenes You've Been Putting Off

There are always one or two scenes you know you *need* to write, but never *do* write until you absolutely have to. If you have any scenes you've been putting off, sit your butt in the chair and write them. Even if they're clunky and messy, at least they'll be down on paper where you can fix them. And if they fight you, maybe that's a red flag you don't need them after all (wouldn't *that* be a relief?).

Step Two: Fill in the Details That Still Require Research

Look for places where knowing a detail wasn't necessary during the first draft, but adding it now *will* make the scene richer and more plausible.

Pick a day when you can focus, then start at the first missing detail and take them one at a time until they're done. At the very least, write the information in another file so you can easily add it when you reach that scene during revision.

Step Three: Finalize Any Shaky Character Backstories

Odds are the main characters have decent backstories and histories (if not, you'll deal with that in Workshop Two), but secondary characters—or characters who turned out to be more important than you originally thought—might not be as fleshed out as needed.

Look at your characters and flesh out any missing histories or defining moments necessary to the plot. Now that the first draft is done, it should

be clear who matters and who needs more oomph to refine their personalities or personal stories. You'll also know what areas or details will add
depth to the existing story and character arcs.

Step Four: Decide on the Final Details or Names

Sometimes you need to live with a name or detail a while before you decide if they're working in the novel or not. And sometimes, you change
them mid-novel and forget, so both versions (or spellings) exist.

If you have any names or details you're not sure about, change them
now so you can get used to the new ones, and change them again if you
still don't like them.

Step Five: Do What You Know Needs Doing

If there's anything you think is going to take additional time or effort, go
ahead and do some work on it first. Maybe you know you're not happy
about the setting, or you wanted to add more symbolism, or you think
the novel needs a subplot—whatever is nagging at you, give in and fix
it. Filling the holes now will make the rest of the revision process easier.

Optional: Hand the Manuscript Off to Beta Readers or Critique Partners

Not every writer seeks feedback at the same stage (if at all). If you prefer to receive feedback before you do your revision, send your draft to
your critique partners when the draft is done. If you'd rather get the
manuscript as finished as possible before looking for feedback, then do
your revision first. When (and if) you seek feedback is totally up to you.

Know When to Revise What

Unless you're one of those rare authors who can write and polish a novel
in one draft, you'll go through several revision passes between the first
and finished drafts. How many passes depends on both the novel and
the writer, and you might do as few as two or as many as twenty. No
matter how many drafts a novel needs, you *can* make the process more
efficient. For example, it doesn't make much sense to polish the text if
you're still figuring out the story.

In this session, the goal is to understand the most effective way to do your revision so you're not revising text you've already edited.

Early Draft Revisions

These revisions take the most rewriting, so tackle them first. They change how the plot and story unfold, who the characters are, maybe even the theme, but don't typically affect how the text itself reads (unless you decide to change narrative styles, such as past tense to present tense or first person to third). In early draft revisions you will:

Get the story the way you want it: This is the story you wanted to tell, even if it still needs some work. It illustrates your idea and conveys the concepts you wanted to explore. If the story isn't working, the most beautifully written prose in the world won't save it.

Get the plot the way you want it: Everyone in the story has the right goals and is generally doing what they need to do. Revising your plot is all about moving the pieces around so they're in the best possible places to achieve the strongest impact. For example, you might know you need a scene where the protagonist discovers her best friend betrayed her, but not know exactly where that scene best fits in the novel.

Get the characters the way you want them: Characters change over the course of a novel, and not just in the story. You might start a character with one personality and end up changing it as the novel develops. Or you might decide two minor characters should be combined into one, or kill off a character altogether. Make sure you have the right story people in the right places.

Middle Draft Revisions

Once you've dealt with the macro issues, move on to the text itself. Middle draft revisions include issues that require rewriting on a smaller, scene-by-scene level. These edits don't change the plot or story, but clarify or enhance how the information is conveyed to your readers. In middle draft revisions you will:

Flesh out or cut descriptions: Descriptions almost always need revising. You'll trim heavy areas and bulk up sparse ones, fix talking heads in empty rooms, and generally ground readers in every scene. You'll cut descriptive elements that aren't working to dramatize and/or set the scene.

Adjust the pacing and scene or chapter transitions: A novel's flow determines how readers experience the story. Awkward transitions and episodic chapters can kill the pacing instead of building tension and drawing readers in. You'll tighten the overall novel and cut out any dead weight dragging it down.

Replace weak words and phrases with strong ones: Some word edits require more rewriting than others, and this is a good revision pass to take right before the final polish pass. You'll tweak the text and make sure everything reads well.

Finished Draft Revisions

The final revision pass is all about the last-minute review, fixing the elements that have been nagging at you, or clearing up any messy areas. Most scenes require little more than a cut here and there or moving a sentence for better narrative flow. In finished draft revisions you will:

Tweak little aspects: Minor tweaks, such as moving a comma or changing a word, gets smoothed over.

Drive yourself crazy deciding if it's done or not: We all do it. The manuscript seems finished, but self-doubt nags you and you start second-guessing every decision you made. If it's only general fears, you're ready to go. If they're specific, your writer's instinct is likely trying to tell you there's still a problem to address. Go examine it further and either fix it, or put those doubts to rest.

Read the manuscript one last time: A final read is useful for catching leftover edits or details that no longer apply. It's also good to check the final flow of the story and how it all unfolds. This pass is particularly useful after letting the manuscript sit for a few weeks so you can read it with fresh eyes and see what's actually on the page. You'll make one last pass before you stop messing with the story and turn to the copyedits.

Final Draft Polish

Once the manuscript is working and everything reads smoothly, it's time for the final polish to put the shine on the prose. These edits that don't change the story, plot, or understanding of either, just how the text itself reads. The goal in this final pass is to focus on the copy editing and proofing.

Check for oft-used or repeated words: We all have favorite words or phrases and we tend to use them a lot. You'll read through and trim out anything that sounds repetitious.

Catch any revision smudge: In any revision, you'll find leftover bits that refer or relate to something you edited out. Details change, time of day moves from morning to night, characters refer to something (or someone) that was later deleted. A final read through in one sitting can help make those smudges jump out, especially if you haven't looked at the manuscript in a few weeks.

Check the spelling, punctuation, and grammar: Break out those dictionaries and style rules to catch any technical errors, dropped punctuation, incorrect word usage, and typos—especially those sneaky little homonyms such as their, there, and they're. If you're unsure of a rule or word, look it up.

Check any spellings or details unique to your novel: If you've created names or items, it's not a bad idea to check to ensure every instance is spelled the same way and used consistently. This is a must if you changed the name of anything midway through writing the draft. Odds are you missed one somewhere.

Working from the macro to the micro issues can make the revision process go more smoothly, regardless of how many drafts you do. It also gives you a structure that makes revising a little less intimidating. You know what to worry about when, and you can ignore elements that don't need your attention in that revision pass.

Mentally Prepare Yourself for the Revision

Not every writer dreads a revision, but if the thought of revising is daunting or even frightening, it helps to mentally prepare for the work involved, especially if you know you have a lot of rewriting to do. By the time a novel is written, the characters feel like family, and anything you do to alter that family *can* be rough. Even if you enjoy revising, it's helpful to prepare for it.

In this session, the goal is to put yourself in the right mindset to have productive and effective revision sessions.

Don't Be Afraid of the Delete Key

I learned long ago that trying to force in a favorite line or scene makes that line or scene *sound* forced and it ends up not working anyway. Remember, your words aren't set in stone. You're the writer, you *can* change the text however you want, and that's okay because you're still *writing*. Delete chapters without a thought if they need to go; cut favorite lines if the scene changes and they no longer work. It's still a work in progress until you decide it's done.

It's the Story That Matters

Focusing on the story makes it easier to accept any big changes you might need to do. Plots change all the time, but the heart of the story usually stays the same. Don't be afraid to re-plot or make drastic changes if it will make the story better. The plot is only a series of events that illustrate the story, and you have tons of options for getting to the same place.

REVISION RED FLAG: If you find yourself changing the *story* as well as the plot, you might have a core conflict issue or story premise problem. It only becomes problematic if you're changing the plot and story so much, every revision reads like a whole new book. You're basically trying to write and revise the draft at the same time, which is bound to cause frustration. Nail down the story you want to tell first, *then* go back and create the plot to show that story.

First Drafts Are for Ideas

A first draft doesn't need to be perfect, or even be the book you expected. Stories evolve, plots change, so feel free to move around major plot events to see how they play out. Decide what you want to do, and if you like the new direction, proceed to revise. If it's not what you want, keep drafting until it is. No one says you have to revise the *first* first draft.

Making the Story Better is a Good Idea, Even if it Takes Work

"But that'll be so much work" is a common reason not to make a change, but it's a bad one. You've already put a ton of work into the book, so why not make it the best it can be and give it the best chance to sell? Embrace the work, because "writing" isn't only done during the first draft. Some of the best writing can come *after* several drafts when you can see how all the pieces work together.

REVISION RED FLAG: If you find yourself adding more and more extraneous plot points or story arcs to the novel to "make it better" and very little of it affects the core conflict of the novel, you probably have too much going on. Don't add more to add more—make sure what you add is serving the story you're telling.

Think Macro Until You're Happy With the Story

The big elements determine if a novel will work—the core conflicts, the character goals, the stakes, the premise. If these aren't working, no matter how much you polish the scenes or the writing, the story will feel *bleh*. Major inherent story flaws need to be fixed before the book as a whole can work.

Trust Your Gut

If you think something needs fixing, it probably does. If it nags at you that a certain character does a certain thing, go fix it before you put a ton of work into revising. If that big reveal doesn't have the impact you think it should, change it. If anything bugs you, trust your writer's compass and work it out until you're happy.

Revising taps into a slightly different part of the writer's brain, so the better you mentally prepare, the easier your revisions will be.

Stay Organized During the Revision

How much feedback the manuscript gets before you start revising will determine how much you have to keep track of. Detailed critiques from your ten best beta readers will yield a lot more information than looking at the first draft with no outside comments. How many changes you plan to do also plays a role, as well as the state of the manuscript at the start. Keeping track of it all *can* be challenging.

In this session, the goal is to determine the best way to organize your thoughts and keep track of what you want to do.

Step One: Gather Your Materials

Some writers like index cards and tape flags, others use three-ring binders and highlighters, and still others use software with electronic files instead of manila folders. Whatever your preferred manner, get everything you'll use so you'll have it handy when you need it. Don't forget about the non-writing essentials—your favorite drink or snack, reference guides, links to blog posts with helpful advice (such as Fiction University). If you think you'll need it, put it within reach.

If you don't have a preferred method yet (or don't think your current one is working), try one or more of these options:

Software: Collect all your notes and critiques in one file (or folder) in your favorite program. Microsoft Word's Document Map feature is a handy way to create a table of contents to quickly scan through for what you want. Scrivener allows you to add text sub-files with everything you need right there per scene or chapter. Note-taking software, such as Microsoft's OneNote or Evernote, is another way to keep everything in one place.

Three-ring binders and paper: For those who prefer a more hands-on approach, a binder with paper you can add to and group how you like it can be the perfect fit. You can easily add pages, move pages as needed, and take notes anywhere. You might even have a separate binder for the manuscript itself, with notes and ideas written on the pages.

Tape flags and printed pages: If the idea of everything written and marked on the manuscript appeals to you, print out your manuscript and use different colored tape flags for different aspects of the revision. Tape additional sheets of paper to pages for extra notes, or write on the backs of the pages. Don't forget scissors and tape if you go this route. Highlighters and colored pens are also useful.

Step Two: Gather Your Notes

Hunting through files or pages to find the feedback comment you want to address can be both time consuming and annoying. Collect everything in one place so you can easily access it when you reach that section of the revision. Create a story bible with important details to maintain consistency.

If you don't have a preferred method yet (or don't think your current one is working), try any of these options:

Put the notes into the manuscript file: Copy all the comments you want to address directly into the manuscript, so as you read through each scene, you'll see what needs to be done. Macro comments might be added at the start of each chapter or scene, or in the beginning of the file. If you have multiple critiquers, you might use a different color per person. Or you might use a different color per type of problem to address, such as green for point-of-view issues and red for places where you're telling and not showing.

Create a master revision file: A master file with a summary and list of what you want to revise can provide a nice, step-by-step guide to follow—and a checklist to cross off when each aspect is done.

Print everything out: Hard copies you can physically flip through could be a better option for those who prefer to edit from paper.

Use index cards: A popular organization method is to write out what needs to be done per scene on a index card, referencing page numbers or chapters. You can put everything on one card, or use a different color for each character or option.

EXTRA TIP: *Decide how you'll identify what comments have been dealt with. Delete them? Move them to another file or folder? Change the color, or simply cross them off a list? It'll help when you're not sure if you've made a change or not.*

Step Three: Gather Your Thoughts

There's a reason the previous session in this book is called Mentally Prepare Yourself for the Revision. Revising a novel is a lot of work, and being in the wrong head space can affect how productive it is. It's not uncommon to try to tackle too much too fast, and end up frustrated and feeling as though you're not getting anywhere (or worse—that you're ruining the manuscript). Take the time you need to be in the right frame of mind to revise your novel, review your plan, and have fun with it.

Let my advice, tips, and questions help you focus, stay on track, and guide you through your revision so you don't have to worry about what you're forgetting.

Types of Revisions

Not all revisions are created equal. You'll write clean first drafts that fall out of your head onto the page as if they *want* to be written, and drafts that fight you every step of the way until you whip them into submission and make the novel work. Other drafts you'll write and revise countless times until they become a tangled mess (even though you still *love* that story and *swear* you'll make it work).

Approaching one of the less common types of manuscripts often requires a different tack than the average draft—and a little more effort to make it work. But the results can be worth it if it turns that mess of a manuscript into the book of your heart.

Different Types of Revisions

Most writers will have a first draft that's ready for revision. These will be split between manuscripts no one but you has seen, and manuscripts that have been through a round of beta readers or critique partners. The more uncommon revision will be a novel you've revised countless times to make work and need extra help to finally get it there.

In this session, the goal is to determine the type of revision you're facing, and determine if you need to take a slightly different approach. Feel free to skip the specific in-depth sections if you're not facing that type of revision.

Revising on Your Own

This is a typical first-draft revision, where no one but you has seen the manuscript. You either want to work out all the bugs before you show it to anyone, or you want to make sure it's as complete as possible before asking for feedback. For a more in-depth discussion on this revision type, see page 21.

Revising From Feedback

This is a draft that's been through critiques and has feedback to help guide you in your revision. It might be a first draft or a later draft. The hard part here is figuring out what feedback to heed and what to ignore. For a more in-depth discussion on this revision type, see page 22.

Revising Overly Revised Manuscripts (The Frankendraft)

The more troublesome manuscripts are those you've revised over and over. You've changed so much you often forget what story you were trying to write in the first place. These revisions require a slightly different approach than a typical revision. Until you decide what you want, you won't know the steps to take to get there. For a more in-depth discussion on this revision type, see page 28.

Revising From Multiple Drafts

If you've been revising for a while, you might have several drafts that explore different directions. This is especially true if you weren't sure how the story might unfold and needed to write a draft or two to figure it out. Problem is, you're now faced with several drafts that all contain scenes and ideas you like, and you have no clue how to merge them all into one draft. For a more in-depth discussion on this revision type, see page 31.

Revising Half-Finished Manuscripts

These manuscripts have stalled, often somewhere in the middle of the novel. They require more effort because they're often inherently flawed—which is why they're giving you so much trouble—and until you fix that flaw you can't get the novel to work. You love the story, but you don't want to scrap the whole thing and start over—though sometimes this is the only way to get this type of novel to work. For a more in-depth discussion on this issue, see the Bonus Workshop on page 325.

Preparing yourself for the revision at hand helps ensure you revise your novel in the most effective and productive way possible.

If you've identified the type of revision you face, move on for a more in-depth discussion, or jump ahead to Workshop One: Revision Prep if you're ready to start now.

Revising on Your Own

You've finished a first draft, seen how the story unfolded, and are ready to move on to draft number two and strengthen the story and/or fix any problems you've found. You know what it needs and want to get the manuscript into decent shape before you send it out to beta readers or even agents and editors.

In this session, the goal is to separate yourself from your work so you can look at it objectively.

One of the toughest aspects of writing is the ability to look at your work without an emotional attachment to it. Since you wrote it, you understand elements that might not be clear to readers, and you often overlook any flaws your instincts say need to be fixed. To get the most from a revision, you have to look at your work as if you didn't write it.

Give Yourself the Freedom to Stink

First drafts don't always stink, but a lot of them do, so don't worry if yours is one of them. It's normal. Pretty much every writer writes a bad first draft at some point, and it doesn't mean the manuscript is a failure. That first-draft brain dump can be messy, and the revision is how you clean up the mess.

If you're revising on your own, you have to rely on your eyes and instincts to spot issues and fix them. This can be hard if you're too emotionally invested in the work, and every little "mistake" can feel like the end of the world.

It's not.

As you go through your manuscript, remember: You're not finding mistakes, you're finding places to improve the manuscript.

Approach it as if You're Doing a Critique for a Friend

It can help to look at your manuscript and pretend it was written by a friend. What advice would you give that friend about this story?

Take it a step further and pretend it's a good friend who wants you to tell it like it is and not hold back. They won't take anything you say personally. Then critique the manuscript to the best of your ability.

Be a good friend and be ruthless. The tougher you are, the better the manuscript will be.

Don't Worry About the Time it Takes to Revise

Unless you're on a deadline, worrying about when you'll get a revision done can be stressful and sap your creativity and energy. You want to get your book done as quickly as possible so you can send it out, but rushing the work never results in the best work, and this can hurt you and your novel in the long run.

It's okay if it takes longer than you expect to make your novel shine. And if you're *not* worrying about it, you often wind up getting done more quickly anyway, because all that energy is going into the revision, not the worrying.

Revising on your own is a useful way to get your novel the way you want it before showing it to others. You're happy with it and aren't being influenced during the drafting process by outside advice.

Revising From Feedback

Writing is a solitary endeavor, and it's common to fall in love with your words. You've spent a lot of time and effort on your book, so sometimes the thought of changing a single word can be disheartening. It's even harder when other people ask for major changes you're not sure the manuscript needs. But revisions are a part of publishing, and you'll have to find the best way to apply any editorial advice received.

In this session, the goal is to look at ways to best use any feedback received to revise your novel.

It's important to remember that *you* are always in control of your work. You *can* say no to changes—whether they come from critique groups, beta readers, agents, or editors. You decide how you want to handle feedback, and you might find that you can find ways to satisfy critiquers *and* do something you never expected with the book.

First Look at a Critique

Everyone has their own process for handling critique feedback and diving into revisions, but when faced with pages of information and comments, sometimes it's hard to know where to start. A good first step is to simply read them with no expectations. Make no judgments here. If anything pops up that seems totally out of left field (and there's always something unexpected), let it slide on by.

Once you've read everything, ask your critiquers any questions you might have. Sometimes you'll need clarification on a point, or someone will say something that resonates with you and you'll want them to elaborate. After that, let the critique sit for a few days.

The sitting is an important aspect. You no doubt have hopes and dreams for your story, so any negative comment can trigger a knee-jerk reaction and the need to justify *why* you did something. "They're missing the point," you cry. (For the record, they usually aren't.) Letting the feedback soak in helps you evaluate it objectively.

Dealing With Feedback From Critique

When you get a critique it can be easy (and tempting) to ignore what you don't like and accept only the comments that praise the manuscript. But you asked or the "critique" part, so treat any feedback with the respect it deserves. It was given to help you discern where any problems lie in your manuscript, and to give you opportunities to make the work even better.

Take every comment seriously: Even if it seems out of left field or flat out wrong, someone thought it based on what you wrote. Ask yourself *why* the critiquer said it and try to see the underlying problem, *then* decide if it's a comment that needs to be addressed or not. Often, comments that come out of left field are your critiquers picking up on a subtle problem, but even they're not sure what that problem is. They know something is wrong, but guessing as to the real cause. A totally wrong comment *can* be missing the point, but it's still valid since it's what the critiquer felt. It's your job to determine what made that critiquer feel that way and then decide if it needs fixing.

If you agree with a comment, make the change: Sometimes you'll agree with something, but don't want to do it. It'll be too much work, it'll cause another problem later, etc. Do it anyway.

If you don't agree with a comment, don't make the change: It's your book; do what you think is best. Even great ideas or suggestions can be wrong for your novel. As long as you understand why the comment was made and have solid reasons for not addressing it, you can ignore it. It's the comments you disagree with but can't say why that can come back to bite you.

If you're not sure about a comment, think about what the critiquer is trying to point out and why: Think about why you're resistant to the comment. Sometimes feedback requires an edit that scares you, asks you to change something you love, or even needs a skill you're not sure you have to fix. Or it might suggest something you hadn't thought about before, but there's something in the comment that resonates with you and you hesitate. It's as if your subconscious knows there's a gem in that comment.

If you trust the critiquer had that issue, but know in your heart the scene or detail is right: Sometimes critiquers spot a problem and know something is off, but the trouble spot isn't where they see it—it's all in the setup, so the resolution isn't coming through correctly. Critiquers see the *symptoms* of the problem, but not the true cause, and your gut is telling you they're wrong, but...still right. If you fix the issue where they mention it, you don't fix the problem and might even create a new one. But if you consider why they feel that way, you can trace those symptoms back to where you went off track.

If it's a grammar or punctuation rule and you're not sure if the comment is right, look it up: People remember rules wrong all the time, especially when things such as commas *can* be a personal preference. Overall, if a punctuation change makes the sentence read better, make it. If not, don't.

If it's a clarity issue, fix it, even if you think it's clear: If a reader was confused, something wasn't clear. Sure, you may have left hints, or even talked about it two chapters earlier, but if your critiquer read those chapters a week apart (like a reader might) and forgot a key bit of information, another reader will likely have the same problem. You might not need to go deep into anything, but a quick word or two as a reminder usually fixes the uncertainty.

Do whatever serves the story best: Even good ideas can be the wrong ideas if they don't fit the story you're trying to tell. Adding or doing something that seems cool just *because* it's cool *can* hurt your novel. It can hijack it, add unneeded subplots, and confuse the core conflict.

Don't Try to Do it All

As tough as revising can be, the hard part is reviewing your critiques and not being sure what to do with all that advice. It's not uncommon to want to do everything everyone says, but listening *too* hard can *cause* problems. Sometimes it's better to hear what they're saying and identify the problem that made them say it in the first place.

For example, you might get comments such as:

> *Nothing's happening in this scene, you should cut it.* (This could indicate a problem with an unclear goal, and simply making that goal more clear would fix it.)

> *I don't understand why this character is doing this.* Maybe explain what they're really after? (This could indicate a problem with motivation, but explaining the specifics too much will give away the secret and kill the tension.)

> *I don't believe he'd do that here.* (This could indicate a failure to lay the right groundwork leading up to that choice, not a problem with the character's actions.)

It's helpful to consider the source when reviewing your feedback. A mystery fan might nudge you to create more mystery or drop more clues, which might not be appropriate for your romantic comedy. The romance fan might encourage you to develop the sexual tension between the leads, even though there's no romance in the novel. A thriller fan might ask you to pick up the pace, even though a historical fiction fan might prefer a slower pace.

It's possible you're getting such comments because:

- The mystery reader doesn't care about characters and only wants a twisty puzzle to solve (and your novel is a character-driven story).
- The romance reader wants to see the two leads fall in love (and your novel is an adventure story with no romance).
- The thriller reader wants an adrenaline rush with high stakes (and your novel is more suspense with personal stakes).

These readers want what the book is not, and their comments would only push you to write a different type of book than what you intended.

However...it's *possible* you're getting such comments because:

- The mystery reader feels the plot is too predictable and she's getting bored.
- The romance reader feels there's no chemistry between your lead characters and they feel flat.
- The thriller reader feels the stakes are too low to make him care about the story.

The details of the comments might be off base, but they point to a problem that *does* exist. It's up to you to determine if the problem lies with the book not being the right type of book for that reader, or an issue you want to address.

Remember, not being the book a particular reader wants to read is not the fault of the manuscript.

On the flip side, you can still benefit from critiques outside your genre. *Would* a little mystery add humor or tension to your romantic comedy?

Maybe tension between the leads in your thriller is exactly what you need, only not the sexual kind. Perhaps a few scenes in your historical could benefit from a little excitement. It's fine to ignore advice that doesn't serve your story, but consider it first.

Trust your instincts to know when a comment is good for your book, bad for your book, or good, but not right for your book. Listen to what your critiquers *felt*, as well as what they said.

But (and this is a biggie)...

If you notice you ignore *a lot* of advice, you might want to examine why.

Are You Ignoring Advice That Can Help You?

Every writer gets at least one rough critique, and it's only natural to ignore words that hurt or sap your confidence. The danger comes when you consistently ignore the very advice that can help you just because it hurts or you don't like it. If you've been revising novel after novel (or the same novel multiple times) and don't think you're getting any better, step back, look at the situation objectively, and ask:

Are you getting the same advice from multiple sources? If a lot of the feedback says the same thing, there's something in the writing or story that needs fixing, especially if it's a larger issue that crops up no matter what piece you're working on. That suggests it's a skill problem, not an individual story problem.

Is the amount or quality of feedback you're getting declining? It's frustrating to spend a lot of time critiquing someone's work, only to have that advice ignored time and time again. People don't want to waste time on writers who brush them off and keep making the same mistakes. If you used to get detailed critiques back, and now you're getting short summarized reviews, you might want to think about *why* no one is bothering to help anymore.

Do you feel as if you ought to do it, but you're blowing it off because "that's what editors are for"?" It happens—writers think problems in their work will be fixed once they sell it, and their work only needs to be "good enough" to land an agent or an editor. Not true at all. The manuscript needs to be as perfect and as polished as you can make it *before* it goes to an agent or editor (and that goes double if you plan to self or indie publish).

With any critique, trust your writer's compass. Focus on the story and keep asking what will make it better. You might take a few side trips getting there, but you'll work it out eventually.

Revising Overly Revised Manuscripts (The Frankendraft)

A Frankendraft differs from a draft you know needs heavy revising. It's been cut and stitched together so many times the scenes no longer work together, and the story is either so deeply buried or so watered down that it doesn't make a whole lot of sense anymore.

In this session, the goal is to determine if you have a Frankendraft, and discuss options for what to do with it.

Often, there's not much you can do with a Frankendraft, so be prepared. Your objectivity is gone since so much of the story is in your head that you no longer notice it's not on the page. Sometimes, it's so terribly flawed that it's best to be merciful and pull the plug. But all hope is not lost, and you *can* take steps to bring this monster back to life.

Step One: Say Goodbye

Accept that the Frankendraft is dead and put the manuscript in a drawer. You created this mess by revising it over and over, and it's time to start fresh. Forget the text you already wrote and focus on the *story* you wanted to tell. Rewrite it from scratch in a clean file. No more editing. No more trying to make *this* manuscript work. Treat it as if it were a brand-new idea and run from there.

It's usually worth taking some time at this stage to brainstorm as if the novel you wrote never existed. Take another look at the idea, maybe run through some exercises to inspire the muse and get a different perspective (I suggest my book, *Planning Your Novel: Ideas and Structure* to help you here).

Step Two: Trim the Fat

Decide what's needed in the story and what's not. What's the single most important goal in the plot? That's your core conflict.

Remember, you're looking for an achievable goal here, not a premise. Something tangible, not a vague concept, such as "the romance between so and so." Look for what the protagonist wants, such as, "Bob wants to win Jane's heart."

What events are *critical* to resolving that goal? If they weren't there, there would be no story. List those events, but no more than ten. Now revise with your core conflict and those plot points and get rid of everything else.

I strongly suggest doing an outline here, even if you're not an outliner by nature. It'll help you see if your plot is working and if you have all the right pieces to write a solid novel without writing the actual novel. If there are glaring holes or problems, they'll show up here.

Step Three: Kill Some Characters

Hard as this will be, eliminating characters will go a long way toward stripping out what's unnecessary. Who is the single most important character in the story (that's your protagonist)? Who is their antagonist? Now get rid of everyone else (don't panic, you'll add some back!).

Make a list of all the other characters. Go through the list and ask if the two critical characters (protagonist and antagonist) absolutely totally need that person to resolve the story goal. It's okay to have a "maybe" list here, as you'll need some minor characters down the road.

REVISION RED FLAG: Watch out for "zombie" characters who might turn this draft back into a Frankendraft—look for anyone who brings a serious subplot with them. If their story risks overshadowing or hijacking the core conflict, they do not need to be there. Save them for their own novel, or cut that subplot out. In most cases, it's better to cut the character as well, so you're not tempted to return to that subplot.

Step Four: Go Five for Five

What are the five critical events that have to happen to resolve the core conflict? Who are the five (or fewer) critical characters necessary to achieve those goals?

Take those five plot events and spread them out over the course of the novel. Which one is the best starting place? One of the critical events in your story should be the inciting event. If it's not, go back to step four and try again. Which one is the ending? You should have figured out this event from step two.

Now, of the remaining three events, which one is the best midpoint reversal event? It should be large enough to sustain your middle, and interesting enough to keep readers guessing. (A midpoint reversal is something that happens in the middle of the novel to surprise readers or change how the story unfolds. It also gives you something to plot toward from the beginning, then deal with in a way that gets you to the ending).

Finally, take each of the two remaining events and put one on either side of the midpoint. These might make good first and second act endings.

You might say, "But I can't do that because the chronology is off now!" but don't worry about that. Just organize and look at those turning points. Is there a way to rework the chronology so that these events fall in that order? Forget what you *already* wrote. Don't try to slip in details you remember you like.

Look at the first event and determine a way to get to the second. Then to the third, and so on. Brainstorm. Think outside the box and imagine what your characters would do. These notes can be rough and sketchy— just try to get an idea of how *this* book can play out.

Those who have trouble plotting might get snagged here, so if you're not sure what to do, try a shift toward the characters and write out their front story. What are their roles in the novel? What do they do? How do they help? Follow their character journeys as if the novel were their story and see what happens. After that, look back and see where this journey overlaps the core conflict and where the plot points might occur.

You'll have a much tighter story and a clearer look at how that story might unfold. You can always add in more scenes or turning points to flesh it out, but be wary of sewing dead pieces back on and creating another Frankendraft. The goal here is to start fresh and breathe new life into the story, not fix the old manuscript.

Most times you have to bury a Frankendraft to keep it away from the villagers, but once in a while, you *can* save it and turn it into something wonderful.

Dealing With Multiple Drafts During a Revision

Some manuscripts go through several drafts before you find the best way to tell your story. Problem is, you can end up with multiple drafts containing good writing in every one. Finding a way to piece together all the best parts and still tell a cohesive story can be a challenge—and risks creating a Frankendraft.

In this session, the goal is to find the most effective way to manage multiple drafts during a revision.

Lists can be incredibly helpful at giving you an overall look at your novel, especially if it's in several pieces. Start figuring out which pieces contribute to your core conflict and which don't. You can hit the critical details in all the scenes you plan to use and see how they flow together. Maybe even use that one-line summary that describes the plot so you can see how they connect to the overall story arcs.

It can also help to create a new file and start pasting in all the scenes you want in the order you want them in. The story won't make a ton of sense since the scenes will likely be disjointed, but they'll be in place and give you a sense of how they flow and work together (and let you see where you might need to write more or cut back). For those using the Three Act Structure, this is quite helpful in determining where your major set pieces fall, and if the right scenes are in the right places. You might find you have too much setup in Act One and not enough scenes for Act Three (or vice versa), and will need to adjust.

Rethink Your Darlings

In multiple drafts, you'll likely have favorite moments you want to include, and you'll probably work hard to get them to fit. But just because it's a great scene doesn't mean it belongs in the final story or plot. Difficult-to-place scenes might not be the right scenes for the book. Forcing a scene can create a stumbling block for readers—it doesn't flow, it doesn't quite make sense, it doesn't advance the story.

This doesn't hold true for every tough bit to fit, and once in a while, you come up with a seriously cool way to make it work that you wouldn't have thought about otherwise. But if you find yourself beating your head against a scene, it might be time to file it away and save it for another story. Look at those favorite scenes and ask:

Does it advance the core conflict? No matter how good the scene is on its own, if it's not advancing the plot, it probably doesn't need to be there.

Does it offer new and relevant information? Often, a favorite scene is similar to one already in the manuscript. The idea appeals to you, and you write it multiple times or multiple ways. It's a good scene, sure, but it does nothing new.

Beware of Revision Smudge

Revision smudge is those bits and pieces left behind that reference something no longer in the story. Maybe you switched which characters were in the scene with your protagonist, or you changed a location of scene, or a goal shifted slightly and the stakes were altered. Reading these scenes feels right, but when you look closely, you realize the details refer to a part of the story that is no longer there. That reference was cut, changed, or moved to a new location. Some things to keep an eye out for:

- Are there any leftover names or details that don't belong?
- Is anything referenced that is no longer there, or has changed?
- Are there extra characters in a scene who aren't anywhere else in the story?
- Is the information revealed new, or has it been added elsewhere?

Check for Repeated Information

Repeated description and backstory often cause trouble when merging multiple drafts. A scene that originally introduced a character in chapter two might now be in chapter five, and readers already know that character by that time.

To help fix out-of-order or repeated details, search for each character's name (or a key detail of backstory) and verify where you revealed it first, then check if it was also mentioned any other place. This can be time consuming, but by the end, you'll know exactly where you wrote what about a character.

Revise Chronologically

Revising chronologically also helps see the story as it unfolds, since you can easily flip back and double check details. Even better, having just read it, the text will be fresh in your mind. You might even make an easy-to-check list of details you changed that need to be edited overall.

Piecing together multiple drafts can be tricky, but a little planning can save you a lot of time and effort, and direct you to the right areas to spend additional time on during your revision.

Workshop One: Revision Prep

The Goal of This Workshop: To organize your thoughts, analyze the manuscript's needs, and determine what revisions you want to do with this manuscript.

What We'll Discuss in This Workshop: How to evaluate a manuscript and determine what it needs, how to create editorial and character arc maps, and how to create a revision plan.

Welcome to Workshop One: Revision Prep

Before diving into a revision, it helps to know what you're working with and what shape your manuscript is in. Novels often change during a first draft, so any outlines or summaries could be outdated by the time you're ready to revise. Your goals for the novel might have changed as well, or even the direction you originally planned to take. Scheduling a day or two to take stock of what you've written and how that compares to your original vision can save you time and effort later.

It's tempting to skip these steps and dive right into the revision, but with all the work that goes into a draft, it's worth the extra effort to understand what you want from your revisions, and the best way you can accomplish your goals.

Take a Look at the Big Picture

You had an idea for this novel when you started it—a vision for what you wanted it to be. Maybe you never wavered from that path and the first draft is exactly what you expected it to be, but often the story changed and evolved as you wrote it. New ideas excited you and your original plan isn't so clear. You need a little reminder as to why you wrote this novel in the first place, and who you wrote it for.

In this session, the goal is to clarify what you want your novel to be.

Step One: What Do You Want This Novel to Be?

This may seem like a simple question, but it's more than "a YA fantasy" or "a futuristic thriller." Do you want it to be funny? Scary? Romantic? Do you want it to fall into a certain genre or subgenre? This is important if you plan to submit it to agents or publishers. Do you want it to entertain or do you want readers to think deeper thoughts? If so, what thoughts?

What type of novel you want to create will help guide you on what aspects to revise, whether it's adding humor, romance, tightening the pacing, raising the tension, or something more fundamental. A character-driven literary novel requires different elements than a hard-core thriller. Just as you wouldn't write them the same, you wouldn't revise them the same. Think of it like adding spice to a meal—you want to bring out the right flavors in your story.

REVISION RED FLAG: If you're not sure of the tone, style, or even genre you're aiming for, or you have multiple (and conflicting) tones and styles, that could indicate you haven't decided what type of novel this is yet. Try exploring the different genres your novel might fall into. Is the core conflict of your novel clear? Does it contain the common elements for any given genre or subgenre? Are the tone and mood consistent with your chosen genre?

Step Two: What Story Are You Telling?

You have a core story about something that intrigues you as a writer, perhaps even a general theme. What core idea is at the heart of your story? What themes are running through it? Forget plot, forget characters, forget details specific to the plot. Think about the general underlying story—at its heart, what is it?

That heart will be the unifying force tying your entire novel together (and often the theme). It will give the overall novel cohesiveness and make it about more than just the plot. Finding your core idea will give you a story compass that will guide you as you revise.

REVISION RED FLAG: If you have no theme or greater concept, don't fret. Not every novel has a theme or poses a greater, universal question. But it *is* an opportunity to make your novel stronger, so it's worth considering how a theme might improve your story. Are there common elements to your story that might further tie the plots or characters together? Is there a greater message beyond the "protagonist solves problem" aspect of the plot?

Step Three: Who is This Novel For?

We like to think our books appeal to "everyone who loves to read," but sadly, that's not true. Readers have their own likes and dislikes, and the better you understand your readers, the better your chances at giving them a book they'll love. Trying to be all things to all readers results in a mishmash of *bleh* that doesn't satisfy anyone.

Your intended audience has varied tastes and needs, and what a middle-grade-adventure lover wants to read is different from what a political-thriller reader wants. If your reader wants a fast pace, you'd want to revise to raise the stakes or tension, cut the fat, maybe add more hooks. If your reader is looking for more word pictures or inner journeys, you might revise to elaborate on your descriptions and character arcs, and build deeper emotions that connect readers more strongly to the characters.

Readers also expect to see elements common to a novel *of* that genre. Knowing those tropes helps you tailor your novel so it satisfies readers looking to read a good tale in their chosen genre.

🚩 **REVISION RED FLAG:** If you can't identify a basic target reader, that could indicate you're not sure where your novel belongs in the market or who it's for. While this isn't always a problem, it can make it hard to revise, because there's no clear direction of what the novel should be. Is it a mystery with romantic elements or a romance with a mystery? Each story appeals to a different type of reader and requires different revision paths. What type of reader is this novel trying to attract? Who do you see reading it?

Once you've clarified the type of novel you want yours to be, you'll have a better idea of what aspects of your manuscript you want to develop and what can be trimmed. You're now ready to examine your manuscript more closely and identify exactly what's in it and how it unfolds.

Create an Editorial Map

Even if you're a fast drafter and completed a manuscript in a few weeks, odds are you don't remember everything that happens in every scene. Without a clear understanding of what's in your novel, it's harder to know the best way to revise. Doing an editorial map (also called an edit map or book map) lets you know exactly how the novel unfolds and where it needs tweaking. It's also a handy reference tool when you need to check when or how something happens and don't want to search the entire manuscript.

In this session, the goal is to map out what happens in your novel to create an easy reference guide for your revision.

As you create your editorial map, keep an eye out for weak spots and scenes you want to work on later. Add revision notes at the end of your scene summaries, such as: "Needs stronger goal," or "Fix character arc." This can make it easier to organize your thoughts for more productive revision sessions.

Please note that this map is to determine what happens when, so don't worry if the plot events don't line up with a particular structure or template. If that's your goal for the revision, you'll fix it during the plot and structure sessions.

How to Create an Editorial Map

Go scene by scene and summarize the important aspects of

Step One: Identify What Happens in Every Scene or Chapter

Determine what happens in each scene, especially the plot-driving goals and conflicts, as these elements create the novel's plot. You can either list them or just think about them at first (we'll summarize next). If plot mechanics are a common weak area for your first drafts, I recommend listing the goals and motivations of each scene. It'll force you to be specific, and the act of writing them down crystallizes your intent, especially if you have trouble articulating what a scene is about or the goals driving it. Ask:

- What is the point-of-view character trying to do in this scene? (the goal)
- Why is she trying to do it? (the motivation for that goal)
- What's in the way of her doing it? (the conflict and scene obstacle)
- What happens if she doesn't do it? (the stakes)
- What goes wrong (or right)? (how the story moves forward)
- What important plot or story elements are in the scene? (what you need to remember or what affects future scenes.)

REVISION RED FLAG: If you're unable to answer any of these questions, that could indicate you're missing some of the goal-conflict-stakes plot mechanics. Make note of these areas, as you'll want to return to them later when it's time to strengthening these elements.

Step Two: Summarize What Happens in Every Scene or Chapter

Once you identify the core elements of the scene, summarize what happens—the actions and choices made. This will be a huge help in analyzing the novel's narrative drive and pacing.

REVISION RED FLAG: If you can't summarize the action in the scene, that could indicate there's not enough external character activity going on. Perhaps this scene has a lot of backstory, description, or infodumps in it. Be wary if there's a lot of thinking, but no action taken as a result of that thinking. Make notes on ways to add the character's goal back in, or how to possibly combine the scene with one that's weak on internal action.

Step Three: Map Out the Entire Novel

Go scene by scene and summarize the novel. By the end, you'll have a solid map of how the novel unfolds and what the critical plot elements are. You'll easily see where/if a plot thread dead ends or wanders off, or any scenes that lack goals or conflict.

REVISION RED FLAG: If you discover some chapters or scenes have a lot of information, while others have a line or two, that could indicate scenes that need fleshing out, or are heavy with non-story-driving elements that might need pruning. It could even show places where *too* much is going on and readers might need a breather. Mark the areas that need work, adding any ideas that might have occurred to you as you wrote your summaries.

REVISION TIP: *Try highlighting your notes in different colors to denote different elements, such as green for goals, red for tension. That makes it easy to skim over your editorial map and see where and what the weak spots are.*

Revision Option: Make Notes for Later

Get a head start by taking additional notes on elements you'll look at later. Some things worth identifying:

Story questions per scene or chapter: Look for the elements readers will wonder about.

Reveals of secrets or key information: When do characters discover important information? When do readers?

Key moments in any subplots: Add a line or two that shows any subplots and how they unfold. It's also useful to note how they connect to the main plot.

Revision Option: Map Out Any Additional Arcs You Might Want

Aside from the core plot elements, you can also include the pacing of reveals, discovery of clues or secrets, how multiple points of view affect each other, or whatever else you want to track. For example, a mystery might have one paragraph per chapter that covers what the killer is doing, even though that's never shown in the novel.

These additional details can be woven into the scene summary or kept as bullet points or a subparagraph if that's easier. You might even have two or three paragraphs per scene: One for the plot, one for the character arcs, and one for information *you* need, but the characters don't know yet.

This additional information is useful for tracking subplots or inner conflicts, as well as critical clues or what the antagonist is doing off-screen that's affecting the protagonist. Timelines can also appear here if you need to know when events happen to ensure everything works together and you don't have any twenty-seven-hour days. Try adding a simple time reminder at the top of every scene, such as: Day One, Morning.

REVISION RED FLAG: If you discover you have no other arcs, that could indicate there's not enough happening in your novel. A lack of plot could mean you have too many non-story elements bogging down the novel, such as an overload of description, too much world building, heavy infodumps or even an excess of internalization. It could also indicate a repetition of too-similar scenes, creating a plot that feels as though it moves forward, but it's the same basic scene goal and stakes repeated in multiple ways.

The beauty of an editorial map is that once the hard work is done and you have it all mapped out, it's a solid guide to the novel. If you get stuck during revisions you can open it up, see what happens when, clarify where the story needs to go, and get back on track.

Now that your editorial map is done and the novel is clear in your mind, it's time to see how the protagonist's character arc is unfolding.

Create a Character Arc Map

Some novels have strong character arcs (such as a character-driven story about a single person), while others have characters who barely arc at all (such as a plot-driven series). Whichever side your novel falls on, there should be *some* kind of change for the protagonist after going through the experience of the novel. If not, that's a red flag that the plot events don't matter to the life of the protagonist. She's no different at the end of the story versus the beginning.

In this session, the goal is to map out how your characters emotionally change over the course of the novel and create a guide for your character arcs and emotional turning points.

As you create your character arc map, keep an eye out for how your protagonist changes or grows over the course of the novel and where she changes. You don't have to develop a strong character arc if it would hurt your novel, but consider how much a basic arc will benefit the story. You can also develop character arcs for other characters if you wish.

How to Create a Character Arc Map

Step One: Identify the Scenes That Show Who the Protagonist is and/or How That Character Changes

Determine which scenes show important aspects of the protagonist's personality or key moments in her life, especially the events that force a change in views or beliefs. You can either list them or just think about them at first (we'll summarize next).

If character growth is a common weak area for your first drafts, try listing the motivations of each decision that causes change to clarify what's triggering that growth (positive or negative). It'll force you to be specific, and the act of writing it down crystallizes how that character grows, especially if you have trouble articulating why a character suddenly changes her ways. Some things to ask:

- What type of person is the character at the start of the novel?
- What type of person is the character at the end of the novel?

- What happens to create this change?
- When did these revelations or changes in behavior occur in the novel?
- What does the character believe at the start of the novel?
- What is believed by the end of the novel?
- What brings about this change in view?
- What is the character hiding (or what is hidden from her) at the start of the novel?
- What is revealed by the end of the novel?
- What emotional sacrifices are made over the course of the novel?

REVISION RED FLAG: If you're unable to answer many of these questions, that could indicate you're missing some of the motivations or reasons for character change. Make note of any unanswered questions, as you'll want to return to them later when it's time to strengthen these elements.

Step Two: Summarize How the Growth or Change Occurs

Once you've identified the key growth moments of the novel, summarize what happens in those scenes—the choices made and how they affect the protagonist. Aim for showing the direct steps that transform the character from who she is on page one to who she becomes by the last page.

REVISION RED FLAG: If you can't summarize why a character makes a choice that changes her, that could indicate there's not enough motivation or plausible reasons behind the change. Be wary if the change is significant and affects the plot but has no solid groundwork leading up to that change. Make notes on ways to strengthen the motives or add reasons for the character to act in a life-changing way.

Step Three: Map Out the Character Arc

Go scene by scene and summarize the protagonist's character arc in the novel. By the end, you'll have a solid map of where and how the character grows and changes, and what causes those changes. You'll see where/if the character changes for no reason, or where the reasons for the change required feel weak.

🚩 **REVISION RED FLAG:** If you notice most of the changes occur in the last act or around the climax of the novel, that indicates there's not enough growth occurring, and the character is changing because it's *time* to change. Also be wary of any areas where a lot of growth happens in a short amount of time, as this might indicate weak or missing motivations. Mark the scenes that need further development, adding any ideas that might have occurred to you as you did your summaries.

Revision Option: Map Out Any Additional Character Arcs Needed

Depending on how many characters you have, or who is important enough to grow, you might have other arcs to track. Map out the change moments for any additional characters you want to evolve in the novel. For example, you might want to track the love interest arc, or the best friend, or the antagonist. Even if the arcs are small or just show a change in attitude, views, or beliefs, characters who grow bring depth and texture to a story.

These arcs can also come in handy to fill holes or slow moments in the plot, or layer in extra tension where needed.

🚩 **REVISION RED FLAG:** If you discover no other character grows, that could indicate that the supporting characters do nothing but supply information or aid to the protagonist—and often, these characters seem flat because they have no lives of their own.

A character arc map is useful for referencing when, why, and how characters change over the course of the novel. Braiding the character arcs with the plot help ensure that something interesting (and story-moving) is happening in every scene.

Now that you've finished your editorial and character arc maps, analyze what's working in the overall novel and what still needs work.

Analyze the Draft

After doing your editorial and character arc maps, you should have a general idea of where the manuscript is weak and what you'd like to do to make it stronger. Use your maps as guides and conduct a more detailed analysis to pinpoint the areas to focus on.

In this session, the goal is to get a solid overview of where the weak spots lie in your novel, and provide you with the best guide to revise those issues.

If your first draft is clean and the plot is working, you might be ready to revise after doing the editorial and character arc maps (if so, you can skip this session). If the manuscript needs more attention, spend some time analyzing its strengths and weakness and decide what will best serve your story and help turn your manuscript into a nice, healthy novel.

You don't need to fix the problems now—this analysis is for identifying problem areas and directing your revision. Once you know what's weak or missing, you can devote more attention to the workshops aimed at those areas.

Things to look for (potential issues include, but are not limited to):

▶ **Weak goal-conflict-stakes structures:** This could indicate a plot or narrative drive issue.

▶ **Lack of character motivation:** This could indicate a character arc or credibility issue.

▶ **Sparse or missing descriptions:** This could indicate a clarity or world-building issue.

▶ **Heavy (or missing) backstory:** This could indicate a pacing or character issue.

▶ **Too many infodumps:** This could indicate a pacing or show-don't-tell issue.

▶ **Slow or uneven pacing:** This could indicate a narrative drive or pacing issue.

▶ **Lack of hooks:** This could indicate a tension, narrative drive, or premise issue.

▶ **Faulty logic:** This could indicate a plausibility or plotting issue.

▶ **Weak or missing foreshadowing or clues:** This could indicate a tension, tone, or description issue.

▶ **Areas that need more emotion:** This could indicate an internalization issue.

▶ **Weak characters and character arcs:** This could indicate a character or internal conflict issue.

▶ **Weak scene structure:** This could indicate a plot or structure issue.

▶ **Lack of narrative drive:** This could indicate a pacing or goals issue.

▶ **Inconsistent point of view:** This could indicate a narrative, character, or show-don't-tell issue.

▶ **Weak dialogue:** This could indicate an infodump, dialogue, or character issue.

If you're unsure what specifically to look for, try answering these questions (be as objective as possible):

▶ Is the point-of-view character(s) likable or interesting enough to read about?

▶ Are their goals clear so there's narrative drive in the story?

▶ Do the characters seem real?

▶ Are there strong and interesting stakes?

▶ Is there too much back story, exposition, or description?

▶ Is the overall structure holding together?

▶ Does the opening scene have something to entice readers to keep reading?

▶ Do the scene and chapter endings entice readers to turn the page?

▶ Is the pacing strong?

▶ Are the plots, stakes, and goals believable?

▶ Does it read well overall?

▶ Do the sentences flow seamlessly or do any stick out and read awkwardly?

▶ Are the dialogue tags clear?

▶ Does the world seem fleshed out?

After the analysis, you should have a good idea of what areas need work. The next step is organizing your notes into a solid revision plan.

Create a Revision Plan

A revision plan helps you get a head start on what you know you want to revise so you're not spending time later deciding what to do. It's a good way to organize your thoughts and look at the overall project before you start, giving you a chance to spot any pitfalls before you stumble into them.

It's easy to get caught up in the story, or worse, chase a new shiny idea that mucks up the novel. The story can, of course, change as you revise, but a revision plan can give you that extra layer of protection against adding more because it's new versus developing what's already written.

In this session, the goal is to help you organize your thoughts and create a plan to revise your novel in the most effective way.

If you made enough notes in the previous steps and feel confident about your revision goals, you can skip this and move on to the next workshop. If you want more organization or guidance on how to approach the revision, continue with step one.

Step One: Condense Any Feedback or Critique Notes

If you sent the manuscript out for critique, read through the feedback you received and make notes of what you'd like to address. Perhaps highlight or copy into a notes file anything that requires broad strokes to fix—such as reworking a scene or changing something on a macro level.

It's also helpful to copy line comments directly into the manuscript so you have everything in one file, especially if you receive several different comments on the same scene. This could point to a slightly different problem somewhere else that your readers are picking up on.

Also review any notes you might have made on elements you want to change. The goal is to get your thoughts and feedback into one place so you can easily review it.

Step Two: Make Notes on Any Revisions You Want in Each Scene

Break out your editorial map and scan though each scene. Look for any notes or comments you made on known problems or aspects you want to work on. Add any feedback from your critique notes, and anything you noted during your manuscript analysis.

Putting these notes in a different color can help immediately identify what to do with each scene. It's also helpful to write out what needs to be revised or added in the scene summary, such as:

> Just as Bob thinks he's zombie breakfast, Sally rushes in with her gun (does it make sense she'd do this?) and shoots the zombie. It has little effect, but does distract it long enough for Bob to get a few inches out of biting range. He yells to go for the head and Sally does, killing the zombie. Bob is happy to be alive, and then panics when he remembers Jane is all alone at the office with these things on the loose (make sure his emotional shift is logical). He has to get to her. Sally takes in the scene and starts yelling at Bob for his poor choice in weaponry and what was he thinking? (Layer in subtext that relates to their failing marriage.) He's just about to lay into her when they hear more moaning from outside. A lot more. (Could this "need to tell her off" be part of his inner arc?)

If this style doesn't appeal to you, take notes in whatever format works for you. If it helps, summarize what needs to be done in each scene, chapter, and/or the entire manuscript.

Even small reminders of problem areas will make it easier to find and fix these areas.

Step Three: Plan Your Approach

Once you know what you want to do, decide how you want to approach your revision. Are you a one-chapter-at-a-time writer who likes to get that chapter perfect before moving forward? Or maybe you prefer one item at a time, such as checking for goals in the entire novel, then looking at description, then looking for trouble words? Maybe you're more of a large chunk of several chapters at a time reviser and like to get one act done before moving to the next. However you prefer to revise, knowing what you'll work on each session keeps you focused.

Step Four: Make Your Revisions

Some edits are easy to do—fixing the typos, changing a name or term, clarifying an ambiguous pronoun. If you need a little warm up before you get to the tough edits, do these first—they take the least amount of brain power and offer a sense of accomplishment. Momentum helps a lot in a revision.

Some revision passes work better when you look at the entire manuscript vs. smaller chunks, so feel free to vary how you review your manuscript. For example, continuity checks are harder to do in chunks, since you might forget what happened between reads. Reading the manuscript in a short timeframe keeps the details fresh in your mind and makes it easier to spot where something is off.

After you're done, re-read your notes and critiques to see if you've addressed everything you wanted to. Double check any feedback that you ignored to see if you have a new opinion on it now (it happens). Tweak as needed.

Step Five: Gain Some Perspective

Once the revision is done, schedule some downtime so the manuscript can sit for a while and the details can fade from your memory. I like to give it a month, but aim for at least a week, longer if the changes were extensive. You want to give your brain time to forget what *was* there so when you look at it again, you'll see what *is* there. There's always some revision smudge that slips into the text that refers to something that changed or was cut.

When you're ready, read through the manuscript once more and make any changes that jump out. Most of it will likely be small edits, a word change here and there. It's not uncommon to cut sentences or even paragraphs that slow the story down now that you've been away and can spot the dead weight. However, if you're still making large changes and rewriting sections, you might consider going back to step four and reworking those trouble spots.

Step Five: Polish the Manuscript

After the story is as good as you can make it, it's time to polish the text until it shines. This is where you'll address individual word choices, copyedits, and grammar goofs you might have made. These elements don't affect the story, but focus on the technical aspects of writing.

Don't be afraid to mix it up or change the order of these steps if that works for you. Some folks might prefer to do the larger issues first and finish up with the easy edits and that's okay. The whole goal of a revision plan is to keep you focused and provide a way to track your progress.

Now that you've refreshed the intricacies of your story in your mind, and planned out what needs tweaking and how you want to approach it, it's time to move on to the manuscript itself.

This book tackles characters first, but pick a different aspect to begin with if that suits your process better.

Workshop Two: Character Work

The Goal of This Workshop: To ensure you have strong, memorable characters readers will love, or love to hate if that's the goal.

What We'll Discuss in This Workshop: How to analyze the characters and character arcs for weaknesses, and discover ways to strengthen those weaknesses. We'll take a look at overall character development, character arcs, backstory, character description, and theme.

Welcome to Workshop Two: Character Work

There's an old saying: plot might bring readers to our stories, but characters keep them there. This underscores the importance of well-crafted, compelling characters in a novel. One of the most common reasons readers put a book down is, "I didn't like the main character." This is why I like to tackle them first during a revision. Amazing characters can overcome other writing flaws, so it takes some of the pressure off (just a little though—you don't want to slack off on the rest of the novel).

How much revising you'll need to do with your characters depends on how much work went into them beforehand. Character-focused writers will likely be strong in this area, requiring little tweaking to bring their characters to life, or they might have gone overboard and need to reel some of that information back in. Plot-focused writers typically find character development a weak area, and need to spend extra time fleshing out the characters now that they know how the novel unfolds.

No matter which side you fall on, the goal of this workshop is to strengthen weak characters and fix character issues found during your manuscript analysis.

Analyze the Characters

You often see two kinds of characters in a first draft: shallow ones who did what they were told without caring why, and overly developed ones who are too wrapped up in their own lives to pay attention to what you wanted them to do. One side needs development, the other needs some personality pruning.

In this session, the goal is to analyze your characters and determine which ones need further development and which ones need pruning.

In the next sessions, you'll also look at the character arcs, backstory, and theme.

If you think your characters aren't living up to their full potential, analyze who they are and how they fit into the story. Look for any characters who aren't pulling their weight, might not be needed, or who need more development to turn them into three-dimensional people.

At this stage, focus on analyzing what you want to do and making notes to guide you afterward.

Run through some basic character questions and determine where the weak spots lie. Start with the most important character (the protagonist) and work your way to the smaller ones, so you'll have a better understanding of what traits will support and/or conflict with your main characters.

If you already know what's missing from the characters, then jump right into your revision session.

Step One: Determine if the Right Characters Are in Place

Though it's rare, sometimes you write an entire novel and realize you had the wrong characters. The protagonist is wrong, the antagonist is flimsy, or a smaller, throwaway character turns out to be the most important person in the story. Sometimes you *have* the right character, but the personality is throwing off the whole novel.

Go through the following questions to see if the novel has the right characters for the story you want to tell:

▶ **Do you have the right protagonist for this story?** The right protagonist has a strong reason to drive the plot, and the story would fall apart or change significantly if this person wasn't part of the tale.

▶ **Do you have the right antagonist for this story?** The right antagonist has good reasons for acting, and is in conflict with the protagonist. She's also a worthy foe for the protagonist to ensure every win is earned.

▶ **Do you have the right number of characters?** Readers can keep track of only so many people at a time. Too many characters make it hard for readers to follow the story; too few make it feel coincidental or contrived.

The right characters in the right places can make the story world feel real and plausible, and create compelling people a reader wants to follow.

🚩 **REVISION RED FLAG:** Pay attention to any characters who showed up as weak on your character arc map, or who don't seem to do a lot for the story. Also note any characters you don't immediately remember who they are and what they do. Those are strong candidates for cutting.

Problems Found?

If you find the wrong characters or number of characters, spend some time doing the exercises in If You Want to Adjust the Roles or Number of Characters on page 61.

Step Two: Determine if the Characters Are Working Overall

Readers don't typically enjoy reading about people they don't like (though people do seem to enjoy *watching* characters they don't like. Go figure). An unlikable character is a major reason novels don't work, so pinpoint what it is about your characters (especially your main characters) that will connect with readers. Make sure they're people readers can relate to, sympathize with, or be fascinated by.

Go through the following questions and see if the characters are the kind of people readers will want to read about:

▶ **Do you like the point-of-view character(s) or find them interesting?** If the main characters aren't piquing interest or tugging heartstrings, they'll need a little more development. Pay particular attention to the protagonist and antagonist. Is their story worth reading about? Are *they* worth reading about?

▶ **Do you care about these characters enough to read their story?** This can be tough for the author to answer, since we usually love our creations, but look at it objectively. Did you give readers a reason to care about the people in your story? Are they worth rooting for? If you didn't know their backstory, would you still care? Remember, readers don't know what you know about these people.

▶ **Do the characters seem real?** Readers will suspend disbelief for a novel they want to read, but when characters feel flat, fake, or downright ridiculous, it yanks them out of the story. Characters who act in ways a normal person never would strain reader credibility, as do too-perfect characters who never make mistakes and always have situations work out for them. "Real" can be subjective depending on the genre, but make sure your characters are being true to the people you've created.

▶ **Are the characters believable in their roles?** You don't want to have an expert hacker who gets technical terms wrong, or a world-renowned neurosurgeon who's only seventeen. Readers aren't going to buy a character who flies in the face of plausibility. If there's anything about your characters that stretches credibility, or relies on specific knowledge they wouldn't have, take the time to ensure they're believable in that role.

▶ **Are the characters flawed in ways that affect their decisions in the story?** Flaws make characters feel real and help readers connect to them. They're also key elements in developing the plot, as flaws often cause a character to make mistakes, and determine what a character needs to overcome to win in the climax.

▶ **Do they have virtues that affect their decisions in the story?** Characters need both good and bad traits. Virtues guide them, even if they're doing the wrong thing for the right reasons. No matter how bad a character might be, there's something redeemable deep inside.

▶ **Do they have contradicting beliefs, both with themselves, and the other characters?** Inconsistency is part of life, and characters can (and should) have conflicting beliefs and opinions. If everyone believes the same thing, there's little room to develop the conflict necessary for the plot. Be wary though, if the contradictions stretch credibility.

🚩 **REVISION RED FLAG:** Pay attention to any characters you could get rid of and not miss, as well as any who feel as though they're acting out the plot because you told them to. Aim for three-dimensional characters with strengths and weakness, interesting stories, and intriguing conflicts.

Problems Found?

If you find any flat or boring characters, spend some time doing the exercises in If You Want to Flesh Out the Characters on page 70.

Step Three: Determine if the Character Descriptions Are Working

Part of bringing characters to life is describing them to your readers, but it's not uncommon to get the balance off in a first draft.

Go through the following questions and see if your characters could use a little more, or less, description.

▶ **How much physical description do you want?** How much you describe your characters is a matter of personal taste. You might be satisfied with one or two brief physical details, or you might paint a word portrait for each character.

▶ **Are the main characters adequately described?** Readers should be able to get a good sense of who these people are, and typically, what they look like.

▶ **Is there too much focus on physical details?** If every character has a long list of physical traits and not a lot on who they are as a person, that could indicate weak character development.

▶ **Are the secondary characters described?** If all the focus is on the major characters, secondary characters might be poorly drawn or underdeveloped. While you don't want to go overboard, you want them to feel solid in readers' minds.

▶ **How many details do you use to describe the various characters?** Look at the level of detail in your character hierarchy. Major characters typically have the most description, then it lessens as the importance of the character lessens. If your walk-on characters have the same level of description as your protagonist, that could indicate description that slows the pace or derails the narrative drive.

▶ **Do the descriptions all fit the same format?** Sometimes you get into a pattern with descriptions, describing every character in the same fashion, such as one or two sentences listing off height, age, hair and eye color each time a new character is introduced.

⚑ **REVISION RED FLAG:** Beware of generic physical details that read like something you'd fill out at the DMV.

Problems Found?

If you find the descriptions need work, spend some time doing the exercises in If You Want to Adjust the Character Descriptions on page 79.

Analyze the Character Arcs

The type of novel you have determines how strong the character arc is. Stories focusing on deeply personal character struggles (such as romance or literary fiction) typically have a much stronger character arc driving the plot, while stories that focus on the plot (such as thrillers or mysteries) usually have less need for the characters to grow and change. The strength of a solid character arc is that it overlays beautifully with the plot, providing the necessary tension and motivation for events to unfold. It fills any slow spots in the external plot, and allows you more flexibility in how you handle your pacing.

In this session, the goal is to analyze your protagonist's character arc to ensure it's working the way you want it to. Do this for as many additional characters as you'd like.

In the next sessions, you'll look at your backstory and theme.

Determine if the Character Arcs Are Working

Just as there are major turning points in a plot, there are major turning points in a character arc. These often coincide with major plot moments, and might even be the source of the action, the problem facing the characters, or the conflict tearing them apart.

If you mapped out the character arcs for the novel, you should have a good idea of where the emotional turning points fall and what areas could use more work (if you haven't, I recommend going back to Workshop One and doing the Create a Character Arc Map session).

Go through the following questions to determine if your protagonist has a character arc, and if that arc is achieving the emotional growth you want for the novel.

▶ **What does the protagonist learn over the course of the novel?** The character ought to change in some way between the opening and the ending (some exceptions apply, such as a genre series).

▶ **How does the internal conflict affect that growth?** Overcoming the internal flaw or weakness causes the character to grow.

▶ **What lie is she telling herself or does she believe at the start of the novel?** Frequently, the character believes a lie about something affecting her life and happiness.

▶ **When does she realize it is or isn't true?** The realization of the truth is often a pivotal moment in the character arc, leading to the needed growth that allows the protagonist to win in the climax.

▶ **What does she want most of all as a person?** For the character arc, this is usually something emotional and internal, not the external goal that drives the plot.

▶ **Does the external plot facilitate her achieving this personal desire?** It's by going through the external plot that the internal change occurs.

▶ **What is she most afraid of?** This will help develop or clarify the conflicts she'll likely face in the story.

▶ **When does she face this fear?** This traditionally happens shortly before the climax, or during the climax itself. It's often the trigger for fully realizing that growth.

▶ **Where do the turning points of the growth occur?** These should be spread out over the course of the novel.

Depending on how character-focused the novel is, you might also ask these questions of the other characters. The antagonist, secondary, and supporting characters can have arcs as well, and conflicting arcs add tension to a novel. Look for any scenes in your revision plan that need more tension and consider if an arc turning point would help them. Arcs get other characters more involved in the plot and add depth and richness to the story.

🚩 **REVISION RED FLAG:** If you notice most of these moments exist at the end of the novel, that could indicate that the characters aren't growing, but just change because the book is over. The growth will likely feel false to readers since the characters haven't earned that growth. Try spreading the moments (and growth) out over the course of the novel so the lessons learned are natural to the plot. Use your outline and major turning points to make sure you have gradual and consistent growth.

Problems Found?

If you find any too-static or changes-too-quickly characters, spend some time doing the exercises in If You Want to Strengthen the Character Arc on page 81.

Analyze the Backstory

When done well, backstory can add depth and meaning to a novel. When done poorly, it can bog down the plot, muck up the story, and ruin the pacing, which is why finding the right balance in your novel is critical.

In this session, the goal is to determine how your backstory affects your novel and if you need to cut, add, or revise any of it.

In the next session, you'll look at your theme.

Determine if the Backstory is Working

Despite the common advice that says eliminate all backstory, backstory is not a bad thing on its own. It's only when it hurts the novel that it becomes a problem.

Look at the backstory in your scenes (especially in the first 25 percent of the novel) and decide what information is vital to understand each scene and what isn't.

▶ **Is the backstory relevant to the scene?** Backstory works when there's a reason to have it. If knowing this information does nothing to advance the scene, it can usually go.

▶ **Does this information help readers understand what's going on in this scene?** If readers will be lost if they don't know this information, it can likely stay.

▶ **Will knowing this information hurt the tension or mystery of the scene (or story)?** If learning the history or details of the backstory too early will *answer* questions you hoped would hook readers and keep them reading, it's usually better to cut those early details and let the mystery build.

▶ **What would be lost in this scene if you took the backstory out?** If losing the backstory has no affect on the scene, go ahead and toss it.

▶ **Why do *you* want it in the scene?** Sometimes your subconscious is trying to tell you to add something to a scene. If a bit of backstory *needs* to be there, take a few minutes to understand why. Often, the backstory is key to how the character feels in the current scene and what she'd do or say. You might be able to add that missing element without the backstory—or discover the backstory does indeed need to stay.

🚩 **REVISION RED FLAG:** One of the problems with backstory is that you often think readers "need to know" this information to "really get" the character, so you dump in way more than readers want, let alone need. Yet, wondering *about* a character's history is often what keeps readers reading and pulls them deeper into the novel. For example, if the protagonist has had troubles with the police, then you might show her avoiding an officer on the street, or taking special care to not let an officer see her face. Readers will wonder, "Why is she avoiding the cops?" and be intrigued to read on. If you say right away that the protagonist has a warrant out for her arrest (or worse, what it's for), then there's no mystery anymore.

Problems Found?

If you find heavy or missing backstories, spend some time doing the exercises in If You Want to Balance the Backstory on page 86.

Analyze the Theme

Theme and characters go hand in hand, because people often seek greater meaning in (or through) their actions. We want what we do to matter, and what a character does creates an entire plot. A plot that matters typically has a strong theme running through it that connects it to the character arc.

In this session, the goal is to examine your theme and see how it's working with your characters and plot.

Determine if the Theme is Working

Not every novel has a theme, but even in an action-focused plot, there's usually *something* bigger underneath—it's not just a series of scenes strung together to solve a problem. The connection could be as basic as "revenge" or "justice," or as complicated as, "Are we truly human if we perform inhumane acts?" Identifying the underlying concept behind the story helps you understand what the book is "about" on a grander scale.

Take a minute and consider:

▶ **What is the theme (or themes) of this story?** Look for common ideas or concepts repeated throughout the novel.

▶ **Where examples of this theme are found in the novel?** This helps identify important plot or character arc moments, and even helps judge if the novel is too heavy on the internal journey and light on plot (or vice versa).

▶ **Where and how does the theme deepen the character arcs?** The theme is often illustrated by the character arc.

▶ **How does the theme tie into the resolution of the novel?** It's not uncommon for the climax to show everything the protagonist has learned and how she's grown, reflecting the theme and tying the external and internal conflicts together.

⚑ **REVISION RED FLAG:** Be wary of too many themes fighting for attention in your novel. If the story is about *everything*, then it's not likely to delve deep enough into any one idea to resonate with readers.

Problems Found?

If you find any theme issues (or you're missing a theme), spend some time doing the exercises in If You Want to Develop the Theme on page 89.

If You Want to Adjust the Roles or Number of Characters

Finding the right balance among characters can be tricky, but once you know how the story unfolds, it's easier to see who is doing their job and who needs to be let go. Characters you originally felt were critical turn out not to be, and those you used because you needed a body in a scene end up becoming major characters. And then there are the harder-to-fix issues—having the totally wrong character in a critical role.

The right number of characters in a novel is also subjective. An epic fantasy series is going to have more characters than a contemporary stand-alone piece. Even making a list of your characters isn't always helpful, because many will be walk-on or throwaway characters, and knowing that, they carry less weight in a list. You might not even list them because they're so unimportant, yet they take up valuable room in the reader's memory.

The following sessions will help determine if you have issues with the wrong protagonist, antagonist, or too many characters. Naturally, if you don't think you have a problem in one of these areas, skip that session.

If You Think You Have the Wrong Protagonist

The wrong protagonist is a serious issue for a first draft, but one that does happen from time to time. You have an idea, you write it, and it turns out that the person you thought was at the center of everything really isn't.

In this session, the goal is to find the right protagonist for your story, or a way to rework your protagonist to fit the story.

Step One: Determine Who Has the Problem

Look at the core conflict of your novel and identify any characters severely affected by that problem. If the goal of the novel is to resolve this problem, the protagonist will be the one trying to do so. List all the characters affected.

To fix the existing protagonist: Look for ways to make the core conflict problem apply to the protagonist. How is this problem going to make her life worse?

Step Two: Determine Who Has the Ability to Act

Some problems affect everyone even if they can't do anything about them. Cross off any characters who can't affect the problem. Look next at characters who *are* in a position to do something about it. Maybe they have access, or skills, or know the right people to help solve the problems.

To fix the existing protagonist: Look for ways to make the protagonist able to affect a change.

Step Three: Determine Who Has Reasons to Act

Being able to act is only the first step. A good protagonist also has *reasons* to act to resolve that core conflict. Cross off anyone who doesn't have a personal reason to solve the problem.

To fix the existing protagonist: Look for ways to add a personal motivation to the protagonist.

Step Four: Determine Who Has Something to Lose

If there's nothing to lose, there's nothing to gain, and a lack of stakes is a common problem with weak protagonists. First, make sure failing to resolve the problem *has* consequences, then, cross off anyone who won't lose something important if they fail.

To fix the existing protagonist: Look for ways to give the protagonist personal stakes and serious consequences if she fails to resolve the problem.

Step Five: Determine Who Has Something to Gain

Winning isn't winning if there's no reward (at least in stories). A good protagonist gains something valuable by resolving the novel's problem. Often, it's connected to the character arc and will allow her to be happy. Get rid of any potential protagonists who don't have anything to gain by winning.

To fix the existing protagonist: Look for ways the protagonist will benefit from solving the problem, especially if it also fits into her character arc (if the protagonist has no character arc, that could be why the character isn't working).

Step Six: Determine Who Has Capacity to Change

In most stories, the protagonist goes through the experiences in the novel and is changed for the better (the character arc). Cut any characters from the list who are the same people at the end of the story as they are at the beginning.

To fix the existing protagonist: Look for ways to cause a change in the protagonist. The problems overcome should have a long-lasting effect (you might need to do the character arc exercises for this character).

Step Seven: Determine Who Has a Compelling Quality

Protagonists have something about them that makes readers want to read about them. It could be a skill, a power, an attitude, or even a way of thinking. Cross off any character without that "something special" about them.

To fix the existing protagonist: Look for ways to make the protagonist more compelling. Add a trait or characteristic to make her more interesting.

Step Eight: Determine Who Has an Interesting Flaw

Flaws provide areas for growth, so perfect characters can leave the room. A good protagonist needs a flaw to make her human, and give her something to work on to better herself.

To fix the existing protagonist: Look for ways to give the protagonist flaws that connect to her character arc and the problem at hand.

Step Nine: Determine Who Has Someone or Something Interesting in the Way

The protagonist is only as good as the antagonist in her way. Look at the remaining potential protagonists and get rid of everyone who doesn't have someone or something trying to stop them.

To fix the existing protagonist: Look for ways to give the protagonist a worthy foe to overcome.

Step Ten: Choose Your Protagonist

Look at the list of remaining characters. Hopefully it's a small list (if not, go through these questions again and be more specific and personal about the answers as they pertain to your core conflict). Pick the best candidate to drive your story and put him or her back in as the protagonist. Rework the overall story as needed before returning to the rest of the revision.

To fix the existing protagonist: Is your protagonist now the right person for the story? If so, revise overall to fix the problem areas revealed in the questions. If not, and you're *sure* this is indeed the right person, then the issue might not be the protagonist but the core conflict or premise of the novel.

If You Think You Have the Wrong Antagonist

Having the wrong antagonist is a little more common in a first draft, because you often know the general "badness" of your story problem, but not exactly who will fill that role. You might even wind up with a cardboard villain who's evil for the sake of being evil—which usually results in a boring story without any real conflict or stakes.

In this session, the goal is to find the right antagonist for your story, or fix the existing antagonist to be a better foil for your hero.

Step One: Determine Who Caused the Problem

Look at your core conflict and list any characters (whether they're in the story or not) who created this problem, either directly or indirectly.

To fix your existing antagonist: Look for ways to make the antagonist responsible for the problem.

Note: The antagonist doesn't cause *every* story core conflict, but they will at least try to take advantage of it.

Step Two: Determine Who Benefits From the Problem

Antagonists act with the end game in mind. Cross off anyone who doesn't benefit from this problem.

To fix your existing antagonist: Look for ways to make the antagonist benefit from the problem.

Step Three: Determine Who is Motivated to Cause This Problem

Nobody is bad just to be bad—they have reasons, even if those reasons are twisted and hardly make sense to anyone but them. Cut any characters who have no reason to want to see this problem happen or hurt the protagonist.

To fix your existing antagonist: Look for ways to motivate the antagonist to want to see the problem occur.

Step Four: Determine Who Has Reason to Prevent the Protagonist From Acting

In most cases, the antagonist has a personal reason to keep the protagonist from resolving the problem and fixing whatever is wrong. Get rid of any potential antagonists who don't have *some* reason to stop the protagonist.

To fix your existing antagonist: Look for ways to put the antagonist in direct conflict with the protagonist. Make sure their goals are at odds with one another.

Step Five: Identify Your Antagonist

The antagonist should be the only one left on the list, but if you have several options, pick the one who's the most compelling overall. If the list is still long, go through the questions again with more personal and specific answers that pertain to the conflict.

To fix your existing antagonist: Is your antagonist now the right person for the story? If so, revise overall to fix the problem areas revealed in the questions. If not, and you're *sure* this is the right antagonist, the problem might not be the antagonist, but the core conflict or premise of the novel.

If You Think You Have Too Many Characters

The number of characters in a novel tends to grow as you write it. You discover scenes need extra hands, or a walk-on role turns out to be a fantastic secondary character, or, if you're writing a series, after a few books you realize the cast list has become unmanageable, and you need to downsize a little.

In this session, the goal is to identify and eliminate unnecessary characters.

Step One: Write Down Your Protagonist and Antagonist

Take a sheet of paper (or do this on a screen) and draw two boxes in the middle, evenly spaced apart. Write your protagonist's name in one box, your antagonist's name in the other. Add boxes if you have more than one of either. If you find yourself adding a *lot* of boxes, that's a problem.

Step Two: Add the Other Characters in the Novel

Start adding boxes with the other characters' names in them. Put them below the protagonist if they're directly connected to her, above the antagonist if they're connected to him. To quickly see what level of importance they are, try using different colors per level. List in order:

- Major secondary characters first (friends, sidekicks)
- Important characters (people the plot or story hinges on, but who aren't hanging out with the main characters)
- Minor characters (recurring people who play smaller roles and are seen multiple times)
- Named walk-on characters (people in one or two scenes who don't do much, but have names anyway)
- Any remaining people who interact with your protagonist or antagonist, named or not

For this exercise, let's say a "character" is anyone who is: A) named, as names = importance to a reader and suggest they should be remembered, or B) shown on the page affecting the protagonist (or antagonist). "People" are those who are unnamed, but interact with the main characters. For example, if your protagonist is mugged by three thugs, there are four "bodies" in that scene—one character and three people.

Do this for all the characters and people in your novel.

Step Three: Connect the Characters

Draw lines connecting the boxes. Use a solid line if the character directly interacts with and affects the protagonist, a dotted line if they're connected to someone who is connected to the protagonist. For example, when the protagonist is mugged by three thugs, and only one speaks to her and interacts in a meaningful way, that thug gets a solid connection line. The other two thugs would get dotted lines to the first thug, because they're connected to *him*, but don't directly interact with the protagonist.

What This Should Tell You:

- How many characters are in the book
- Which characters directly affect your protagonist and which don't
- Which characters might be good candidates to cut or combine

REVISION RED FLAG: If you had a hard time finding room for all your boxes, you probably have too many characters. Same if you have a lot of characters who have zero connections to your protagonist, but connections to other characters in the book. Lots of people with dotted lines to one person could be combined into one or two people who fill multiple or similar roles.

This exercise is also useful to see if a particular scene has too many characters in it, especially those hard-to-manage scenes with a group of people all chiming in about something. Look at who matters in that scene and who is there to toss out a single comment.

This exercise forces you to examine the connections between characters. You might think a character is affecting the protagonist, but when you sit down and *really* look at it, he has no direct interaction with her at all. He's more connected to someone who is connected to the protagonist.

Sometimes a visual representation can provide more information than a list, and looking at your stories from a different perspective can allow you to see connections you normally would have missed.

If you discover you *do* have too many characters, you have several options for wrangling them into a manageable number:

Option One: Get Rid of Characters You Don't Need

Deleting characters is by far the easiest way to reduce your cast, though sometimes the most painful option if you're attached to them. Look back at your boxes, or make a list of every character in the novel, starting with the main characters, and move down to the minor named walk-ons.

Who doesn't *need* to be there? Maybe one of the minor named walk-ons can become "the server" instead of Maria the waitress, or the conversation in the diner can be moved to a new setting where another person isn't needed.

Determine what would change if you cut that character. Would it create a problem or would a minor edit here and there fix his absence? If his departure has little to no bearing on the book, go ahead and say goodbye.

Option Two: Show Clingy Characters the Door

The longer a story is, the more likely it is to accumulate extra characters. This happens often in series, where characters with past roles stick around long after they've done their jobs. Story logic says they'd be in a particular scene, but there's no graceful way to get them into the story. They're in the way and might even hijack the plot if you try to give them more to do to justify them being there.

Find the characters who are in the scene only because it feels like they *have* to be. There's a decent chance these characters irritate you, because you know they're mucking the scene up and you're trying to shove them in—such as, the protagonist wouldn't cast off his faithful servant, but he's too much of a hassle to deal with if he's always around.

Look for ways to remove this type of character from the story in a plausible way. Think about why the protagonist *wouldn't* want that servant around. You might even be able to add conflict with his removal, as the heartbroken hero is forced to send her beloved friend away for his own safety.

Option Three: Let an Existing Character Do the Work Instead

Another easy fix is to let an existing character do the job instead of giving it to a new character. Look at your smaller walk-on roles, which can often be fleshed out to include the new tasks needed for the story. If the walk-on won't work, perhaps a more important character can do that task or exhibit that skill, or cause the problem. Instead of adding a character, add a layer to someone already there.

Often, the who doesn't matter as much as the what, and a character is there to do a specific job. If the reasons for a character being in that scene (or book) are general (and not specific to that character), you can likely accomplish the same thing by using an existing character.

Option Four: Reconnect a Smaller Character to the Bigger Picture or Problem

Sometimes you have characters you want to use, but they don't do all that much. You have *reasons* for wanting them in there (often dealing with backstory or world building), but their presence causes more problems than it solves. They feel unconnected to the story because they're unconnected to the plot, and thus stand out. If you give them more to do, they might not feel so useless or extraneous.

With a little creative thinking, they might be able to help solve *other* problems, such as a world-building issue or a plot hole. Maybe give them a history or skill that allows you to show an aspect of the world, or connect them to the protagonist's past to show a critical piece of her history. They could be the missing piece of a puzzle that isn't quite fitting into another part of the manuscript.

Option Five: Check for Unnecessary Subplots

A large cast can be a red flag for a bloated plot, so it's not a bad idea to check the subplots for any extra characters. Kill a subplot and every unique character in that subplot can also go. Not only do you cut down the cast, you eliminate a subplot that was probably bogging down the story anyway.

Streamlining a too-large cast can be tough, but you'll have a much tighter (and better) story once you cut away the dead weight.

If You Want to Flesh Out the Characters

Unless you did little to no character development before you started writing (which is possible), you have at least a basic sense of who your characters are. After all, you needed to know *something* about them in order to write them, even if they still need some work.

In this session, the goal is to further develop any weak characters.

Your character arc analysis will come in handy here, since you'll have a guide on how (and where) your characters need to grow to complete their arcs. Look for any notes on weak or underdeveloped characters and begin with them. You might also take a peek at any scenes with weak goals or motivations—a weak character could be the reason, since you don't know them well enough to know what they'd want in that scene.

Step One: Evaluate the Character's Role

Before you start adding character details, consider what role that character plays and how she affects the novel as a whole. This can help determine the best way to flesh out the character for your novel. You don't want to throw in random "stuff" that does nothing to improve the story, but add the right details to deepen a character in a way that best serves the story.

Explore what the character did: Look at what the character did in the novel (actions, choices, mistakes, goals, issues, etc.) and think about what shaped her to be the person who acted that way or made those decisions.

Explore why the character did it: Look at the motivations behind the actions and add reasons or history as to why those choices were made.

Explore the character's mistakes: Look at any mistakes or bad choices the character made in the novel and work backward to add a flaw that could have contributed to them.

Explore the character's victories: Look for any victories or successes and add positive traits that would logically have helped the character in those moments.

Explore the character's views and beliefs: Look for what the character believes or how she sees the world or events in the novel, and add traits (positive and negative) that helped shape those views.

If you want additional questions to help develop a flat or weak character, look at these specific areas (pick as many or as few as you need). Adapt or adjust these questions to suit your own story:

Personality and Voice

Personality influences how a character will interact with the other characters in the novel. Characters *can* have inconsistencies, but, typically, personality traits blend and support each other, and are based on a character's history and upbringing.

What kind of person is she? If you were describing her to a friend, how would you do it? This helps identify how you see this character.

How does she answer questions? This helps identify how open or forthcoming she is.

How does she present herself to other people? This helps identify how she wants others to see her.

Is her outer voice different from her inner voice? How? Why? This helps identify how much she's concealing about her own feelings.

Which personality traits help her? Which hurt her? This helps identify where her flaws and virtues lie.

How did she get that way? This helps identify the important aspects of her backstory.

How organized is she? This helps identify how she approaches problems.

Does she plan or react? This helps identify how cautious or impulsive she is.

Can she be depended on? This helps identify how connected she is to others, and how trustworthy she is.

Is she outgoing or reserved? This helps identify where she falls on the introvert/extrovert scale, and how she approaches situations.

How compassionate is she? This helps identify how she relates to and empathizes with others.

Is she willing to work with others? This helps identify how controlling or accepting she is.

Is she inherently trusting of people she doesn't know? This helps identify what's hurt her in the past.

Is she helpful or does she worry about herself first? This helps identify how selfish she is.

How excitable is she? This helps identify how she reacts in intense or emotional situations.

How confident is she? This helps identify how strongly she pursues her goals.

How does she handle the unexpected? This helps identify how she reacts to surprises.

How emotional is she overall? This helps identify her general emotional state.

Needs and Wants

What a character needs and wants will determine the goals and motivations for the plot. The character's personality will determine how he goes about getting those needs and wants.

What are his critical needs? This helps identify what's influencing the character's decisions. Look for needs that will help your plot unfold.

How self-motivated is he to act? This helps identify whether or not he'll act on his own or if he requires an outside push.

How much effort will he exert to achieve a goal? This helps identify the types of solutions to plot problems. Will he take the easy way out or do what's right even if it's hard?

How ambitious is he? This helps identify how hard he'll fight to win and what levels he'll strive for.

How assertive is he? This helps identify how direct he is in trying to achieve his goal.

How positive is he? This helps identify his outlook on life.

Does he want to do things on his terms or just follow along? This helps identify how well he works with others.

Hopes and Dreams

A character's hopes and dreams determine the character arc and often connect directly to the internal conflict. These are usually the things she feels she'll never have, but needs to be happy.

What are her hopes, both in general and in the specific story problem? This helps identify her character arc and what she wants from life.

What does she dream about? This helps identify unconscious needs she doesn't feel she deserves.

If she wasn't dealing with the problems of the novel, what would she be doing? This helps identify if she's being oppressed or held back by the story events or elements.

Flaws and Fears

A character's flaws and fears help create conflict in the novel, providing reasons for him to make mistakes and do the wrong things.

What are his flaws? This helps identify places for him to grow as a character, and areas he might make mistakes in.

What does he fear? This helps identify potential areas he can use as excuses or reasons that can cause him to make the wrong decision.

What are his prejudices? This helps identify where he's ignorant or misguided. Prejudices are useful when you need your protagonist to instantly dislike another character for plot reasons and he has no good reason to do so.

What makes him uncomfortable? This helps identify fears and concerns, as well as judge where his moral compass lies.

What makes him furious beyond rational thought? This helps identify what he feels strongly about.

What makes him change the subject or walk away from a conversation? This helps identify his bli

nd spots, or what he's trying to avoid.

Strengths and Weaknesses

A character's strengths typically drive the plot, while her weaknesses drive the character arc.

What are her strengths? This helps identify the positive skills she might use to complete the novel's tasks.

What do you admire about her? This helps identify admirable or redeeming aspects.

What are her weaknesses? This helps identify where she still needs to grow as a person.

What causes her problems? This helps identify common mistakes and flaws.

What are the negative aspects about her personality? This helps identify traits that can get her into trouble.

How does she handle stress? This helps identify how well she'll handle the pressures of the plot.

Views and Opinions

Readers see a story world through a character's eyes. What he sees, they see, what he believes, they believe. These opinions and worldviews form his personality and give him a foundation for his flaws and virtues.

How does he feel about the world around him? This helps identify how he views the world he lives in.

How does he feel about the other characters? This helps identify possible personal conflicts.

How does he feel about the problem at hand? This helps identify how he'll approach resolving the problem.

What doesn't he want to think about? This helps identify what he's trying to avoid.

Does he question the world around him? This helps identify how accepting he is of the status quo.

Does he want to know why, even if the reason is hard to understand or even find? This helps identify how curious he is, and how willing he might be to push for answers.

Does he accept the way things are or what people tell him? This helps identify how trusting he is.

Likes and Dislikes

What a character likes and dislikes makes her feel real to readers and shows her human side.

What makes her happy? This helps identify possible motivations to act.

What makes her sad? This helps identify possible stakes.

What pisses her off? This helps identify ways to cause her to react irrationally.

Ethics and Morality

What a character considers right or wrong changes based on the world he lives in. It's his job as a character to show readers the ethics of the story world.

What are his morals and religious background? This helps identify where his morality might fall, and where his intolerances are.

What does he think is fair? Unfair? This helps identify his sense of justice and what he's willing to accept from others.

Background and Family

Family can have significant influence on who a character is and what she'll do.

Where did she grow up? This helps identify any cultural morals and views.

What was her childhood like? This helps identify how she relates to and interacts with others.

What was the most traumatic thing to ever happen to her? This helps identify deep emotional influences on her behavior.

What was the best thing to ever happen to her? This helps identify positive influences on her, or shed insights into her hopes and dreams.

How did these two events shape her perceptions of the world? This helps identify how she approaches and solves problems.

Who is her family? This helps identify how she handles relationships.

What was her economic background? This helps identify how she values money and wealth, and what importance she places on it.

What was her educational background? This helps identify where her knowledge (or lack thereof) comes from.

What are the key defining moments in her past, both good and bad? This helps identify the events with the most influence on her behavior and decision-making skills.

Friends and Enemies

You can tell a lot about a person by who his friends (and enemies) are. We naturally seek out people with similar views to our own.

Who are his friends? This helps identify different aspects of his personality, and the type of person he is. It also could be a pool of allies to draw from.

Who are his enemies? This helps identify potential antagonists or troublemakers, as well as aspects of his personality he dislikes.

What won't he do to help another character? This helps identify how far he's willing to go, or what lines he won't cross.

What does he like about his friends? Dislike about them? This helps identify his values and what he wants and expects from people. Are they allies or tools?

How large is his circle of friends? This helps identify how likable or outgoing he is.

What types of social situations is he comfortable with? This helps identify how he'll react when faced with the plot's problems.

Is he energized or drained by people? This helps identify how well he works in a group, or if he prefers to work alone.

How are his relationships with other characters? This helps identify potential conflicts, and places for growth.

How easily does he make new friends or allies? This helps identify how hard it is for him to gain allies or help for his problem.

Roles and Obligations

Some characters are created to fill a particular role or show a perspective different from the protagonist's.

What role does she play? This helps identify how she fits thematically and how much she might have to do.

Does she see herself in this role, or does she play it unconsciously? This helps identify how committed to the role she is, or if she's being manipulated.

How do others see her? This helps identify if she's true to herself or changes to suit what others expect of her.

How does she feel about how others see her? This helps identify her level of self confidence.

Characters are both predictable and unpredictable at the same time. Their past can show insights into their behaviors, but their personal quirks and idiosyncrasies mean that they won't always act as expected or be who you expect them to be.

Now that you've worked out what's inside your characters, let's focus a little on the outsides.

If You Want to Adjust the Character Descriptions

There's no rule on how much you need to describe your characters. Some writers will toss out a detail here and there and call it done, while others will give enough details to create an accurate police sketch.

In this session, the goal is to determine the right level of detail, and make sure your character descriptions are serving your story, not bogging it down.

Step One: Make Sure *You* Know What Your Characters Look Like

This might seem like a ridiculous step, but not everyone thinks about what a character looks like on a first draft (I don't, for example). Some writers focus more on figuring out who a character is than what she looks like, and often don't decide on physical details until the second draft.

Look at your character list. For every character who doesn't have the standard police-blotter description (and needs one), go ahead and create it (unless of course, you aren't using physical descriptions in your novel).

This is also a good time to flesh out or create your story bible to keep track of these kinds of details. It's not uncommon to forget what color eyes a secondary character has, or where someone grew up. This is especially useful if you plan to write more than one book with these characters.

Step Two: Add or Strengthen Descriptions When a Character is Introduced

The first time readers meet a character is typically when she's described. For point-of-view characters, these details are often spread out over the scene or chapter. For non-point-of-view characters, it's common to see the details in a quick summary from the point-of-view character in that scene.

The more details you add, the more you'll want to keep it in your point-of-view character's head. Let *her* judge what she's seeing so the details do more than just describe. They'll also characterize and do some world building at the same time.

When fleshing out the descriptions, consider:

What are the obvious physical details about the character? The classic hair, eye, height, etc., details.

What are details that only the point-of-view character would notice? Describe anything that gives you an opportunity to share a little insight into the point-of-view character. What does *she* see and how does she feel about it?

What details suggest or hint at what's unique about that particular character? If the character is a world-class pianist, maybe the point-of-view character notices long, graceful fingers. If he's ex-special forces, then maybe there's a scar or military bearing that stands out.

Readers remember what they see first, so pick the critical details you want associated with the character.

Step Three: Revise Any Clichéd or Stereotypical Descriptions

Clichés and stereotypes are information shorthand, so they slip into first drafts all the time. Go through your scenes and rework any descriptions that rely on clichés or stereotypes.

Some common clichés to look for:

Characters describing themselves in a mirror: Unless you've come up with a unique way to have the character look in a mirror (or any reflective surface) and describe themselves, look for other ways to show the description.

Characters introducing themselves to readers: Another common cliché is to have the character introduce themselves and then say what they look like. "I'm your average gal, five foot four, brown hair, blue eyes," or, "I'm nothing special, six foot, black cropped hair and brown almond eyes."

Characters slipping in a detail: It's not bad to see a detail slipped in casually, but it can read awkwardly depending on the narrative distance. For example, "I brushed my long, blond hair" can sound too self-aware. Who remarks on the length and color of their hair when they brush it?

Overdone physical traits: There's a bit of a joke in young adult fiction that a large percentage of best friends have red hair (and yes, I'm guilty of it, too). Villains are often dark haired with dark eyes, while sweet, innocent characters are blond and pale, and funny sidekicks are brunettes with quirks. It's not a bad idea to look at your descriptions and think about *why* you chose them. Are you inadvertently using a stereotype or cliché?

Characters with stereotypical defining details: Be wary of having one particular detail that defines a character in a stereotypical way. Not all Asians are martial arts experts, not all southerners are slow, and not all Christians are Bible thumpers.

Yes, people *can* be stereotypes in real life, but it's the writer's job to find a fresher, more original way to portray the characters.

Step Four: Trim Any Extraneous Character Description

Not every writer will need to add description—some will have too much and will want to do a little trimming. Trust your instincts on this, and if it feels like too much, cut back a little.

If you're not sure what can go, cut back wherever you use more than three details in a row. If you notice you use multiple details a lot, try reducing them by half and see how it reads. Add more details as needed.

At this stage, you've strengthened who your characters are and what they look like. Next, let's work on what they want out of life (and this novel).

If You Want to Strengthen the Character Arc

At the heart of every character arc is the internal conflict. Your characters feel conflicted, and that emotional struggle is preventing them from getting what they want and being who they want to be. The goal of the character arc is to put them through the grinder so they learn the lessons necessary to become the people they feel like inside. No matter how much or how little the protagonist arcs, the internal conflict will drive her and affect her choices in the novel.

In this session, the goal is to develop any weak internal conflicts to create stronger character arcs.

Step One: Examine the Internal Conflict

The internal conflict is the problem the protagonist is facing on the inside. It's often a personal struggle that deals with the protagonist's belief system—something she values, something she was taught, something she "knows" is true.

What is keeping your protagonist from being happy or feeling satisfied? What's the one thing she needs to feel fulfilled? Unlike the external goals, this goal can be vague or even something the character isn't aware of yet, such as: the need to feel safe, though she doesn't yet know where her unease is coming from.

What's the internal problem your protagonist is facing? This is usually due to personal self-doubt, uncertainty, or a flaw she has to overcome. It often relates to the external plot issue, such as: The protagonist's goal is to move overseas for a new job, but she has a fear of flying.

How is this inner problem forcing your protagonist to make an impossible choice? This can help determine the major character growth points—the moments where the internal forces act on the external in a big way.

How does this inner problem directly oppose the external problems? The inner problem or flaw usually causes the character to make mistakes. For example, if the problem is trusting others, it could result in the protagonist not heeding the advice that will help her at a crucial moment. Letting the inner problem negatively influence the protagonist at key moments can turn weak scenes into strong, high-stakes scenes.

 REVISION RED FLAG: If the protagonist has no internal conflict, that could indicate a lack of stakes or personal motivations for her to act in the novel. There should be pros and cons to every choice she faces, usually driven by this internal issue. If this is weak or missing, consider doing the exercises in If You Want to Flesh Out the Characters on page 70 to determine what drives the character, or try the exercises in Workshop Three: Plot and Structure Work on page 92 to strengthen the backstory, goals, conflicts, stakes, and/or motivations.

Step Two: Determine the Beginning and End of the Character's Arc

Once you're clear on where the internal conflict lies, focus on how you see that character evolving over the course of the novel.

Where does the character end up? A strong arc will show the lessons learned or flaws overcome during the novel. Look for how the character becomes a different person (for better or for worse) by the end of the book. Identify the personal changes, and what caused those changes. Look for the moments in the novel where these changes occur to see where the arc advances.

How much does the character need to suffer to achieve this change? Nobody changes for the fun of it. A good character arc will make the character reevaluate her behavior and realize she needs to make a change or else. If the character is going to evolve in a major way, the events that force that change will be equally major. Look for the moments or triggers that force these changes.

Who or what brings about that change? The character usually exhibits the behavior that needs changing and it turns out badly for her early on in the novel. Eventually, she'll behave the right way and be rewarded. Typically, this takes many small steps in a longer process to make the character take a hard look at herself and her life. Identify the clear path (even if there are setbacks) between the beginning and the end of the novel.

How does the change reflect the premise or theme? Odds are the arc is going to connect to the theme or premise, since character growth is a common vehicle for illustrating theme. Look at what the story is about on a more conceptual level, and if the character arc can help illustrate that idea. Pinpoint where the character arc illustrates the theme.

REVISION RED FLAG: If you have trouble identifying or answering these questions, that could indicate where the weak links in the character arc fall. How and why a character changes are the two most common areas of weakness.

Step Three: Check That the Character Arc is Arcing

Once you've identified all the right arc points, verify that they're unfolding in the right places throughout the novel. Refer back to your character arc map and fill in any missing or weak spots. Some variation is normal, so if the arc is unfolding over the entire novel at a good pace, you don't have to hit every single point exactly as stated. These are guidelines, not rules.

Identify where the protagonist's flaw is established: This is usually seen in the opening scene or first few chapters. If not, look for ways to add an example of the flaw in this area.

Identify where the protagonist makes her first mistake: This usually happens on or around the inciting event, and might even cause the event. If the protagonist makes no mistake, look for ways to add that to this area.

Identify where the attempt to grow fails: The first attempt to change usually doesn't go well, and is often seen around the end of Act One when the plot problems start putting pressure on the protagonist. If there's no growth attempt, or the attempt to grow fails, look for ways to add the attempt or have attempt to grow not turn out as expected. Show the character trying and failing to be a better person.

Identify where the protagonist is blindsided by weakness: It's common for the flaw or weakness to cause unexpected failure, often around the midpoint of the novel. Is there a moment when the character is surprised or caught off guard because of her flaw? If not, look for ways to create something unexpected (good or bad) around the midpoint.

Identify where there's a major screw-up or rejection of growth: This usually triggers the classic Dark Moment of the Soul just before the climax (Act Three) starts, and it's the personal demon the protagonist must face in order to move forward. If you have no moment of despair, look for ways the character's flaw might emotionally destroy her right before she needs to be her strongest.

Identify where the protagonist realizes she's grown: This is the culmination of everything she's learned and experienced over the course of the novel, and the result of the soul searching she did during her dark moment. If there is no realization, look for ways the character arc can influence and aid (or hurt if it's that kind of novel) how the climax unfolds.

🚩 **REVISION RED FLAG:** If you have trouble identifying or answering these questions, that could indicate the arc isn't arcing. Consider returning to your character arc map and adjusting where the arc moments occur in the novel.

Step Four: Overlay the Character Arc With the Plot Arc

The ebb and flow between the external and internal conflicts helps control the pacing and narrative drive of the novel. Examining how the two sides interact can reveal structure or pacing problems.

- A traditional dual-conflict arc has these common turning points:
- Establishing the protagonist's flaw occurs on or around the opening scene
- Protagonist's first mistake occurs on or around the inciting event
- Attempt to grow fails occurs on or around the end of Act One (Act One problem)
- Blindsided by weakness occurs on or around the midpoint reversal
- Major screw-up or rejection of growth occurs on or around the end of Act Two (Act Two disaster, the All is Lost moment, the Dark Night of the Soul)
- Realization of growth occurs on or around the climax

🚩 **REVISION RED FLAG:** If these moments are way off, or the character arc has no bearing on the plot arc, that could indicate the internal conflict isn't working with the external plot arc. Consider focusing on how the two conflicts (internal and external) relate to and affect each other so they work together to bring about the character's change. If they mostly line up and it feels right, it's likely working as intended.

While you don't have to stick to this basic structure, it's a proven way to see how the inner conflict and character growth can aid with plotting and increase the tension and conflict for the entire story. Adjust as needed, but if you want a little extra guidance, this format will give you a solid structure to work with.

You should now have strong, well-developed characters with solid character arcs, so let's take a moment to see how they became that way.

If You Want to Balance the Backstory

Everybody has a backstory. In fiction though, that past isn't always relevant, even if it *is* interesting. Readers like to see a story moving, and stopping to explain a character's history tends to bog down the narrative. Too much backstory is high on the list of why agents reject a manuscript, and many advise to cut all backstory from the first fifty pages. This is why it's critical to find the right backstory balance.

In this session, the goal is to eliminate any unnecessary backstory and find the right balance for your novel.

If you made notes in your editorial or character arc maps on scenes with too much backstory (or not enough), start with those.

Step One: Eliminate Unnecessary Backstory

Once you've identified any unnecessary backstory for a scene, you have three choices—cut it, move it to where it *is* relevant, or make it relevant in that scene. Your character arc map can show the most relevant aspects of the character's personality, and guide you in gauging the backstory needed.

If you're unsure if the backstory is unnecessary, consider:

How does it affect the scene's goal? Backstory that affects motivation seems natural because it has a place in the story. If the backstory has no bearing on what the protagonist is trying to do in that scene, either directly or by affecting a decision made in that scene, then it's probably not needed.

Were any of the scene's characters involved in the backstory? If the backstory changes the way readers (or even characters) see the scene, it might be worth keeping. Unless of course, that change steals tension or reveals a secret better left a mystery.

How does the point-of-view character feel about the backstory? People think about the past when it has relevance to the present. If the point-of-view character doesn't care, or isn't affected by the backstory, there's no need to reveal it.

Step Two: Revise Backstory to Show, Not Tell

Take a look at the remaining backstory and ask: Is it showing or telling the information? Backstory is a common place for told prose to sneak in as you explain the history and why it matters to the character at that time.

REVISION RED FLAG: Look for common telling words, such as "in order to" or "because" or "which" or "once" to help spot backstory. If you're stopping the story to explain something, it's telling, not showing.

Revision Option: Ways to Hide the Backstory

If you have backstory that needs to be there, try slipping it into the text in small bites, or disguise it as something else.

Background the backstory: Hiding the backstory in plain sight is a handy trick to get the information into the story without stopping the story to explain it. For example, if you wanted to tell readers about the terrible past of your protagonist, and that she spent nine years in an underground prison, consider how might she might behave *because of* that experience. Is she extra sensitive to the light? Claustrophobic? Skilled at getting around when she can't see well? By putting your backstory in the background (backgrounding), you can flesh out your characters and show their history without stopping the story to explain it. Better still, you'll leave enough tantalizing hints that readers eventually *want* to know the whole story.

Drop teasing hints: Instead of revealing all of a character's past, try dropping hints here and there to tease readers into *wanting* to know the history. Look for places to toss in a casual comment or exhibit an interesting skill that's never explained. After a while, readers will be so intrigued they'll have no problem with the story pausing while this history is explained in more depth.

🚩 **REVISION RED FLAG:** Be wary of being *too* vague with hints and clues. Find the right balance between a tease and being too cryptic to be understood, which can turn readers off and confuse them. Make readers think, "Oooh, what's *that* all about?" not "What the heck are they talking about?"

Revision Option: If You Need More Backstory, Not Less

There *are* rare instances when a novel needs *more* backstory, so if analyzing your backstory reveals certain scenes require additional information to be fully understood, go ahead and flesh out those details. Just make sure what's being added is truly necessary.

Red flags that a scene needs more backstory include:

Readers are having a hard time understanding the importance of the scene: If your beta readers or critique partners aren't catching the significance of a scene, or don't know why something matters, you might need a little backstory to explain the motives or significance.

The critical information has never been discussed or shown: While most of a character's past can be shown in how she interacts with the world, sometimes the only way to convey that information is by telling the backstory of that character.

The backstory is complicated: In genre novels with a lot of world building, it's more common to see an above-average amount of backstory. It's much harder to glean clues from how a character acts when the world isn't a world readers are familiar with.

Backstory isn't just explaining the characters' history; it's showing the experiences that shaped their lives and made them act the way they do.

You want to mention what's *driving* characters to act, not just events that happened in their pasts. Pick what's important both to the character and to the story itself.

After doing all this character work, the final step is to connect it all and give it greater meaning through your theme.

If You Want to Develop the Theme

If plot is a novel's skeleton, and characters are the muscle, then theme is its soul. It's what the book is *about*, and without it, a story can feel shallow at best, pointless at worst. Themes keep readers thinking about your novel long after they've put it down.

In this session, the goal is to look at your themes and see how they can guide you to a stronger story.

Step One: Strengthen the Theme(s)

Go through your editorial map and look for examples that reflect your theme.

Are there any weak scenes that could be improved by adding a thematic layer? Look for any decision-making scenes, scenes where the characters face a consequence for their actions, or scenes involving a moral or ethical dilemma.

Do thematic scenes coincide with major plot points and character growth moments? Not every turning point needs to reflect the theme, but if none do, that's a red flag the theme doesn't truly affect the story.

Are any of the scenes a stretch to fit the theme? If so, clarify how and why that scene reflects the theme.

Step Two: Eliminate Competing or Conflicting Themes

For every story that has no theme, you'll find one with too many themes. While you can have more than one theme (story themes plus character themes), if you find yourself with a long list of what the novel is about thematically, it's probably trying to do too much and not giving any one concept the attention it deserves.

A general rule of thumb: aim for no more than one theme for the story itself, and one theme per major character. If those character themes can fall under the story theme, so much the better. For example, if the story theme is "justice," then character themes might be, "Where's the line between justice and revenge?" or, "How far will you go for a loved one?"

Also be on the lookout for any themes that conflict. If the story theme is, "Love conquers all" and the protagonist's personal theme is, "You can't fight city hall," that could pose problems identifying what the story is about. Should they fight or not?

Step Three: Use Your Theme to Guide Your Revision

Theme can help you decide what details you want to use, and what ideas you want to show. For example, if you're fleshing out your setting, you can use details that show the world and also convey the theme. If the protagonist is looking for justice, you might show examples of the injustice of that world and why this is a noble pursuit. Or you might show examples of other people finding justice to illustrate why the protagonist needs it so badly. If love is the theme, there might be red roses, or hearts, or other details that suggest love scattered about.

Revision Option: Adding a Theme

If you don't have a theme and would like to add one, start by examining what you already have in the novel. There's a good chance you have a theme lurking in there that needs drawing out. Ask yourself:

What larger concepts did you explore with your novel? Theme is often found in the conceptual level of your story.

If you had to pick one cliché or adage to describe your novel, what would it be? Clichés capture a thematic concept and show a larger idea with just a few words.

What are common problems in your novel? Do they point to a theme? Look at the various issues your characters are facing. The types of problems they face often point to a common theme.

What are common character flaws or dreams? Themes are frequently found in what the protagonist wants or dreams about, or even what she wishes she could overcome.

Themes can connect every aspect of your novel and tie the characters and the plot together. Now that the first half (your characters) is strong, let's move on to developing your plot.

Workshop Three: Plot and Structure Work

The Goal of This Workshop: To strengthen and clarify your plot, story structure, and narrative drive.

What We'll Discuss in This Workshop: Ways to analyze your plot, story structure, and narrative drive, and ways to fix any issues found during the analysis.

Welcome to Workshop Three: Plot and Structure Work

Stories are about interesting people, solving interesting problems, in interesting ways. Workshop Two covered the interesting people, so now let's look at the interesting problems and the ways your characters solve those problems.

Plot and structure work together to create the foundation for your story to flourish, giving it the support and guidance it needs. It's also where a lot of common first-draft problems surface, because a good plot requires you to think on your feet, be original, and constantly surprise your readers.

Your plot illustrates your story to your readers and lets your characters act. The plot is how they interact with each other and how they resolve the problems thrown at them in the novel.

The novel's structure provides the framework for the plot to unfold, while the individual scenes make up the plot, and the narrative drive ensures every piece flows smoothly (and compellingly) from one to the next.

Outliners (those who prefer to outline a story and know the details before they start writing) and plot-focused writers will likely be stronger in this area, while pantsers (those who prefer to dive in without knowing or planning their story) and character-focused writers will probably need to do more work here.

A good plot is like a well-crafted puzzle. Each piece is vital to the bigger picture, connecting to each other to tell the larger tale. Too many pieces are too hard to keep track of, too few create too simple a puzzle.

Analyze the Story Structure

No matter what structure you use, the general storytelling format remains the same. A protagonist discovers a problem, decides to solve that problem, has a hard time doing so, but eventually overcomes the obstacles and faces the antagonist in the end to resolve the problem. Key turning points exist in these moments, and this framework from beginning to end provides the structure for the novel. How you choose to develop that structure and story is up to you.

In this session, the goal is to examine your basic story structure for any missing or out of place turning points that might throw off the flow of the novel.

In the next sessions, we'll look at your plot and subplots, scene structure, narrative drive, tension, hooks.

A note about structure: As you go through these questions, keep in mind that the terms used are meant in a general, conceptual way. For example, the "final battle" doesn't have to be an actual battle, or even a fight; it's the final moment when the two conflicting sides (protagonist vs. antagonist) resolve the conflict.

Determine if the Story Structure is Working

What makes story structure so valuable is that it provides solid, proven turning points that can help you decide what events need to happen when to get the most out of your stories. It also helps you find holes in the plot, and places where the stakes might need to be raised.

Grab your editorial map and look at the novel as a whole. Ask:

▶ **Are all the pieces in the right places?** Key turning points in the plot keep the story moving forward. Put the right piece in the wrong turning point, and the novel can drag, or feel rushed if events happen too early.

▶ **Does the opening scene present an intriguing problem or mystery to draw readers in?** The goal of the opening scene is to pique readers' interest and make them want to read on. Is there something interesting happening on page one that makes you want to read page two?

▶ **Is there an inciting event within the first thirty pages (or fifty pages for longer manuscripts) that puts the protagonist on the path to the rest of the novel?** In every story there's a moment early on that changes the protagonist's life forever by putting her on the plot path—if it hadn't happened, the plot wouldn't unfold as it does and the story wouldn't have happened.

▶ **Is there a moment in the beginning where the protagonist makes the *choice* to pursue the story problem?** Near the end of the beginning (around the 25 percent mark in a traditional Three Act Structure), the protagonist has the option of saying "no" and not pursuing the core conflict goal, but makes a choice to move ahead with the plot and venture into the unknown.

▶ **Do the stakes escalate at this time?** Good story structure provides opportunities for the stakes to escalate at major turning points of the plot.

▶ **Does something happen in the middle of the book that changes how the story problem is viewed or approached?** The middle of the book often gets harder for the protagonist and plans start to fall apart—whether she realizes it or not. Or truths might be revealed which change how the entire story thus far has been viewed or understood.

▶ **Are the stakes raised again around this time?** Stakes typically become more personal and the risks get higher at the midpoint, and the protagonist is now more invested in resolving the problem.

▶ **Is there a dark moment or setback right before the ending starts that raises the stakes again?** As obstacles get tougher for the protagonist, it becomes uncertain if she can win. Shortly before the ending (around the 75 percent mark in the Three Act Structure) everything is (or has been) stripped away, and the protagonist loses all hope and doesn't see a way out of the problem.

▶ **Are the stakes raised yet again?** Often, this is when the highest, most personal stakes come into play—an all or nothing, do or die consequence.

▶ **Does the protagonist make the decision to continue the fight despite the risks or sacrifices?** This is a critical moment that triggers the climax, sending the protagonist to face off against the antagonist to resolve the novel's core conflict.

▶ **Is there a clear win for the protagonist at the climax? Something that must be done in order to succeed?** The final battle uses everything the protagonist has learned so far, and what must be done to win is clear (though *how* is often still a mystery).

▶ **Does the ending resolve itself in a way that satisfies the story questions posed in the beginning of the novel?** Not every loose end needs to be tied up, but the core conflict and the major plot threads should be answered to reader satisfaction.

▶ **Is the ending satisfying?** A satisfying ending equates to a satisfying novel, since it's the last thing readers see. It's the ending readers have been waiting for, and it gives them what they wanted—though not always in the way they expect.

REVISION RED FLAG: If you're missing any of these points, that could indicate the structure is off or out of alignment, and a critical plot moment is still needed.

Problems Found?

If you think your story structure needs adjusting, try the exercises in If You Want to Adjust Your Story Structure on page 107.

Analyze the Plot and Subplots

Every scene in your novel should move the story forward, building on the individual goals to resolve a conflict, which in turn forms a cohesive story. Plot isn't a series of dramatized moments from someone's life, but characters making choices and acting in ways that affect them and others.

In this session, the goal is to analyze the plot and subplots to make sure they're advancing the story through solid goals, clear motivations, strong conflicts, and high stakes.

In the next sessions, you'll look at your scene structure, narrative drive, tension, and hooks.

Step One: Determine if the Plot is Working

With so many moving parts, plotting can be a tough element to analyze, especially when every plot is different. Trust your writer's instinct and let it guide you during your analysis.

▶ **Does the plot make sense?** Confusion is never good in a story, and it's one of the harder aspects to check in your own writing—you *know* what it all means. If you *didn't* know how these events all interconnected, would it make sense? Do you need to explain anything for others to understand it?

▶ **Is there a clear core conflict driving the plot?** It should be clear by the end of the beginning (Act One if you use the Three Act Structure) what the main problem of the novel is, even if some details are still a mystery.

▶ **Are the characters' actions believable?** A quick way to lose readers is to have characters behave in ways that strain credibility. Check if your plots feel unrealistic, contrived, or coincidental. Make sure it makes sense for the characters to be doing whatever they need to do in the novel.

▶ **Was the plot predictable?** No matter how well-written a novel, predictability will hurt it. If readers can see what's coming long before it happens, there's no reason to keep reading. Do events turn out exactly how anyone would expect them to? Are there enough twists and turns to keep readers guessing?

▶ **How often does the protagonist have to make a choice?** Choices drive a plot. If the protagonist isn't making a lot of decisions and is just going along with whatever happens, that indicates a reactive protagonist and a plot with no goals, conflicts, or stakes.

▶ **Are those choices difficult?** Easy choices aren't real choices and indicate a lack of true conflict in a scene. There should be consequences, both good *and* bad, with every choice the protagonist has to make. The bigger the turning point, the higher the cost, and the tougher the decision.

▶ **Does the protagonist have approaches different from the other characters' toward solving problems or looking at situations?** Different opinions about how to resolve the story's conflict make for more unpredictable plots. If everyone always agrees with the protagonist on how to proceed, that could indicate a predictable plot.

▶ **Are any leaps in logic or the decision-making process plausible?** Look for places where characters suddenly figure out an important clue or plot point without solid groundwork to back it up. It's not uncommon in a first draft for characters to "magically" know the answer to a problem even though they didn't earn it.

▶ **Do coincidences work to aid the protagonist instead of hindering her?** If so, that could indicate a lack of real conflict and no struggle to complete goals.

▶ **Are the protagonist's motivations plausible?** There should be reasons the protagonist is willing to risk something to resolve this problem. Look for any spots where the protagonist is acting only because the plot said so.

▶ **Is someone or something opposing the protagonist?** A weak antagonist often leads to weak plots, because there's no worthy foe trying to stop the protagonist.

▶ **Does the antagonist have a plan, or does he cause random trouble when the plot needs it?** If the plot feels a little random or coincidental, look at what the antagonist's plan is. If the actions aren't the result of *his* pursuit of *his* goal, he might be tossing pointless obstacles in the protagonist's way.

▶ **Is the antagonist trying to win, or does he sometimes act stupidly so the protagonist can win?** Look for any spots where the plot events hinge on the antagonist making a stupid mistake or acting like an idiot. The tougher—and smarter—your antagonist, the better the plot will be, because the protagonist's victories will be earned.

▶ **Do the choices create conflict between the protagonist's internal and external goals?** Strong plots put the protagonist's external goal at odds with the internal goal, creating difficult or impossible choices.

▶ **Is the protagonist asked or forced to do something that goes against her beliefs?** If beliefs are never tested or strained, that could indicate a weak character arc and a protagonist who doesn't grow or change.

▶ **Are there strong stakes?** Even when the protagonist has goals, without consequences for failure, they can seem flat and uninteresting. Check for consequences if the protagonist fails to get what she wants. Make sure what she wants matters, and not achieving that goal has serious repercussions.

▶ **Do the stakes escalate as the novel unfolds?** Problems should get worse and worse for the protagonist as she struggles to complete her goals. Look for places where the stakes never change, such as every scene having the same risk ("the protagonist's life is at risk" is a common non-escalating stakes issue). In essence, it's the classic "how can you make things worse?" question.

▶ **Will the protagonist's life change if she fails to achieve her goal?** Even if the change is small, every scene should affect the protagonist. If not, the scene can feel pointless and unnecessary.

▶ **Do the stakes affect the protagonist personally?** Sometimes the stakes seem high (such as the lives of thousands of people), but since they don't affect the *protagonist*, readers don't care.

▶ **Is it impossible for the protagonist to walk away from this problem?** If she can, that indicates the stakes aren't personal enough. Consider raising the stakes and making the consequences for failing harsher.

▶ **Are the stakes clear from the beginning of the novel?** Sometimes the stakes aren't obvious and the reasons behind a character's actions don't make sense. Look for places where your characters can discuss or consider the risks—even if you never plan to have them happen. It's the fear of what *could* happen that helps raise the stakes.

▶ **Are the stakes big enough to be worth the reader's time?** Someone can write the best book ever on a man choosing which sushi restaurant to dine at for lunch, but unless readers care about the consequence of that choice, they won't care about the character or the novel. Just having stakes isn't enough if the stakes are minor or inconsequential.

Problems Found?

If you find any plotting issues, spend some time doing the exercises in If You Want to Deepen the Plot on page 151.

Step Two: Determine if the Subplots Are Working

Subplots work with your plots to layer in complexity and emotional growth, shedding more light on different aspects of the characters, and showing deeper meaning to the plot events.

▶ **What's your goal (as the author) for the subplot?** If you're devoting time to this subplot, what do *you* want it to do? How will it enhance the novel?

▶ **Are the subplots contributing to the core conflict or character arc?** The role of a good subplot is to add layers and emotional depth to the story, often on a more personal level than the main plot. For example, a romance subplot is quite common, even in non-romance genres. Look for any subplots that feel extraneous to the core conflict and do nothing to enhance the story in any meaningful way.

▶ **Will this subplot make the story better, or just longer?** If all it does is delay the time it takes for the protagonist to complete her goal, it might not be a worthy subplot. It should affect something in the story, plot, or character arc, otherwise it's just "stuff" the protagonist has to slog through to get anywhere.

▶ **If you took the subplot out, what's lost?** Consider how the story would unfold without this subplot. What would be lost? What might be gained? Would it change the way readers see the story? Would it change the way the characters see the problem? If the protagonist or another major character won't be changed by *not* going through this experience, you probably don't need it.

▶ **Does it explore a new problem (and likely raise the stakes) or repeat a similar scene or idea you've already done?** At the resolution of this subplot, will the protagonist be worse off than she was before, either internally or externally? Be wary if this subplot only shows yet *another* way the protagonist's life is threatened, or has the same stakes you've already established.

▶ **Does it require more attention (and words) than the main plot?** Often you start to question a subplot because it feels as if it's hijacking the story. If you're spending more time on it than on the core conflict, that's a red flag you might have the wrong main plot, or this subplot is too strong for this story.

▶ **Is your protagonist trying to do too much in too many subplots?** Having too many subplots can make it hard to know what the story is about. What does the protagonist learn or gain from solving this mini-problem (this might relate to the inner conflict or character arc), and how does it help solve (or make it harder to solve) the core conflict? If it doesn't do either, cut it.

▶ **Is the subplot compelling enough that readers won't mind the delay in getting back to the main goal, or will they think you're dragging your feet to keep making the problem worse?** If readers don't care about this subplot, they'll get bored and start skimming, wondering when you'll get back to the real story. Make any side stories just as intriguing as the main plotline, and offer compelling story questions to keep readers invested in the novel.

Problems Found?

If you find any subplot issues, spend some time doing the exercises in If You Want to Deepen the Plot: Developing the Subplots on page 173.

Analyze the Scenes

Scenes are the relay racers of plot. Not only do they need to have their own goals, conflicts, and stakes, they need to build off a previous scene and hand off the story to the *next* scene. When they stumble, the entire plot can stumble.

In this session, the goal is to examine the individual scenes to make sure each one is contributing to the story as a whole.

In the next sessions, you'll see if the narrative drive is moving the story, and examine the level of tension and hooks.

Determine if the Scenes Are Working

Begin by looking at your editorial map. Start with scene one and go scene by scene to the end of the novel, pinpointing the plot-driving aspects of the scene. If plotting is a weak area for you, write these down. Being specific will make it clear when something is missing from a scene.

If the scenes are structurally sound, you should clearly see how they move the plot forward. Some scenes will take small steps, others will make giant leaps. Ask:

▶ **How does this scene serve the story?** Something in the scene should cause a change somewhere. Otherwise, the scene can feel pointless. Make sure each scene affects plot and story movement or reveals new information.

▶ **How does this scene serve the protagonist's character arc?** Not every scene will affect the growth of the protagonist, but be wary if you see few scenes affecting the character arc.

▶ **How does this scene serve the *other* characters' arcs?** It's not all about the protagonist. Sometimes the best way to serve the story is to let another character illustrate one part of it through actions, choices, or options. Even what the antagonist is doing can force your protagonist to consider different options that reflect your story.

▶ **Where does this scene take place?** The setting should be clear and benefit the scene somehow.

▶ **What is the point-of-view character trying to do?** The goal should be clear and the bulk of the scene should revolve around trying to achieve that goal.

▶ **What goes wrong? What's the problem or challenge?** The conflict should be clear, with enough obstacles or challenges to make the struggle to achieve it worthwhile, as well as uncertain.

▶ **Why is this important and how does it potentially hurt the point-of-view character?** The stakes should be clear and of high enough consequence to cause reader concern if the character fails.

▶ **Who else is in the scene?** Make sure readers know who's in the scene early on so the "sudden" appearance of a character doesn't throw them out of the story. This doesn't apply if the whole point was to shock them.

▶ **What happens right before this scene?** The previous scene should lead to this scene (opening scenes are exempt, of course). In multiple-point-of-view novels, the previous scene in that point of view is the most likely lead in.

▶ **What does the point-of-view character do next?** The scene should suggest where the plot needs to go and give the protagonist a new goal or task if the current goal is not met.

▶ **If you took any scenes out, would the plot change?** If nothing about the plot would change if a scene is cut, that indicates you don't need that scene, or it needs a reason to be there.

⚑ **REVISION RED FLAG:** Pay attention to scenes that feel aimless or slow, especially any scenes you wanted to skim (or did skim) while re-reading the manuscript. Wanting to skim a scene is an indication that it's uninteresting and not worth re-reading. It's also common to skim a scene because it feels "fine" and needs no work, but upon a later re-read, you discover it does have issues or doesn't need to be there. Also take a closer look at any scenes you think *need* to be there, even though your instincts say it's not the most interesting scene. There's a good chance there's necessary information there, and if you move it, that scene can go.

Problems Found?

If you find any scene issues, spend some time doing the exercises in If You Want to Develop the Scenes on page 184.

Analyze the Narrative Drive

Narrative drive is the force that moves the story from beginning to end. It makes the plot seem as though it's going somewhere and isn't a bunch of scenes wandering aimlessly looking for a point. A weak narrative drive leads to a story that rambles and a plot that encourages skimming.

In this session, the goal is to analyze the narrative drive to see if the story is advancing in a compelling way.

Your editorial map can be a good first step here and help you pinpoint larger trouble spots, but you should also do a scene-by-scene analysis.

Determine if the Narrative Drive is Working

Look at your novel and focus on the reasons readers will want to keep reading. Find the elements pulling them through the plot and keeping them hooked in the story. Ask:

▶ **Are the character and story goals clear so there's narrative drive in the story?** Plots are all about characters acting to achieve goals, and their actions should move the story forward. Even if the details are still a mystery, there should be a sense of a story unfolding toward a resolution.

▶ **Is the protagonist doing something in every scene?** A plot that moves forward has the protagonist trying to accomplish tasks, even if she fails.

▶ **Is there a story point (author's perspective) to every scene?** What are *your* reasons for a scene to be there? Look for the important elements that you wanted to show as the author.

▶ **Is there a story question (reader's perspective) in every scene?** Questions keep the story moving. Look for the puzzles readers will wonder about and want answers to.

▶ **Are these points and questions clear from the start of the scene?** Good narrative drive makes it clear where the story is going, even if the details are still unknown. Readers can see the plot is progressing, and there are still plenty of puzzles to solve.

▶ **Is the protagonist moving toward something?** If there's a lot of "stuff happening" *to* your protagonist, and not a lot of her *doing* anything, it could signal a reactive plot brewing. It might be a good idea to do a goal check and see what's driving the protagonist to act.

▶ **Do the scenes and chapters build on one another or are events happening one after another?** Scenes should affect other scenes or the story can feel episodic. Is the plot a cohesive story or a series of scenes stuck together? Does it have a point?

▶ **Where is the critical information revealed?** Information will be spoon fed to readers the entire book, but you'll usually find a handful of shocking plot twists, surprises, or big reveals in every novel. Where do your surprises and twists fall? Do any fall too close to another major plot point or character arc moment? If they're clumped together, perhaps space them out more to keep the tension high.

▶ **Is the protagonist feeling too much?** If your scenes focus more on emotions and not so much on action, you might be short on external goals. Look at the goals and make sure there's enough for the protagonist to do to keep the plot moving.

▶ **Is the protagonist debating too much?** If you have a lot of sections where the protagonist is figuring out information or debating what to do next, this could indicate not enough plot events. You might look for ways to get the protagonist moving and trying to accomplish tasks, *while* struggling with inner turmoil or figuring out a puzzle.

REVISION RED FLAG: Scenes that lack narrative drive often illustrate an aspect of the story or world, more like extended infodumps than plot-driving events. If you find the same basic goal, that could indicate nothing new is happening and the story might feel repetitive.

Problems Found?

If you find any issues with the narrative drive, spend some time doing the exercises in If You Want to Strengthen the Narrative Drive on page 192.

Analyze the Tension and Hooks

When a scene feels like nothing is happening even when you *know* things are, the most likely culprit is a lack of tension. The scene is predictable and readers can guess how it's going to turn out, even if they don't know the details. Adding hooks and increasing the tension will create a sense that something is about to happen, whether that's a plot turning point, a secret revealed, or an answer readers have been waiting for.

In this session, the goal is to examine your hooks and make sure there's enough tension to keep readers in the story.

Determine if the Hooks and Tension Are Working

Grab your editorial map or manuscript and look at how your scenes and chapters start and end. Identify the hooks meant to draw readers in, and the elements that will keep them reading. Ask:

▶ **Is there a sense of something about to happen in every scene?** There should be a sense of anticipation about something no matter what is going on. Look for places where you frequently skim or read quickly, as these are often where the slow, tension-weak areas lie.

▶ **Are there unanswered questions in every scene?** If you marked these on your editorial map, it should be easy to see what you have and where they fall. If not, look for places where you posed questions that still need to be answered.

▶ **Is there tension on every page?** Though time consuming to do, it's a good idea to go through the novel and make sure there's a sense of something being held back, something about to happen, or a potential problem brewing on every page.

▶ **Is there tension between characters?** There should be differences of opinion and problem-solving approaches. Look for tension-weak places where characters all agree.

▶ **Is there tension in the setting?** Inherent conflicts in the setting can create tension in a scene. Look for places where the setting isn't doing anything besides giving the scene a place to happen.

▶ **Are there moments when the protagonist is relaxed?** A relaxed protagonist is a big indication there's no tension in that scene.

▶ **Are there big reveals and discoveries throughout the novel?** Aim for a new discovery or reveal every chapter. It doesn't have to be huge, just something new. Also look for a solid arc between big moments that raise tension for the entire novel.

▶ **How many reveals are plot-related?** This can indicate pacing issues, as things are (or are not) happening to move the story along. Few plot reveals or discoveries suggest too many similar scenes or a novel that's episodic in nature.

▶ **How many reveals are character-related?** This indicates how the character growth arc or internal conflict is moving along. If the protagonist isn't learning or revealing new details about herself, she might not be growing. Few character reveals suggests nothing is changing about that character and she's not trying or learning new things.

▶ **How many reveals are backstory or world-building related?** If you have a lot here (or the balance is way off in favor of this), it's a red flag that your protagonist might not be driving the story. The focus is on telling the history of a place or person, not on what the characters are doing. Some backstory reveals are fine since readers will want to know that history if it bears on the plot or a character arc, but if a lot of the reveals or discoveries are "cool" aspects of the world or situation, it could mean you have a premise novel on your hands.

🚩 **REVISION RED FLAG:** Too many reveals at the start of the book often indicate too much backstory or exposition. Heavy reveals at the end could indicate a lack of discovery during the story, or that you're holding out on readers and not giving them enough reveals to keep them interested.

If You Want to Adjust the Story Structure

Stories have a beginning, a middle, and an ending—three points that frame a novel and offer a compelling tale to your readers. What you put into that frame can (and does) vary wildly, and you're not beholden to any one structure or format. Even if you love a particular structure, you have the freedom to vary it and adjust it to suit whatever story you're telling at the time.

In this session, the goal is to adjust any out-of-alignment structures, and make sure the story is unfolding in the strongest possible way.

You'll also explore common problems with beginnings, middles, and endings, and how to fix them.

Step One: Create a Structure Outline Template Using Your Preferred Outline

It's a good idea to get a sense of how the structure is working over-all and where the major turning points lie. Using your editorial map and your preferred structure format, write what happens at each of the major turning points of your novel (plotters and outliners will likely already have this in their files). These moments are typically external moments, with the protagonist acting to move the plot forward. Aim for at least a sentence or two that summarizes what happens.

REVISION RED FLAG: If you have a lot of "is told information" or "bad things happen *to* the protagonist" moments, that could indicate a reactive protagonist who's not driving the plot.

Don't Have a Structure Style?

If you don't have a preferred structure style, try using the classic Three Act Structure to start. It allows for plenty of flexibility while still providing a solid framework on which to hang your plot. The Three Act Structure uses the following major turning points:

Act One: The Beginning (The first 25 percent of the novel)

Opening Scene: How the protagonist and world are introduced.

Inciting Event: When the protagonist is first pulled onto the plot path (typically occurs within the first 10 percent of the novel—somewhere in the first thirty or fifty pages for longer novels).

Act One Problem: When the protagonist first realizes there's a problem and must make a choice to move forward (typically occurs on or around the 25 percent mark of the novel).

Act Two: The Middle (The middle 50 percent of the novel)

Act Two Choice: When the protagonist makes a choice and decides to act (typically occurs right after the 25 percent mark of the novel).

Midpoint Reversal: When the situation unexpectedly changes (typically occurs at or around the 50 percent mark of the novel).

Act Two Disaster: When the worst happens and the protagonist wants to give up (typically occurs at or around the 75 percent mark of the novel).

Act Three: The Ending (The last 25 percent of the novel)

Act Three Plan: When the protagonist decides to risk it all to fix the problem (typically occurs just after the 75 percent mark of the novel).

Climax: When the protagonist faces the antagonist and resolves the problem (typically occurs at or around the 90 percent mark of the novel).

Wrap Up: Where the protagonist goes from here (final scene of the novel).

Step Two: Move Scenes and Turning Points as Needed

Major plot turning points don't have to fit a template exactly, but structure is a proven way to craft stories for readers. It covers the natural rise and fall of stakes, pursuit of goals readers have come to expect from a novel.

Major plot events that fall way outside the general structure format usually indicate problems with the overall structure of the novel.

Be concerned if:

A turning point falls more than 20 percent outside the general range: This can indicate a pacing issue, or too much information in the story (infodumps, backstory, subplots, exposition, etc.). Variances of 10 percent are normal, but the farther it goes beyond that the more likely there's a problem.

A turning point is missing altogether: This can indicate a narrative drive or plotting problem. For example, if there's no Act One problem, then what transitions the protagonist from the beginning to the middle? Chances are the middle is bogging down or wandering because there's no clear goal driving it.

A turning point occurs in a different section: This can indicate a plot that's out of whack, with pacing and stakes issues, and likely a narrative drive issue. For example, if a typically high-stakes turning point occurs too early, the novel can peak long before tensions have time to build, leading to an anticlimactic ending.

Multiple turning points occur close together: This can indicate there's not enough plot to flesh out the entire novel, or it might have a pacing issue. Turning points work because they support the plot and story and allow for waves of tension and reveals to build over the course of the novel.

As you work through your structure, you might also discover a chapter, scene, or elements of a scene that fit better elsewhere. Reorganize the manuscript so it unfolds in the strongest way possible.

Structure holds a novel together and takes some of the guesswork out of revisions. If the structure is out of alignment, it throws off the entire story, but once you get it adjusted, what you need to do to strengthen your stories is much more clear.

Step Three: Fix Problems With the Beginning

Beginnings contain a lot of setup and introduction, so it's not uncommon for them to start off wrong, or take too much time to get going.

If a beginning isn't working, it's usually due to not grabbing readers' interest, either by lack of a compelling problem, nothing happening to draw readers in, or taking too long to get to the story. For more in-depth discussions on these issues, see Fixing Common Problems With the Beginning on page 116.

Common beginning problems include:

Starting in the wrong place: If you're worried the novel is starting too soon, look for scenes where the protagonist is going through a lot of normal day routines without a goal, conflict, or problem. In too-late beginnings, look for a lot of action and characters in dire straits without a clear reason, sense of who they are, or context for what's going on.

Too much (or not enough) setup: Too much setup results in slow beginnings full of infodumps, backstory, and too much setting the scene to "get readers ready" for the story to start. Not enough setup leads to confusing beginnings that lack enough information and ramp up for readers to understand what's happening and why it matters.

Lack of story questions: Beginnings that aren't grabbing readers often lack hooks or narrative drive. Things may be happening, but nothing makes readers care enough to wonder how it turns out.

An unclear or reactive protagonist: Confusing or slow-to-start beginnings can be the result of an unclear or reactive protagonist. Look for multiple points of view with characters all acting, but no one person, or one problem, is standing out as the main problem of the novel. Since it's not clear what the point is, or who has the problem, readers can't tell what they're reading or who they're reading about. And since no one is actively doing anything, no hero emerges.

⚑ **REVISION RED FLAG:** If your beginning doesn't "end" until the middle of the novel (from a page count perspective), that's a good indication that there's too much unrelated information in the front of the novel. Maybe there's excess backstory, or scenes that don't move the plot, or even too many of the same kinds of scenes that aren't serving the story. Conversely, if your beginning ends right away, that could indicate there's not enough setup and the story is starting too fast.

To fix a beginning, you sometimes need to look at (and write) the ending. Once you see how the story ends up, it's clearer where and how it needs to start.

Step Four: Fix Problems With the Middle

Most of the plot happens in the middle as the protagonist tries and fails to resolve the story problem, while the antagonist makes those tasks harder and harder. For more in-depth discussions on these issues, see Fixing Common Problems With the Middle on page 128.

Common middle problems include:

Boggy middle syndrome: Since the middle is half the novel, it's common for plots to drag and wander without direction. There aren't enough goals to drive the plot to the climax. A boggy middle is often solved by adding a major turning point in the middle of the book (the midpoint reversal). Boggy middle syndrome creates most of the problems found in middles.

Repetitive scenes: Too many similar scenes can bloat a boggy middle as you try to fill up all that space—such as, multiple chase scenes, several attempts to solve the same problem, repeated interactions between characters, and way too many conversations around a kitchen table. Repetitive scenes can indicate a middle that's light on plot, or one that needs to vary how the protagonist accomplishes the goals so the scenes are different.

If your middle is suffering from this problem, consider doing the exercises in If You Want to Develop the Scenes: Revision Option: Making Similar Scenes Feel Different on page 190.

Unnecessary subplots: Subplots often bloom as you flesh out a middle by sending the characters running around, killing time. It might add words, but it's not adding any value. For more on fixing subplots, do the exercises in If You Want to Deepen the Plot: Developing the Subplots on page 173.

No payoffs: In an effort to pile on the problems, sometimes you forget to reward both the characters and the readers for sticking with the plot. Constant failure can make a plot feel as if it's not getting anywhere, but a few victories (even if they're small), can make the plot feel like it's moving toward the end.

No surprises: You set up the beginning, you know the ending, and the middle is all about getting there. But it unfolds exactly as readers expect without any surprises, twists, or discoveries, so readers start skimming to find out how the story ends. Add in a little unpredictability and make readers want to stick around.

Dumping on readers: Now that readers are hooked, you dump all the backstory you held back from the beginning into the middle. You explain, you flashback, you infodump—and the pace slows to a crawl. If you think your middle is dumping a lot, consider doing the exercises in Workshop Five: Description Work: If You Want to Eliminate Unnecessary Infodumps on page 237.

Stagnant stakes: Bad things happen all through the middle, but the stakes never escalate. The protagonist faces exactly the same danger by the end of the middle as she did when she started it. If you're concerned the stakes in your middle aren't escalating, consider doing the exercises in If You Wanted to Deepen the Plot: Developing Conflicts and Stakes on page 160.

No character arc movement: The protagonist solves problem after problem, but nothing is learned by it, and she's making the same mistakes she made at the beginning of the novel. Let the protagonist learn a few lessons and suffer a few failures.

🚩 **REVISION RED FLAG:** A good place to start looking to fix a boggy middle is to check how your internal conflict and character arc affect your external plot arc. If these two aren't causing trouble for each other, that's a likely trouble spot.

Middles are notorious for bogging down, so if you discover you have a lot of reworking to do in yours, don't worry. It's a common problem. As you review your middle, also keep an eye out for anything new to share with your readers, or a different way of looking at the story or world.

Step Five: Fix Problems With the Ending

The ending resolves the core conflict of the novel and puts the protagonist up against the antagonist. It's the moment readers have been waiting for the entire book (no pressure), so the most common problem is not living up to that promise. For more in-depth discussions on these issues, see Fixing Common Problems With the Ending on page 134.

Common ending problems include:

The ending is too short: The story is rushing to the payoff and not letting enough tension build, trying to wrap it all up too quickly. This indicates the climax might not be fleshed out enough and needs to be dramatized more—description, internalization, dialogue, etc.

The ending is too long: A too-long ending rambles on after the climax is over, or it takes too long to get there. It could also be that there's too much description or infodumping as you tie up loose ends. Liberal use of the delete key typically fixes this problem.

It doesn't resolve the core conflict: While getting the protagonist into and out of trouble, you forget what the point of the novel was and end up solving a problem in the climax that doesn't fix the problem posed at the beginning of the story—and the one the protagonist has been trying most of the book to solve. Try letting the climax solve the core conflict instead.

The ending doesn't fulfill the story promise: A close cousin to not resolving the core conflict is when a story changes somewhere in the middle and the ending isn't the promise made at the start of the novel. Maybe it started out as a political thriller and turned into a romance, or started as an adventure that turned into a story of self-reflection. The story promise made at the start is not kept. Keep the promise.

It doesn't involve the protagonist: The climax comes and goes and the protagonist isn't the one who finally defeats the antagonist and saves the day (however that unfolds in your novel). If the protagonist isn't the hero, then why have readers been following her all book? Put the protagonist back in the driver's seat and let her solve the problem.

There's no end for the character arc: The protagonist goes through all the deliciously evil things you did to her to get through the novel and by the end—she learns nothing, and is no better or worse off than when she started (this applies only to novels with character arcs). Give the protagonist a character arc and a reason to experience the plot of the novel.

Too many loose ends: Readers reach the end of the novel with way too many story questions left unanswered. It feels as though half the interesting problems were forgotten or shoved under the rug. Start tying up those loose ends early.

Not enough loose ends: On the flip side, endings that tie up every single loose end often feel too pat, as not everything needs to be explained and wrapped up with a bow. Leave a few questions unanswered or ambiguous (just not the ones readers *want* you to answer).

It's not satisfying to readers: Readers expect a payoff worth waiting for and this ending isn't it. Sometimes it's a matter of expectations, or the buildup was a promise that couldn't *be* kept. If you can't raise the ending to meet the promised payoff, maybe lower the expectations so the payoff works.

The stakes don't go up: The climax should be the highest stakes in the novel, but if nothing gets worse or costs more to win in the end it's not as satisfying. Try raising the stakes and making them more personal to the protagonist.

It comes out of the blue: Something or someone appears from nowhere and fixes whatever is wrong (*deus ex machina* endings). There's been no groundwork for it, no clues that it was possible, it just "magically" works itself out (often with little to no help from the protagonist). Let the characters solve the problem—don't swoop in and save the day.

It just stops: The climax happens and then it's over. There's no denouement, no wrap up, and it feels like the last few pages of the book were torn out. Another variation is an ending that reaches a certain point, resolves the last goal, and then ends. No climax, no big finish, it answers the story question and quietly fades away. Give readers a chance to come down after all that excitement, or give them the excitement they waited for.

The ending is often what determines how much readers like the novel, so do your best to craft a satisfying end.

Revision Option: If You Have a Major Plot Event That's Not Working

Sometimes you have a plot event you love, maybe even looked forward to writing the whole draft, but it just flat out doesn't work when the book is finished. It can be heartbreaking to cut it, but a necessary evil.

Here are some clues you might need to cut a critical event from your novel:

Your writer's instinct says so: You often know (even if you don't want to admit it) when something isn't working. This is a different feeling than those "is this working?" doubts we all get from time to time. Being unsure of a project is normal, but that keep-you-up-at-night dread that it's *just plain wrong*? Your instinct is on target. Trust yourself.

You're doing plot gymnastics to make it all work: Plot events should flow naturally from one to the next, and it should seem inevitable, not forced. Sometimes you get the best plots from trying to make two ends meets, but if you're working too hard to *force* it to work, it's probably better to cut or change it.

The reasons to arrive at that event aren't plausible: If you can ask one or two questions about the protagonist's motives and the whole scene falls apart, you're probably on shaky ground here. Same as when you answer those questions with "Because that has to happen for X to happen."

Resolving that event doesn't help the story: It *feels* like a major part of the book, but it doesn't resolve the problem the protagonist needs to fix, and it's not driving plot.

There are no real stakes for that event: You probably *have* stakes, but they're likely to be the large, yet vague "Lots of lives will be lost" type. On first glance they seem high, but your readers (and often your characters) don't care if it happens or not, because they're not invested in it. If this event can happen and nothing changes one way or the other for the main characters, you might want to take another look at your stakes here.

That's Not Working

Realizing there's a fundamental flaw in your plot is never fun, but if you look at it objectively, you can usually find the answer and fix the problem. Even if that's banging on the delete key in a big way.

Cut it: It'll be hard, but the story will be the better for it. Allow yourself to follow where your plot naturally leads. Save the original scene(s) in another file to make the cutting easier. You still have it, and can always add it back if you find a way to make it work.

Move it: Sometimes moving a plot event to another part of the novel fixes the problem. Perhaps that event will work better as a trigger to another plot point instead of the result of one.

Change who's in it: The same event might work better if it happens to or with different characters.

Change what triggers it: Maybe the event itself is fine, but how it comes to pass is wrong. Look for ways to have this same event happen, but through different means.

Change the outcome: If the event causes a problem down the line, try adjusting the results of resolving or dealing with the problem.

If you need more in-depth work on the beginning, middle, or ending, continue on to the next sessions. If these are working, skip ahead.

Fixing Common Problems With the Beginning

For these exercises, the beginning means the first 25 percent (roughly) of the novel. It's the setup and the introduction of the problem and everything that happens to get the protagonist into the main plot path and to the middle of the book.

Revision Option: If You Think You're Starting in the Wrong Place

Plenty of first drafts start in the wrong place, so don't worry if yours is one of them, or if it's taking you a few drafts to find the right opening. It's common to not know the right opening until you've written the ending.

Step One: Examine the Opening Scene

Analyze your current opening, which will be either the first scene or the first chapter if it's only one scene:

Describe how the story opens in the first few pages: Does it start with description, internalization, action, etc? What's the first thing readers see? Try to sum up your opening in one or two sentences and capture the essence of what it's doing.

Describe the goal in the opening scene: What's the protagonist in this scene trying to do? Even if the scene has nothing to do with your core conflict, the protagonist should be trying to achieve something.

Describe the conflict: Goals don't mean a lot if there's nothing in the way of getting them, so who or what is keeping the protagonist from what she wants to do? What type of conflict is creating the tension in this scene that will hook readers and draw them into the story?

Describe the stakes: What risk is the protagonist facing? No matter how small the goal, there should be a consequence for failing that will keep readers interested. If the protagonist isn't the one at risk, who else might be?

Describe in one paragraph or less what happens next in the scene: How does this opening move the plot forward? A short description will force you to look at what's going on in that scene and help you pinpoint the goal-conflict-stakes structure.

Describe how the first scene or chapter ends: This event transitions into the next scene or chapter, and is the "oh, no!" moment that will either hook readers or not. How did the previous events in the scene get readers to this moment? Where will the plot go from here? Is there a reason for them to turn the page?

Step Two: Connect the Beginning to the End

Next, step back and look at the story as a whole to see how this opening connects to the rest of the book, especially the ending:

What's the core conflict of the novel? The beginning is all about getting the protagonist started on the journey to the end. Consider both the internal and external conflicts, as the opening scene might focus on the character arc first (internal conflict) and introduce the external conflict in a few chapters.

When is the protagonist brought into this core conflict? It can be small, and it can be something the protagonist doesn't even know connects to a bigger issue yet, but there's a moment where if the protagonist turned left instead of right, she never would have had this thing (the inciting event) happen to her. That moment is when she makes a choice or acts in a way that sets her on the plot path. This is the bridge moment that connects the opening to the rest of the novel (if the opening scene isn't the inciting event itself).

What's happening when the protagonist triggers that moment and steps onto the plot path? Stories typically start in the normal world of the protagonist's life, so the protagonist will likely be doing something normal that doesn't go as it usually does. What is she doing when this plot path moment occurs?

How does this event connect to the core conflict? You should be able to make a step-by-step list that shows how this event leads to the end of the novel. If you can't, that's a red flag that this isn't the inciting event, and that's likely the problem.

Is the opening the inciting event? If so, and you still think something is off, the story might be starting too early and needs more setup or a few more scenes before you reach this point. Try creating a smaller problem that introduces the protagonist and the world and *leads* to the inciting event.

If the opening does nothing to get the protagonist onto the plot path (the inciting event), or onto a path that directly leads to the inciting event, that's a strong indicator that this isn't the right opening for the novel.

If it does, then you're probably starting in the right place.

If you *are* starting in the right place, but think the opening isn't as strong as it should be, look closer at your goals, conflicts, or stakes in the scene. If those look good, move on and examine the narrative drive. Consider doing the exercises in If You Want to Strengthen the Narrative Drive on page 192 for more insights.

If the drive still feels off or weak, look back at your opening scene analysis. Is there anything you didn't answer, or half-answered (be honest)? If so, this is likely the problem. Answer those questions again with the core conflict in mind, and this time dig for the honest answers.

If this doesn't fix the problem, and everything looks good but something is *still* off, look at (and be ruthless):

The first few pages: What is the protagonist doing on page one? Is she active or is there more description or narrative that sets the scene? Perhaps there's too much setup and that's bogging the scene down. If you're not sure, try highlighting in different colors what lines are action, internal thought, description, backstory, and infodumps. Look at the color balance. Where is there too much? Not enough? Make the protagonist active and give her something to do that will get her to the first step of the core conflict.

The opening scene goal: Is the goal apparent from the first page, or is it a goal that appears later in the scene or chapter (or several chapters in)? Sometimes the protagonist is doing something unrelated at the start of a novel to setup the scene, and the real goal is mentioned several pages in, delaying the beginning of the story. Show the goal right from the start and make it clear what the protagonist is trying to do.

The opening scene stakes: Even if it's clear what the protagonist is doing, if readers don't care if she succeeds or not they won't be curious enough to keep reading. Are the stakes worth worrying about (again, be honest)? Even a mundane scene can have meaningful stakes if the protagonist cares enough about the outcome. For example, not buying milk when a character knows it'll cause a huge fight with the spouse does matter, even if it's just about milk. But stopping off for a latte that has no repercussions at all doesn't give readers a reason to stick around.

If the current opening scene isn't getting the protagonist to the inciting event or core conflict, look at the *next* scene and evaluate that one as a potential opening scene. Keep moving forward until you find the right opening scene, or you determine what scene puts the beginning back on track.

Revision Option: Dealing With Too Much Setup

Every beginning has setup in it, but there's a difference between good setup and bad setup.

Bad setup explains the story, typically using infodumps, flashbacks, and backstory. It stops the story because there's no goal or reason for it to be there aside from dumping information.

Good setup refers to the elements that flesh out the story and lay the groundwork for the plot. It's conveyed in a way that establishes a character, world, or situation all while moving the plot and story forward at the same time.

Step One: Eliminate Unnecessary Infodumps

If the information isn't needed to understand what's going on in that scene, and does nothing but dump in facts and explain, it doesn't need to be there and is likely bogging the beginning down.

For example, if you want to set up that being out on the street after dark is dangerous, show the protagonist being nervous about going out after dark, or have her think about it being a bad idea. Show how someone afraid to be out after dark would *behave*, and avoid a paragraph-long infodump about the *reason* it's dangerous to be out after dark and why that reason exists.

Ask, "What is the reason for this infodump?" If it's to *show* X, look for a way to show it. If it's to *explain* X, cut it and see how the scene reads without it.

If you find a lot of infodumps in your beginning, consider doing the exercises in Workshop Five: Description Work: If You Want to Eliminate Unnecessary Infodumps on page 237 at this time.

Step Two: Eliminate Unnecessary Flashbacks

Look for any flashbacks added so readers will "get" an upcoming scene. Instead of flashing back, use details that will suggest how the flashback affected the character.

A good flashback is a revelation, not an explanation. A subtle difference, but it changes how readers absorb the information. If they're figuring something out, they'll read on. If they're being told what's important in the story, they'll likely start to skim to get the key plot details.

Fixing Weak Flashbacks

If you have a flashback that needs to be there, but it's weak, here are some options to strengthen it:

Flashback to events readers *want* to know: If you've teased readers with a secret for a while, and they're *dying* to know what happened, a longer flashback will usually hold their interest. Pique curiosity first, then give them the information once they crave the answers.

Make the flashback relevant to the situation: Information revealed in a flashback should advance the plot and move the story forward. It can also be something relevant to the character's development. Using a flashback to trigger a realization can be quite useful.

REVISION RED FLAG: If the flashback doesn't do these two things (it's not relevant to the scene and readers won't care about the information), there's a good chance you can cut it and insert the information another way.

Keep the flashback short: The longer readers stray from the main narrative, the higher the chance they'll start skimming to get back to the main plot.

Keep flashbacks in the character's voice: If there's a reason for a character to flash back on a memory and she remembers it in her voice, it will feel more natural.

Give longer flashbacks the same drive as a regular scene: If the flashback has its own goal-conflict-stakes structure, it will draw readers in and make them curious to see where it goes. The longer you ask them to pause the main storyline, the more responsibility you have to entertain them during that side trip.

Flashbacks can be an effective tool when used well, and they can help eliminate backstory. A few lines of memory can often dramatize a past fact a lot better than exposition, and help characterize to boot.

Step Three: Streamline the Focus on the Protagonist's Normal Life

Common writing advice says to start with the protagonist's world before you change that world. The problem comes when there's no conflict for the protagonist to encounter, so the "day in the life of" is just watching the protagonist go about her (often boring) day until something "suddenly" happens and she's dragged into the plot. In a beginning, this is deadly.

REVISION RED FLAG: Look for the words "suddenly," "without warning," "out of nowhere," or something similar just before a big action scene. Odds are, this is when the action starts and everything before it is bad setup you can trim back or cut entirely.

Often, you'll find backstory and infodump mixed in with the "typical day" as well, trying to add some excitement or interest to what your instincts are telling you is a boring setup scene. Trust those instincts and cut what isn't vital.

Revision Option: Not Enough Setup

Stories that start too early usually need *more* setup to ground readers in the world and introduce them to the protagonist. Too much too fast is thrown at them and they have a hard time keeping up and understanding why what's happening is important.

Step One: Add Necessary Groundwork to Set the Scene

A little groundwork goes a long way. As long as readers understand the general gist of what's happening, and they find that compelling, they'll keep reading to see what happens next. If they're lost, they'll stop trying to figure it out. Make sure:

It's clear who's in the scene: Faceless people can be hard for readers to absorb, especially if they're not sure who the protagonist is. "The man" or "she" with no hints as to who these people are can put readers at a distance and not let them connect to the story as they should. After all, if the character isn't important enough to name, why should the reader care?

It's clear where the scene takes place: Readers need to be able to picture where they are, and a sense of location allows them to ground themselves in the setting.

It's clear what's happening in the scene: Show the goal and what the protagonist is trying to do to give a sense that something is happening and the story is moving on page one. The specifics can be a little vague if you need to maintain mystery, but give readers the basic details to understand the context of what's going on. For example, you don't have to say the characters are breaking into a bank, but let readers know it's a robbery. Or, let them know the building is a bank and going in there is creating tension between the characters, but surprise them with the robbery.

It's clear why it matters: Stakes create interest and give readers a sense of where the danger lies. They can't worry about the protagonist if they don't know what she's risking.

It's clear where it's going: Setup is a lead in, so it needs to lead somewhere. If there are no hints where the plot is going, it can feel aimless and uninteresting.

Adding setup doesn't have to give secrets away or explain anything you don't want it to. Readers want the mystery and the wonder, but they also want context for it. Often, all a scene needs is a few specific words or lines to provide that context.

Revision Option: Fixing a Lack of Story Questions

Story questions can mean any number of things—a literal question a character asks, a situation that suggests a question, a mystery that makes readers and characters wonder, the meaning behind an odd detail or bit of dialogue—whatever works for the story. They're *not* the questions readers ask because of confusion about what's going on. Confusion does not equal suspense, and problems with story questions usually fall into this area.

Step One: Add Story Questions to Hook Readers

Look for places where you want readers to question or wonder something, and either add a question, or tweak what's there to nudge readers into thinking and wondering about it.

🚩 **REVISION RED FLAG:** Watch for questions posed right in the text. It's common in a first draft to state outright what you want readers to wonder about instead of maintaining a little mystery. Sometimes this is good; sometimes it bangs readers over the head and is too obvious.

Add literal questions: These are questions posed by the characters. The protagonist might say or think, "Where's Papa going with that axe?" and then readers will want to know as well. Literal questions make readers wonder the same thing as the character, then tag along to find out the answer.

It's not uncommon to see literal questions within goal statements, such as, "Did Bobby kill that boy? I had to find out." They're flashing lights that tell readers what the plot is going to focus on for a while.

🚩 **REVISION RED FLAG:** Too many literal questions can hurt the tension, so use them carefully. They work best when they're questions the character would logically ask at that moment, not a rap on the head by the author telling readers what to wonder about.

Add situational questions: These are questions created by an unusual situation that draws readers in and makes them curious about what's going on. Who are these people with guns lurking outside a school? Why is that woman agreeing to be put to death? The clues that provide the answers to these questions are missing and readers will read on to find out what this is all about.

This type of "what's going on?" is different from the confusing type, though. With a situational question, what is *happening* in the scene is clear, but the *reasons* behind it are a mystery. It's more about discovering the who or why than the what. For example, readers can see that armed men are studying a high school, but who they are, why they're studying it, and what they plan to do is uncertain.

A confusing "what's going on?" scene would show the same people planning an attack on a building, but not mention it was a school or that they had guns. The compelling parts are missing, and there's not enough context to understand what's going on at the basic level.

Add emotional reaction questions: These are questions created by emotions. Something is brewing in the story that will cause the protagonist (or another character) to react emotionally in a way readers anticipate—both negatively and positively. Dread is just as strong as hope in these types of questions (often stronger if the stakes are super personal).

If the protagonist is clearly headed toward something bad (or even good), readers will hold their breath to see what will happen and how the character will react to it. Readers might even fear that outcome, knowing what it's going to do to the character they love.

Add information questions: These questions focus on the discovery of information. Usually the type of information the protagonist is looking for is clear, and revealing that information is the goal—such as the protagonist discovers a coworker broke into her office and searched it, and she sets out to discover why. Sometimes it's more subtle with clues dropped by the author that only readers see—such as hints that suggest the protagonist doesn't know the truth about herself; perhaps she's adopted, or she has a special ability.

How something came to be is another example, and one commonly seen in genre fiction. How does a world that forces its children to fight to the death on TV happen? Why is everyone scared of an eight-year-old girl? Readers want to know how or why something is the way it is and they'll read on to find out.

Add teaser questions: These are questions posed when answers to previous questions lead to *other* questions. Readers get an answer they've been dying to know, but it only opens the door to more mysteries, more delicious reactions, more unknowns. Perhaps the protagonist finds proof Howard shot the sheriff, but readers *know* Howard was in another state at the time.

REVISION RED FLAG: Questions that drag on and *never* get answered can weaken the suspense of other questions (because why worry about something if the author has proven they won't answer it?). They also have less impact because readers don't fully remember why they wanted to know the answers in the first place.

Story questions are important, but be wary of posing too many of them at once. A flood of questions can leave readers struggling to remember details and undo all the work you put into creating those mysteries. Just like your plot and character arcs move the conflicts, a solid arc of questions that build and lead to more keeps the overall novel moving forward.

Revision Option: Fixing a Reactive Protagonist

You often wind up with a reactive protagonist when you're not sure what the protagonist wants from the novel. You know the premise, and what must be done to explore that premise, but there's no main character with a problem working within that premise.

Step One: Make the Protagonist Act to Create the Plot

The protagonist drives the plot. She makes it happen through the choices she makes and the results of those choices. Revise the beginning so that:

The protagonist makes choices that affect how the plot unfolds: Look for places where the protagonist acts only because an outside element forces her to. Find ways to make the outcome be her choice instead— even if outside elements *create* the need for that choice.

Those choices cause events that would not have happened had she not made that choice: Look at the choices the protagonist makes. Edit any outcomes where it made no difference which option she chose. Find ways to make the choice affect what happens at that moment, down the line, or even better—both.

The protagonist plans and acts out those plans to achieve a desired result: A proactive protagonist is trying to solve a problem and achieve goals. Look for places where events are happening *to* the protagonist, and find ways for her to get into that trouble by her own choices and actions.

The protagonist has goals to strive for: Find tasks for the protagonist to do. Look for places where she's just reacting to whatever is happening in front of her and adjust it so she's more in control (even if things are out of control). If everything is going crazy around the protagonist, she should still try to act, even if you know it's pointless and will do nothing to help her. It's the act of trying that matters.

The choices the protagonist makes and the actions she takes create the plot for the novel. Without those choices, the protagonist is just along for the ride.

Revision Option: Fixing an Unclear Protagonist

An unclear protagonist is most commonly found when:

The focus is on the problem: The core conflict and problem to solve in the novel aren't personally connected to any one character—so there's no personal goal to drive a protagonist and no stakes to motivate her.

The focus is on the idea: The novel is trying to explore an idea more than solve a character's problem. In premise novels, the concept is all that matters, and any old character will do as long as you can tell readers all about this cool idea.

In essence, it's when you forget you need a character to solve a problem within an idea.

To clarify who the protagonist is, look for ways to connect her to the core conflict, and give her a series of goals to solve to avoid an unpleasant consequence. If you have multiple point-of-view characters (common in these cases), one character typically stands out as the main character, even if the points of view are balanced, such as in a romance with both parties as point-of-view characters. Ask yourself:

Who is the character with the most to gain and lose? This is typically the protagonist.

Who has the ability to act and effect change? The protagonist drives the plot and creates the story.

Who must be there for the story to happen? The protagonist is the only character who must be in a novel for it to work. Even the antagonist can sometimes be a non-character, such as in a Person vs. Nature story.

An unclear protagonist is frequently a character issue, because the protagonist isn't fleshed out enough yet to be that "person with a problem." If this is the case in your manuscript, consider doing the exercises in Workshop Two: Character Work on page 51 at this time.

If not, then focus on adding details and goals to make it clear who the protagonist is. A lack of internalization might be the problem here, so consider doing the exercises in Workshop Four: Point of View Work: If You Want to Streamline the Internalization on page 212.

Beginnings can be tricky, but it helps to remember that their job is to pique your readers' curiosity, sweep them away in your story world, and prepare them for the plot ride ahead.

Fixing Common Problems With the Middle

For these exercises, the middle means the center 25 percent to 75 percent (roughly) of the novel. It's the efforts and failures of the protagonist to resolve the core conflict, and everything that happens to get the protagonist to the climax in the last 25 percent (roughly) of the novel.

Revision Option: Unclogging a Boggy Middle

Middles tend to sag because a lot of time and effort is spent setting up the story, and an equal amount of time and effort is spent on the climax and ending, but the middle gets less attention. It's like an airport terminal where the characters wander around, grab some food, and hang out until the call for the climax is heard.

Not a good recipe for a happy middle, let alone a happy ending, since readers have probably wandered off to do something else by now. Luckily, a boggy middle can be fixed by giving the protagonist problems to solve—or else.

Step One: Add a Midpoint Reversal

The midpoint reversal is a major event in the middle of the novel that provides a goal for the protagonist to work toward, thus providing narrative drive through the middle, and something exciting for readers to anticipate (or be surprised by).

A good midpoint reversal:

Reveals new information that changes how the protagonist views her world and problem: The midpoint can also work as a fake out, where the protagonist thinks she's won, but the truth is the exact opposite. The protagonist gets everything she *thought* she wanted, but it turns out that's the worst thing that ever could have happened to her. "Success" has terrible consequences she was completely unprepared for. Or "failure" is exactly what will lead her to victory in the end.

Takes the story to a new level by raising the stakes and piling on the pressure: The first half of the novel gets the protagonist into trouble (of her own making, naturally), and after this point, the trouble gets piled on (often by the antagonist) and she must reap the consequences of every mistake made so far. The midpoint is the beginning of everything about to go horribly, horribly wrong for the poor protagonist.

Starts stripping away the protagonist's support system: As the antagonist gets the upper hand and the stakes get higher, people the protagonist has relied on (and used as a crutch) are no longer there for her. Sometimes her own actions cause the problem, but it can also be because she never truly knew the extent of the problem and now she does. Characters who were willing to help no longer can, or are no longer willing to. Assets are taken away. Access to necessary resources vanishes.

Starts a ticking clock: It's not uncommon to introduce a hard deadline during the midpoint to help raise the stakes and make the situation harder on the protagonist. The full extent of the problem is often revealed here, and now the protagonist knows what's barreling toward her at high speed.

If you're stuck with a boggy middle, ask:

What is the absolute worst thing that can happen to the protagonist in the middle of the novel? Now consider what choices it is *actually happens.* How does it affect the scenes leading up to the middle? Does it give the protagonist more to do? Does it tighten the pacing since all the scenes now lead to this big event? If not, keep brainstorming ideas until you find one that offers you a solid plot path to get there and keep the middle moving.

Is there a way to make the protagonist's inner goal clash with the outer goal in a disastrous way? Midpoint reversals are excellent places to have a victory in one area (say a plot win), but a loss in another (say a character arc loss). The second half of the middle is dealing with the ramifications of that loss (or the unforeseen consequences of that win).

What's the one thing that could happen that would make the protagonist give up? Make that happen in the novel's middle, then devise a reason why she *won't* give up. The second half of the middle often has the protagonist slipping farther and farther away from her goal, driving her to the dark moment just before the climax. Finds ways to force her to that low point.

Are there any deep, dark secrets that could be revealed and ruin everything? Information that changes everything characters (and readers) thought they knew can shake up a boggy plot and get it moving again.

Can you mirror the climax? Sometimes a midpoint reversal will foreshadow what's to come, either by showing the protagonist failing or hinting at what she'll need to do to win.

The midpoint reversal is a major turning point in a novel that welds the front and back half together. Everything that came before it has led to what occurs after it, and it's all in jeopardy (which is why it's so much fun to write).

Structuring a Middle

If you're not sure of the best way to structure your middle, plan out a few turning points and build a plot foundation. You probably have three to five big plot events that happen in the middle (if not, this is a problem). One launches it, one surprises readers in the middle, and one ends it, and often you'll see two more points between the beginning and the middle, and the middle and the ending. These are usually smaller plot points or subplot moments.

It typically looks like this:

Start of Act Two problem – minor problem one – midpoint reversal problem – minor problem two – end of Act Two problem.

Start of Act Two problem: This is the problem created by trying to solve the inciting event or story catalyst from the beginning. The protagonist spends the first half of the middle trying to resolve this problem.

Minor problem one: The plan to solve the Act Two problem runs into a snag. It's common to see a subplot around this time, often connected to the character arc.

Midpoint reversal problem: A major problem is discovered, possibly sending the story in a new direction or shaking things up.

Minor problem two: A snag occurs in the plan to fix whatever problem occurred at the midpoint. Often, the midpoint changes the situation so all the protagonist's plans are useless and she has to come up with a new approach. It's also common for the antagonist to cause the reversal, and now the protagonist is struggling to stay ahead and not fail spectacularly.

End of Act Two problem: The protagonist discovers a major problem that will be the focus of Act Three, and will lead directly to the climax of the novel. This is typically the lowest point in the protagonist's arc.

The middle is all about deepening the story, allowing the beginning and the ending to come together in a way that satisfies your readers.

Revision Option: Fixing a Lack of Payoffs

In an effort to pile on the problems, sometimes you forget to reward both characters and readers for sticking with the plot. Constant failure can make a plot seem like it's not getting anywhere, but a few victories—even if they're small—can make the plot seem like it's moving toward an end. See what wins you can give your protagonist that move the plot without making the obstacles seem too easy. Maybe the wins can be from a subplot or emotional aspect to provide the payoff.

Revision Option: Adding Surprises

Middles can easily turn into a "here's how the plot unfolds" series of *how* the protagonist solves the problem, not *if* the plan will work. They become too focused on getting readers to the ending and forget that the middle is why readers picked up the book in the first place—to see what happens as the protagonist struggles to find the answers and solve the problems.

Surprises keep the monotony out of plotting, defying your readers' expectations and making them want to read every word, because they never know when something new or unexpected might appear.

Look through your middle and find the scenes where something happens in the plot. Ask:

Was it obvious this was going to happen? Some plot points *are* going to happen as expected, but there's a difference between predicable and inevitable. Inevitable feels like the hand of fate arranging situations despite how hard the protagonist tries to fight it. Predictable feels like the protagonist is following directions. Look for places where you can do the unexpected and surprise readers.

Did the protagonist do exactly what she said she would do, exactly as she planned? Often, the protagonist lays out the plan and explains everything before she starts in an attempt to establish the goals and stakes (which is good). But it goes too far and ends up sabotaging your middle, because readers now know exactly how it will play out. Look for any planning sessions and cut out everything but the bare minimum to establish the goal and get the plot moving.

Did any of the potential risks or problems occur? Just saying there *are* risks isn't enough if nothing happens, or only the risks mentioned ever occur. Look for ways the stakes and potential dangers might come to pass, but not in the way the protagonist thought. This will alert readers that something bad is brewing, but surprise them with how.

Do the characters behave as expected? Middles are good times for people to screw up, act out of character due to stress and fear, and generally break from the pressure. Look for ways to surprise readers by having a character do the last thing they'd expect.

For more on plot twists, see If You Want to Deepen the Plot: Developing Plot Twists and Twists Novels on page 176.

Revision Option: Restarting Stalled Character Arcs

Sometimes character arcs stall, because you know the protagonist needs to change, but you didn't spend enough time figuring out how. So the protagonist solves problem after problem, but nothing is learned by it, and she's making the same mistakes she made at the beginning of the novel.

REVISION RED FLAG: Check how your internal conflict and character arc affect your external plot arc. If these two aren't causing trouble for each other, that's a likely trouble spot.

A lot of first drafts stumble in the middle, so don't worry if yours needs more work. In most cases, simply adding a midpoint goal is enough to give the plot the necessary drive to ramp up from the beginning, and speed down toward the ending.

Fixing Common Problems With the Ending

For these exercises, the ending means the last 25 percent (roughly) of the novel. It's the final march to the big battle against the antagonist, where the protagonist uses all she's learned and resolves the core conflict.

Revision Option: Fixing Too-Short Endings

Too-short endings typically happen when you don't leave enough time to build up tensions before the climax. You go from Act Two to the end in one or two steps and rush the plot. In the rush, it's common to skip important elements such as description and internalization. The ending turns into a fast-paced, dialogue-heavy whirlwind, or it's one long summary of the action.

If your ending seems too short, look at your plot and consider:

How does the protagonist start her journey toward the antagonist? Common story structure dictates that right before the ending begins, the protagonist will undergo a failure or dark moment when all seems lost. It's the dark before the dawn, the moment when everything comes crashing down. The protagonist makes a decision to move forward and face the antagonist, whoever or whatever that is. The journey to the antagonist is how you create the necessary buildup of tension.

Look at how long it takes your protagonist to reach the antagonist. Odds are the path between the dark moment and the climax is pretty short (making the ending feel short), and adding a few more steps and obstacles will slow the pace down.

If the issue is too much summary, take those described moments and turn them into full-fledged scenes. Dramatize instead of summarize.

How many obstacles are thrown in the protagonist's way? One way to test this is to examine the beginning and count how many obstacles kept the protagonist from stepping onto that plot path in the first place. Beginnings and endings often mirror each other, so the paths might be similar.

Also look for any subplots that need to be resolved before the ending. These are all useful elements to add conflict and give a sense of forward momentum as the protagonist marches to the climax.

🚩 **REVISION RED FLAG:** Be wary about adding obstacles to delay the resolution. Too many of those can create the opposite problem (an ending that's too slow or never ends), and bog down the ending. Aim for plot complications that also reveal something interesting or new in the story, or allow the protagonist to exhibit a needed skill for the climax.

How has the protagonist changed, and what examples show that change and growth (the character arc)? The ending often shows how the protagonist has grown and developed the skills necessary to defeat the antagonist in the end. The previous obstacles overcome and problems solved all show how the protagonist has learned from her mistakes and is now (readers hope) ready to face the antagonist (or show she's still refusing to grow and this is her last chance).

In a too-short ending, this growth might have been left out or glossed over, so those last final growth moments aren't seen. The protagonist changes suddenly to be what she needs to be, but there's not enough of that growth displayed in the end to make it plausible.

Look for situations and opportunities that show this growth, and add them where needed so the protagonist is growing at the same times she's figuring out how to defeat the antagonist.

Can you add one last surprising twist that raises the stakes or reveals critical information? Another reason an ending can feel short is because it unfolds exactly as expected. The predictability makes it feel rushed (even if it isn't) because readers are waiting for something new that never comes.

Look for ways to add a surprise or have the ending unfold unexpectedly. This is when long-held secrets might be revealed as well, especially if those secrets will put the characters in the worst possible mindset for the final showdown.

Even small twists can help create unpredictability, so don't think you need a major twist to make it work. Look at each step in the protagonist's plan and think about your options. Did she choose the most obvious path, or can the plot go a slightly different (and unexpected) way? What might happen if events don't turn out as expected but still keep the plot on track?

How does the protagonist battle the antagonist? Sometimes, the final battle is over too quickly, and all your buildup evaporates in a few paragraphs. This should be the hardest battle, the toughest fight, the most difficult decision the protagonist faces in the novel. If the defeat is a breeze, it cheapens the entire story.

Look for ways to make the final battle harder, tougher, and more developed emotionally. If you're light on description, add more detail and further develop both the setting and how the action itself is conveyed. If you're light on internalization and dialogue, look for places where the protagonist can think about what's going on, toss in a quip, say something, or even talk herself through it.

How does the protagonist win (or lose)? The final moment of resolution is a major event in the story. If this goes by too fast, readers won't feel the emotional impact they need to be satisfied by the ending. If it's too easy, they'll feel cheated. While you don't want to drag this out unnecessarily, if the win is rushed, it can make the whole ending feel rushed and leave readers confused.

Look at how your protagonist wins and see if you need to add more description or internalization, or if it needs clarification of what happens.

How does the story wrap up? Some stories end right after the protagonist wins, dropping readers mid-emotion. It's jarring and can feel like someone kicked them out of a moving car. A little wrap up is a good thing, and helps ease readers down from the excitement of the climax.

Look at how you transition from final battle to last page. If it all wraps up too quickly, it might be leaving your readers behind.

Revision Option: Fixing Too-Long Endings

Too-long endings drag and make readers groan and say, "Will this ever *end*?" You want that sense of events building to a climax, but too many obstacles can make the story feel as though it'll never end because there's always "one more thing" that must be overcome or resolved.

Sometimes, too-long endings result from too many subplots or story questions that need answers before the book ends. There's too much left hanging to fit everything into the ending, so it feels bloated and overdone.

If your ending feels too long, ask:

Are there obstacles that are there only to delay the ending? With so much emphasis on creating conflict and struggle, it's easy to go a little too far and add too much.

Look for obstacles that don't change how the ending unfolds—they just slow down the time it takes to get there. Cut any that aren't critical to the climax.

Are there plot wrapups or denouement events that can come *after* the climax? Some events can wait until the final wrap up to be resolved, such as showing how so-and-so finally reached home. The fate of smaller, yet loved, characters and what happens to them can be a nice way to finish off the story.

Look for resolutions that don't need to be resolved in the climax or even the third act. Some of these resolutions might be better resolved late in Act Two if they help make tasks harder on the protagonist.

Is there an order the resolutions need to happen in? Depending on the importance of the various characters, you could pace your ending by how you arrange those characters' endings. Smaller reveals might build perfectly to the big "oh, wow!" moment.

Look at what you want to resolve in the end and determine what tasks need to go where and why. Think about how these smaller resolutions can make the climax stronger.

What priority are the resolutions? This is important if you have smaller subplots or lesser characters you're wrapping up. Their plot resolutions might come earlier in the third act, because they aren't critical to the plot. Major characters and major storylines would likely be resolved at or near the end, because that's what readers are looking for.

Look for anything that doesn't absolutely need to be there and either cut it or move it out of the ending.

Can any of the resolutions be smaller asides and not full-blown scenes? Not every character in the novel needs a fairytale ending, especially secondary characters. If a subplot can be resolved in a paragraph or two, let it.

Look for mini-endings within your ending, where the focus is on non-protagonists wrapping up their own storylines. The more time it takes to wrap those up, the more likely it is you can cut them back.

Revision Option: Fixing Endings That Don't Resolve the Core Conflict

The core conflict (the point of the book) should be tied up. That's the promise you made to your readers and they expect you to fulfill that promise. This is the reason the story exists in the first place—to solve this problem.

If the core conflict isn't resolved, that can indicate a few things:

You're not sure what the novel is about: This is a tough call to make, because it usually means there's a lot of rewriting to do to fix it (and at this stage, the last thing you probably want to do is more revision). But you can't resolve a conflict if you're not sure what that conflict is. You can't go forward until you fix that problem.

Go back and examining the beginning of the novel. Usually, the core conflict is stated somewhere in the beginning, and it's clear what must be done. Pay particular attention to the inciting event and the Act One problem. These two moments are where the protagonist enters the plot path and becomes drawn into the story proper. The rest of the plot is simply resolving the problem discovered in one (or both) of those moments.

If you realize you don't know what that core conflict is, consider returning to the plot and structure analysis sections and re-evaluating the plot (page 96). You might also want to skip ahead to the If You Want to Deepen the Plot section on page 151 to nail down what your core conflict truly is.

In rare cases, you might need to go back to the planning stage and do some heavy brainstorming to find the conflict (I suggest picking up a copy of the first book in my series, *Planning Your Novel: Ideas and Structure* in this instance).

You don't know what the protagonist's goal is: Depending on how complicated the story is, or how many characters there are, it's possible you lost sight of the goal and forgot what it was all about on a deeper level.

Look at your protagonist and ask what she wants and what she's been after the whole time. Somewhere in the story, the protagonist likely said what she was after and why it was important. If not, that could indicate you have a premise novel on your hands and no one is driving the story. You might benefit from reading through the bonus workshop on page 325, Salvaging Half-Finished Manuscripts, and seeing if any of the common fatal flaws of a HFM are causing your ending issue.

You might also try re-evaluating the character arc, especially if the story is more character-focused. It's possible the growth didn't happen or the ending isn't fixing that internal problem.

You changed what the novel was about somewhere along the way: Sometimes stories change, and what you thought you were writing isn't what you ended up with, so the ending you planned isn't the right ending for this new and improved story.

Move backward from your ending and determine where the shift in story occurred. An idea probably hit you at a precise moment and the protagonist changed focus and goals. What she wanted no longer applies, and you'll need to revise the beginning and/or the middle to add this new plot or direction into the existing storyline.

How extensive the shift is will determine how much rewriting is needed. A small shift might require only a few tweaks here and there to nudge events back on track, but a major shift might require major re-plotting. Re-doing your editorial map with this new direction can help ensure your story is working the way you want it before you do any additional rewriting.

You're not done yet: In some cases, what you think is the ending really isn't. Maybe it's an exciting step on the way to the climax, and it feels right because it's well-written and defeats a major villain, but it's not *quite* there yet and doesn't resolve the whole problem.

Look at your ending and see where the story can move forward to the core conflict ending. Try listing the steps needed to resolve that goal and compare it to the ending you have. What changes? What's missing? How might you combine the two aspects of the story so it all blends smoothly?

🚩 **REVISION RED FLAG:** If the ending *isn't* the core conflict, but you feel strongly that it's the *right* ending, that could indicate the core conflict isn't what you thought it was. Look at the problem the ending resolves, and determine if that's what the novel is about. You might have to go back and re-plot sections of the novel to lead to this resolution instead.

Revision Option: Fixing Endings That Don't Fulfill the Story Promise

Sometimes a story will *technically* resolve the core conflict, but do it in a way that doesn't keep the story promise made to readers at the start of the novel. Often, this happens when the reasons behind resolving the core conflict change, and the protagonist's motives or needs shifts. Maybe she wants to see the killer found, but what was once a story of revenge suddenly turns into a need to put that death behind her. Readers will be thrown when the protagonist forgives the killer instead of taking revenge.

Not only will broken promises cause you revision nightmares, you'll destroy the entire story in the process. Take a look at your ending:

Remember what your core conflict is: Your story is trying to solve a single problem (even if it's complex) for a single reason. There will be other factors that influence this reason, but something is motivating the protagonist to act. Make sure your protagonist resolves *that* problem for *that* reason using the skills and lessons learned over the course of the novel.

If the protagonist's motives need to change in the story, make sure there are hints and clues along the way so the change in focus isn't jarring. Don't promise a story of friendship that turns into something else by the end.

Don't let subplots hijack the real story: Subplots are shiny, they're fun, and they're often filled with emotions, but they're *not* the point of the novel. If one takes over and demands to be the star of the ending, kick it off the stage.

Readers will trust you to keep your promises and give them the story you agreed to tell them. Don't let them down.

Revision Option: Fixing Endings That Don't Involve the Protagonist

Since the protagonist is the one driving the story, and the one facing the core conflict, the ending needs to have her solving the problem.

Look at your ending and ask:

How does the ending affect the protagonist? The protagonist must be affected by the problem or she wouldn't be the protagonist (if not, that could indicate you have the wrong protagonist and might consider doing the exercises in Workshop Two: Character Work: If You Think You Have the Wrong Protagonist on page 62).

Look at how the ending matters to the protagonist and what role she might play in it. What does she need to do to make it all come out right? What skill does she bring, or knowledge does she have that will make all the difference?

How might the *protagonist* solve the plot point of the book? Sometimes you have several characters who are all deeply connected to the core conflict, even though they're not the official protagonist. If another character is facing the antagonist and doing all the work, what happens if you let the protagonist do it instead? A simple shift in who does what at the end could fix the problem with minimal effort.

Look for ways to put the protagonist back into the plot-driving seat and make sure she acts to resolve the problem. Other characters can help, but if she wasn't there, the entire final battle would fail, or maybe not even happen.

🚩 **REVISION RED FLAG:** If the person resolving the core conflict and facing off against the antagonist is the only person who can do it, that could indicate *that* character is the real protagonist of the story.

Revision Option: Fixing Endings That Don't Resolve the Character Arc

In more plot-focused or series novels, the protagonist doesn't grow all that much and there's no strong character arc (so there's nothing to resolve here). But in most other novels, the protagonist learns through the experiences in the novel and becomes a different (usually better) person by the end of the story.

If there's no growth at all, that could indicate a lack of inner conflict, or that the novel's problem isn't personal enough to the protagonist. She's solving the problem because she's told to, not because she cares or has anything at stake.

It could also indicate that the growth stalled and the plot took over. The story is no longer about the protagonist figuring out X while solving Y, it's just focused on solving Y.

Look at your story and ask:

What inner conflict has your protagonist been struggling with all along? Dealing with this inner conflict typically plays a big role in the ending. Either this is the flaw that must be overcome to defeat the antagonist, or it's what's been holding the protagonist back all this time and getting in the way of her happiness.

Look at the flaws, weaknesses, and even dreams of the protagonist. What needs to improve or be fixed? How might that problem be solved by what the protagonist undergoes and faces in the climax?

Also look at how the character arc has been unfolding so far (don't forget to refer to your character arc map). Is there a moment where the growth stopped? Check any notes you made about when and where growth should happen that might have been left off or obscured.

How can you make that inner problem conflict with the outer problem in your climax? Character arcs create tension and conflict, and if the protagonist has to make serious and deep personal changes in who she is or what she believes in order to win, that final showdown will be tough.

Look for ways in which the inner conflict is hindering (or helping) the protagonist as she faces the antagonist. Where might it make the situation harder or the choices tougher?

How might that inner conflict influence what the protagonist needs to do to solve the final problem? Realizations of the "right path to take" are fairly common in a climax, as the protagonist takes that last step of the character arc and grows into who she needs to be. This is frequently a path she never would have chosen had she not undergone and faced the problems of the novel.

Look for ways in which the problems the protagonist overcame to get there can influence how she resolves the core conflict of the novel. She *uses* what she's learned.

Revision Option: Fixing Endings With Too Many Loose Ends

While you don't have to tie up every loose end in a novel, leaving too much unresolved can lead to unsatisfied readers.

Rule of thumb: The bigger a deal you made out of something, the more likely it is you'll need to tie it up in the end. If a good part of the story goes into trying to resolve a conflict, resolve it.

However, series books often have a primary conflict that spans the series with steps to the larger story arc. It's okay to leave those hanging, as you can't exactly give away the ending of book three in book one. If the goal of book one is to get to X so the protagonist can ultimately do

Y in another book, it's okay to leave Y hanging in a series. The point of book one is to solve for X.

If you're not writing a series and think you have too many loose ends, consider ways to:

Identify the plot threads that need tying: Determine which threads should be tied up and which ones can be left dangling. Anything you've spent time teasing readers about will probably need to be dealt with, while smaller throwaway clues can usually stay unresolved.

Connect the threads: Look for any threads that serve the same plotline or story arc. It's possible you can resolve multiple connected questions in one scene. Also look for smaller or less important threads and see if they can be resolved earlier.

Space out the threads: Examine when and where a thread is resolved, as the resolutions affect a novel's pacing. Too much information (such as revealing what it's *really* all about) at once can leave readers confused or unable to absorb (and remember) it all. If a lot of threads need to be tied up, look for ways to space those reveals out so readers get a little bit at a time and aren't overwhelmed.

Tying up plot threads can fix a slow scene, so look for scenes and moments that could benefit from a little information boost. If there hasn't been any new information revealed for a while, it might be the perfect place to tie up that loose end.

Revision Option: Fixing Endings With Too Few Loose Ends

Readers can complain if you wrap up the plot *too* nicely. It's not realistic, because life is messy and problems don't always solve themselves in the end. If your ending is a little too pat, you might:

Untie a few ends: Look through your plot and subplot resolutions and see if any could be left unresolved without hurting the novel. Maybe it's enough to know that the two sidekick characters have feelings for each other, and readers don't need to see for sure that they get together. Or maybe that lost or missing detail remains a mystery, leaving readers to wonder about it after the novel is through.

While a few dangling ends can feel real and create some fun mystery, make sure anything vital to the story is resolved. If it's something that will hurt the resolution of the entire novel, tie it up.

Leave a few mysteries unexplained: Not everything in the story needs to be explained. If knowing how or why something works as it does has zero effect on the outcome of the plot, then perhaps leave it for readers to wonder about.

Not every character needs an ending: You love your characters and you want to show what happens to them, but the farther they are from the protagonist, the less readers will likely care. Sure, they liked reading about them, but they don't always need to know where that minor character will go now that the world is saved.

Revision Option: Fixing Endings That Don't Satisfy the Reader

A satisfying ending is subjective, so it can be hard to know if your ending is doing its job or not. You want your ending to be a surprise, yet still feel inevitable.

For some genres, the ending is obvious and inevitable and *won't* be a surprise (such as a murder mystery or romance). That ending is *why* readers picked up the novel—to see the hero win, the couple united, the child saved.

It's *how* you get there that makes all the difference.

Look at your ending and pose it as a question: For example, will Frodo get the ring to Mt. Doom? Will Bob and Jane find love? Will Nya save her sister?

This is the plot goal of the book, and it'll be a yes or no question. Readers expect the novel to answer this question. What's satisfying to readers are the events that occur between points A and Z—how the protagonist solves her problem, how it affects her, and what price she pays to do it.

If you're unsure if your ending is satisfying or not, ask:

Does it resolve the core conflict of the novel? This is the big "this is what my book is about" question that your protagonist has spent the entire novel trying to achieve.

Does it satisfy the major questions posed in the novel? You don't want to tie up *all* the loose ends, but you'll want to tie up the major issues in the story your readers will want to know the answers to.

Is this the ending most readers are hoping for? This one can waffle a bit, because we've all read books where we wanted one ending, but the book ended another way. If you do have an ending that isn't how readers will likely want it to go, make sure it's clear that that's how it *needed* to go to make whatever point you're trying to make.

What price does the protagonist pay for this resolution? Have you ever been to a sporting event where you didn't care for the sport or either team? Did you care who won, no matter how good the game was? Readers need to care about the outcome, and if the protagonist fails and loses nothing, then the problem is meaningless. Even if failure means something horrible happens to other people—if it doesn't affect the protagonist or characters readers care about, they *won't* care.

What new information is revealed that connects to this problem? Last-minute twists, final reveals to long-awaited secrets or mysteries can happen in the end to surprise readers. The discovery that things weren't what they seemed or there was more to it can add surprise to what is inevitable.

⚑ **REVISION RED FLAG**: However, withholding a key piece of information until the end—a piece that just happens to be the thing that makes everything clear and solves the problem—risks making readers feel lied to and cheated. If there's no way readers could have ever guessed the whole reason behind everything until you told them, you'll have unhappy and angry readers. Surprise them, don't trick them.

Is the ending meaningful? Happy or sad, the ending should *mean* something to satisfy readers. There should be a point to the problem and the effort it took to resolve that problem, and a reward for readers who spent

X hours to read this story. Maybe the resolution is clear, maybe it's vague and ambiguous, maybe it sets up the next step in a larger story—but it *ends*.

What constitutes a satisfying ending is up to you (and the reader I suppose, but that's beyond your control). What you want to say with the ending is also your call. It's your decision what emotions and thoughts you leave readers with when they finish.

Revision Option: Fixing Endings That Don't Raise the Stakes

Some endings don't cost the protagonist anything more in the final battle. For example, her life was in danger before she started the fight, and it's still in danger as she enters the fight. There's nothing else to lose. The stakes *feel* like they've gone up, but they've only gotten bigger and more impersonal, which lowers the risks as far as readers are concerned.

Look at your ending and ask:

Are the stakes more personal or just bigger? Thousands of people suffering is bigger than the protagonist and her friends suffering, but readers don't care about thousands of faceless characters. The stakes look higher, but it doesn't matter if people readers aren't interested in are affected.

Look for ways to make the final stakes more personal to your protagonist. Let it cost more to win, and have greater rewards for that victory (and greater sacrifices for failure).

Is the only thing at stake the death of the protagonist? This is a common "stakes never increase" problem in first drafts. On page one, the protagonist's life is in danger if she doesn't resolve this problem, and by the end, her life is still in danger if she doesn't resolve this problem. It feels huge (life and death usually is), but nothing the protagonist does (or has done) has affected her fate. It's still all or nothing.

Look for ways to work up to the life-or-death consequence, or find other ways to hurt the protagonist besides loss of life.

Does nothing change? In some cases, resolving the core conflict doesn't change anything. It's hard to accomplish, sure, but the protagonist's life is no better or worse off at the end than when she started the journey back on page one. It's common to see life and death stakes here, but since that's never an option it doesn't carry any weight with readers. They know the protagonist won't die, and nothing less has any affect on her life.

This issue usually requires more work to fix, as it's typically caused by an inherent flaw in the story. Look for ways to make what's happening matter to the protagonist, and give her consequences for failure and rewards for victory. Not resolving this issue will have long-lasting effects on her life and cause her pain or suffering on some level, either physical, mental, or emotional.

If you're concerned about your stakes, you might consider doing the exercises next in, If You Want to Deepen Your Plot: Developing the Conflicts and Stakes on page 160.

Revision Option: Fixing Endings That Come Out of the Blue

A *deus ex machina* ending (endings where a larger, unseen force comes in and makes it all work out) are problematic because the author, not the protagonist, saves the day and resolves the problem. There's no way for readers to anticipate or determine what will happen, as nothing the protagonist has done has any effect on the outcome of the story. The "hand of God" reaches down and fixes the problem.

These endings usually feel contrived, often based on huge coincidences or even brand-new information appearing from nowhere. Characters develop never-hinted-at skills, someone or something the protagonist barely noticed back on page five suddenly appears and is the key to everything, the protagonist makes a leap in logic that no one would ever make—whatever it is, it's so unrealistic it makes the ending of the novel feel pointless. The journey to get there didn't mean anything, but the problem is solved by outside forces.

If you think your ending might be coming out of the blue, ask:

How is the ending resolved? Look at how the ending unfolds. Can you see specific actions the protagonist takes to get from problem to resolution? Did those actions affect what happened?

How is your protagonist involved? The protagonist should be the one who makes the ending happen through her actions. Her choices and plans led to this moment.

Could readers have anticipated or guessed this ending? Out-of-the-blue endings usually shock readers (and not in the good way), because there's no groundwork in the story to prepare for them. Key information is either too well-hidden or never shown, and the ending draws on and depends on details that appear moments before they're needed. Or worse—how it happened gets explained afterward.

Is the ending based on coincidence? A good rule of thumb for coincidences is: Coincidences that hurt the protagonist are good, but coincidences that help the protagonist are bad. If events have to work out just right, and characters just happen to be in the right spot at the right time for events to unfold as needed, then the protagonist isn't doing enough to drive the plot and resolve the ending on her own.

Does an outside force or lucky break help the protagonist win? Sometimes these events can fall right on the border of acceptable—such as a person or event that made a brief appearance earlier suddenly arrives at the right moment to help. It can *feel* okay—after all, the protagonist did help that old beggar man in chapter two—but it's so far-fetched it stretches credibility; the beggar man turns out to be the most powerful magician in all the land and decides to lend a hand because the protagonist was nice to him once.

Lucky breaks can also feel this way, though sometimes that Hail Mary pass *does* land, and that once-in-a-lifetime shot hits the mark. These can be tough, because gasp-worthy surprise victories *do* happen. The trick here is to let the protagonist do all the legwork, so that lucky shot feels like the result of hard work, not a lucky break at the right moment.

In most cases, fixing an out-of-the-blue-ending means putting the protagonist back in the driver's seat and letting her cause the ending's events to happen. Spend some extra time doing the exercises in, If You Want to Deepen Your Plot: Developing the Goals and Motivations on page 158 and the exercises in If You Want to the Develop the Scenes on page 184.

Revision Option: Fixing Endings That Just Stop

It's tempting to end the novel after the climax. You've done so much work and you're tired, and you just want it over. But novels that end when the bad guy hits the mat (so to speak) leave readers feeling as though they missed something.

Endings that simply stop are some of the easier issues to fix because they usually just need a little more to wrap the plot up. The climax is over, the core conflict resolved, and it's now time to let the characters take a breath and get on with their lives.

If your ending just stops after the climax, try showing:

The characters' reactions to the victory: The characters have been working all novel to resolve this issue, so let readers know how they feel about winning (or losing if that's the way the story ends). Give readers the emotional payoff they've been waiting for.

How the resolution changed the protagonist's life: If this victory brings about a much-needed change in the protagonist, readers will want to see that change. Look for ways to show how the protagonist is different now, and how that has made her life better (or worse) and changed who she is.

Where the protagonist and key characters go next: While you don't have to lay out the rest of the characters' lives, a hint or suggestion that they're headed in the right direction to get their hopes and dreams is enough for most readers. You can show the first kiss and hint that it will lead to happily-ever-after, or show the sun coming out on a new and brighter day without fear.

Look for ways to let readers know life goes on for the characters they've come to care for and that those lives will be the ones they hoped for all novel.

The larger or far-reaching ramifications of this victory: In some stories, the goal is to make large-scale changes in the world, and readers will want to see if those changes occurred or had any effect. Small examples that indicate the situation will get better will leave readers hopeful that everything will indeed turnout okay.

Look for ways to add clues, or even state outright where appropriate, that life has changed and the world is heading onward on a new path.

Endings often need a few tries to get right, so don't worry if you have some rewriting to do. Keep reminding yourself that the ending resolves the problem stated in the beginning.

If your story structure is now solid, move on to ways to deepen your plots and subplots.

If You Want to Deepen the Plot

There are some plot problems almost every writer runs into in almost every draft. Sometimes you need to write the first draft so you know enough about the story to be able to fix these issues, and they clean up with little trouble. Other times, they're deeper-rooted problems that take more work to fix.

In this session, the goal is to address any plotting issues discovered in your analysis.

If you get stuck, remember the cornerstones of plot: What do your characters want and what are they going to do to get it?

Step One: Fill in Any Plot Holes

A common plot hole is a scene where the characters are doing what they *need* to do for the plot to unfold, but the reasons might be weak or non-existent. Readers don't know why this event or situation is happening, or there's no explanation of how it could happen based on what's been seen so far.

To make it all seem logical, look for:

A previous event or situation that can affect the problem scene: Chances are your scene doesn't exist in a vacuum. If it does, you might want to look at the sessions on fixing episodic chapters in Step Three. Something had to happen for your characters to be at this point. Go back and look at each of the key scenes that led the protagonist in this direction:

- Where did the protagonist make a choice that would affect this scene?

- Where did something unforeseen occur that affected this scene?

- Where did the protagonist miss a clue (or where could she miss one) that would affect this scene?

- Can the antagonist cause a change through her actions?

A character who can act or choose differently to change the outcome: A simple choice can change how a situation later unfolds. This is especially true if the problem scene involves an item, or a piece of information. Having a character find or learn something early on that can simmer in readers' minds until it's relevant can set up what you need to have happen without it feeling contrived.

- Where might a character make a different choice to achieve the desired outcome for that scene?

- Where might new information be revealed that affects a decision?

- Where might information be withheld instead?

A new way to achieve the desired result: Sometimes you need to step back from the scene and look at it objectively. Forget what you wrote or planned. Consider what steps *need* to happen for this scene to work. Then look back and see where any of those steps might take place:

- Where did the plot go off track?

- Where might a clue be discovered to lead it where it needs to go?

- Where might a character do or say something to lead in this direction?

- What might be added to achieve this result?

Don't be afraid to look elsewhere for the real problem. Sometimes it's not the scene you think that's "broken," but what came *before* that scene that's causing trouble. Look at the scenes leading up to the problem and see if adding more groundwork would make the scene turn out just fine.

Step Two: Fix Contrived or Coincidental Plots

Is the protagonist *always* finding the right person at the right time, who happens to have the *exact* item she's looking for? No matter how exciting a story may be, when the plot hinges on coincidences, readers feel cheated. If solutions to problems are falling into the protagonist's lap with little to no work, the plot will feel contrived.

Plots work best when events happen for reasons rooted in character goals and motivations and not because the author wanted it to unfold that way. There's a fine line between situations that read plausibly and those that read like a series of unlikely coincidences.

Unlikely is the key here. Coincidences *do* occur in real life, and often you'll find one or two in a story. It only becomes troublesome when a high percentage of plot events rely on coincidence to make them happen, *and* they get the protagonist out of a jam.

Rework to remove any problem coincidences and give plausible reasons for events to turn out the way they do:

Make sure the protagonist causes this event to happen: Let a goal lead directly (or indirectly) to this event happening.

Let a needed plot coincidence relate to the protagonist's goal: Maybe the coincidence is a result of a choice made, or a result of a previous action. For example, the protagonist chose to ignore A to deal with B, and now A is coming back to bite her in the butt. Or she tried to fix C and that made B happen.

Make sure the other characters in the story, especially the bad guys, have a plan: Antagonists with plans and goals of their own make much better villains, because their actions have motives, and that keep their plans from seeming random. The plan is grounded in strong motivations and goals just like the protagonist's, so even when the protagonist is trying to solve one problem, the antagonist is chugging along on his own, causing trouble.

Find a plausible reason for the coincidence to happen: If two strangers both have kids attending the same school, them running into each other at a school event is plausible, even if the coincidence happens to be the right thing at the right time. But those same strangers running into each other on a random street at a random time will feel contrived. Readers don't need much to maintain believability—they *want* to buy into your story. Show events aren't *entirely* random, and they'll go with it.

If your characters are after something for a reason and their paths cross logically, you reduce your coincidence level considerably. But they also have to *work* for it. They have to uncover clues, overcome obstacles, face internal struggles, complete the tasks that make figuring out the solution plausible.

Step Three: Fix Episodic Chapters

An episodic structure often develops when you have a series of location or goal changes and you lose the thread tying the chapters together. Events are happening, possibly even exciting "doing all the right stuff" things, but information is being put out there and it's not *going* anywhere. There's no cause and effect between chapters, even if there is within scenes.

You might have an episodic plot if:

You can shift chapters around and the plot doesn't change: This is a big red flag, because it indicates the scenes are self-contained and aren't affecting what comes after them. If six chapters can happen in any order as long as it's all before the Act One climax, they're episodic.

Every chapter has a different, unrelated goal: While you want all your scenes to have a goal, if those goals aren't steps in a larger plot, they're not doing much to advance your story. Look at where those goals lead. Is the resolution of one setting up the next? Does the next chapter start with an event or decision created by the previous goal? Does it continue with that previous goal and lead somewhere new?

The early chapters are just setting up later chapters: Foreshadowing is good, but if you have a lot of chapters in a row that are there *only* to set up later events, readers will wonder what the point is. World building and backstory chapters are common culprits here. What happens in them doesn't matter because the point is to show some aspect of the character or the past that will have relevance later. The scene goal is just something to make the scene work since you *need* a goal.

How to the Plot Moving Again

Luckily, reincorporating episodic chapters isn't that tough. It usually just takes deepening the connections already under the surface, and adding a common thread that ties everything back to the plot.

Look for ways to:

Connect the goals: How might you connect the goals in these chapters so they trigger each other? Are there external events pushing your protagonist toward her decisions that can be connected? Look at the major plot event for that part of the novel—what are the steps to get there? How can you make those steps the goals?

Connect the internalization: Can your protagonist have a common train of thought that connects the chapters? Inner conflict can tie the story together if the external conflict isn't linear.

Connect the stakes: Can the chapters all be ways to avoid the same stake? Different attempts to accomplish a similar task?

Connect the conflict: Can you bring forward a conflict that these chapters set up? Maybe foreshadow a later problem or failure?

Episodic chapters can read like random scenes, but there's a reason you wrote them, so pinpointing that reason is often all it takes to fix them. Look more deeply at what's going on and pull out those connecting threads so readers can see the story building.

Step Four: Get Sidetracked Plots Back on Track

Sometimes you can get so focused on creating problems for your protagonist that you forget what they were doing in the first place.

Here are common red flags that a plot has gone off track:

All the problem does is delay what would have happened anyway: This problem exists only to *be* a problem, and doesn't do anything to advance the story. When the protagonist resolves this goal, nothing about the overall story has changed at all. For example, completing Goal B doesn't matter, because she *still* needs to complete Goal A to avoid or prevent a consequence. You most often see this in middles, but it can happen anywhere.

The resolution to the current problem won't affect the overall story much, if at all: The problem might affect the story in a large-scale "the protagonist gets caught" kind of way, but the specific actions don't change anything. These scenes are probably decent scenes, but they're dragging the pacing or feel a little flat as a whole, and making the reader's eyes glaze over.

The resolution to the problem sends the protagonist even further away from the story goal: It's good to waylay your protagonist a little, but a subplot that requires more work than the plot to solve just so the protagonist can get back on track is one you can usually lose and not hurt the story any.

You keep adding more problems to reach a key piece of information for the plot or character: Ironically, if you have strong goal-conflict-resolution skills, you're more likely to find yourself going astray in this way because you're looking for opportunities to make the situation worse. Make sure any problems added keep your plot tight, focused, and riveting.

Fixing a Sidetracked Plot

If you think your plot has veered off track, look at each scene or plotline and consider:

How is this problem hindering the protagonist's goal? In most cases, you'll be able to answer this pretty quickly. "It keeps her from the safe house." "It stops her from meeting Brad." "It puts her life at risk." But look again at those quick and easy answers. Is keeping her from the safe house something that *also* provides a solid conflict for the overall plot, or is it one more thing getting in the way of a step that *does* connect to the bigger plot? If the problem is more delay than real conflict, it could be what's sending the plot sideways.

Is this problem different from what you've already done? It's not unusual to have the same basic scene repeated in various ways. The protagonist has to sneak past a guard to get some vital piece of information. She's trapped and has to fight her way out. She gets captured by the bad guy. Sometimes these tasks *are* important and you can't help a little repetition, but if you find yourself using a lot of similar scenes or goals just to make it harder on your protagonist, you might be throwing too much at her.

What is the protagonist trying to do from a larger standpoint, and how does this smaller step fit into that? Character goals, especially larger story arc goals, don't always start and end in one scene or chapter. They span chapters, with multiple obstacles to slow them down. It's a good idea to look at what the protagonist is trying to do overall (like a major turning point goal) and how the smaller goal fits into that.

The plot is important, especially in genre fiction, but if the story isn't holding that plot up, it just flops around and makes people look away. Keep your story in mind, and how your plot can serve that story.

Compelling characters need something to do, and a strong plot will allow them to show off their skills (and reveal their flaws). A solid plot is also how you illustrate your story to readers.

Let's dig in and develop character goals and motivations next.

Developing the Goals and Motivations

What the protagonist does and why she does it drives the plot. Weak goals or implausible motivations risk making your plot weak and implausible as well. The stronger the goals, and the better the reasons for trying to achieve those goals, the stronger your plot will be.

In this session, the goal is to fix any goal and motivation issues found in your analysis, and look for ways to make the characters' choices harder.

A note about goals and motivations: The focus here is on the protagonist, but this holds true for all point-of-view characters, and even the antagonist (though often those goals are off screen).

Step One: Add or Strengthen the Goals

Add any missing goals first, as they'll directly affect how the plot unfolds, then move on to strengthening the weak or unclear goals. Weak goals are often caused by a lack of motivation—the protagonist seems as though she's following a script—so you might need to focus on the motivation first in some cases.

It's also common for protagonists to have too *many* goals, and the best way to tighten the scene is to trim out the smaller, less important goals. Try moving those extra goals to scenes that need more action or forward movement.

In every scene, make sure:

It's clear what the protagonist wants: Sometimes all it takes is for someone to say it.

The goal is specific: Weak goals are often the result of a too-vague need, such as "finding love." There's nothing to physically do to achieve that, so the protagonist can't act. But "going to the park to meet people" is an actionable goal to drive the plot and eventually find love.

It's the most logical goal for the situation: Implausible goals are frequently spotted in scenes where the easiest, most obvious path is ignored by the protagonist in lieu of some convoluted plan. It's human nature to take the path of least resistance, so if you need the protagonist to work harder to win, make sure she has reasons why she can't take the easy route.

The protagonist acts in ways to achieve that goal: Weak goals sometimes happen because the protagonist says she wants X, and then doesn't try to get it. She phones in the work and then the goal magically drops into her lap—a common problem with contrived or coincidental plots.

Step Two: Add or Strengthen the Motivations

What the protagonist does moves the plot, but why she does it moves the character arc. Goals and motivations work hand in hand to propel the scene forward.

Add any missing motivators first, then move on to the weak ones.

Look at your motivations and make sure:

It's clear why the protagonist wants to do what she's doing: Often, all a scene needs is a line or two of dialogue or internalization to make that motivation clear. There's a reason for it in your head: it just didn't make it to the page on the first draft.

It's what the *protagonist* wants, not the author: Pay particular attention to any motivation that "needs to be that way for the plot to work." For example, if the protagonist is going into the abandoned house so she can stumble across the serial killer's lair, the scene is going to feel forced. There's no reason for the *character* to act, and in fact, they way she's acting is contrary to what any normal person would do in that situation. If you need her to go inside that house for the plot to work, create a plausible reason why she'd walk through that door.

Any leaps in logic or in the decision-making process are plausible: This usually happens when something specific needs to be realized or discovered at that point in the plot, and even if the protagonist hasn't done or learned enough to plausibly figure it out, she does anyway. Common feedback for this problem are comments such as, "This seems a stretch" or, "I'm not sure how she came to this conclusion."

If you have a scene with this issue, look back at previous scenes and identify where the character encountered the reasons, clues, or steps that led her to that realization point. Are they clear? Can readers logically make the same connections the protagonist did to reach the same conclusion? A common issue here is a clue that has meaning to the author, but not the readers, so they're not seeing it the same way.

The protagonist's motivations and choices realistically lead the plot where it needs to go: Protagonists who drive the plot are wonderful things, but sometimes they take over and send the story where you didn't *want* it to go. When this happens, it's not unusual for you to force the plot back on track in a way that forces the protagonist to act in a way that doesn't feel plausible. For example, the wife of a cheating husband has been going to great lengths to eradicate him from her life, but then the plot demands she gives him a second chance, and the rest of the novel depends on it. So she does, even though there's no way she'd do it based on how the story unfolded.

The right motivation can cause your protagonist to do whatever you need them to, even if it's something no sane person would *ever do*.

After your characters are acting with purpose, take a closer look at the obstacles getting in their way—conflicts and stakes.

Developing the Conflicts and Stakes

Sit in on any agent panel at a writers' conference and you're bound to hear at least one say the most common problem with manuscripts they receive is a lack of conflict and stakes. Without conflict there is no story, and without stakes, there's no reason to care about the conflict.

In this session, the goal is to make sure your conflicts are strong and your stakes are high.

Places to Look for Conflict

Conflict—both internal and external—is all around your characters. If you think your novel lacks conflict overall, or in a specific scene, try looking at these areas first:

Family: Are there any family issues that can throw a wrench in the protagonist's plan?

Friends: Can a friend oppose, disagree, or even need help when the protagonist is least able to help?

Self: Are there personal demons, fears, secrets, or other personal issues that could cause trouble?

Work: What problems or issues can come up on the job, or because of the job?

World building: What inherent problems occur in the world?

Health: Is there a medical issue that can cause recurring trouble?

Having a better sense of where the potential conflicts lie will make it easier to add and strengthen conflicts during this session.

Step One: Strengthen the External Conflicts

Conflict is an often misunderstood word. It's easy to assume it means fighting, but conflict is just two sides opposed to the same goal. It can be adversarial (bad guy wants to nuke the city, good guy wants to stop him) or friendly (sister wants to win the race, brother wants to win the race). It can be different approaches to the same goal between friends, or even conflict within the character.

Examine any weak scenes and determine if one (or more) of these options would strengthen the conflict:

Force the protagonist to make a hard choice: Look for places where the protagonist has to make a choice, and make that choice as difficult as possible. If the answer or path is easy, brainstorm ways that aren't so clear or easy.

Let the antagonist work against the protagonist: Is the antagonist causing trouble or doing something that would result in trouble in the scene? Could the antagonist meddle somehow? What if you put them or their cronies in the same room with the protagonist? What would happen? If the antagonist isn't acting for his own reasons, even when the bad guys *are* trying to stop the protagonist, it doesn't feel like their hearts are in it.

Eliminate coincidences that work to aid the protagonist instead of hindering her: Weak conflicts often appear when the plot "just needs to go that way." For example, the author knows the protagonist will escape from jail, so the scene is written as if this is a foregone conclusion. The protagonist gets a lot of lucky breaks, the bad guys get a lot of *unlucky* breaks, and even if bad luck *does* befall the characters, it turns out to be the best thing that could have happened and works in their favor.

This is usually an easy fix—revise as if the protagonist might not succeed. Think about how the other characters or obstacles in the scene would act or work if they truly *were* trying to stop the protagonist. This will force the protagonist to work harder to win and provide real problems that feel natural to the scene.

Consider what the *other* characters want: What often holds a scene back are non-point-of-view characters who know what the protagonist wants (because the author does) so they go along with it or don't try all that hard to stop it. Friends of the protagonist are on her side and support whatever she's doing and how she's doing it. Everyone is always on the same page because that's where the plot is going.

Who might want something different from the protagonist in the scene? Are there differences of opinion in how a plan is to be enacted? Are there any ethical differences that can come into play?

Put the protagonist in an emotional or ethical bind: Doing something the protagonist knows or believes is wrong can cause a lot of trouble. It hurts, it makes her feel guilty, it could cause her to overreact about something else. Look for issues that might give the protagonist a reason *not* to act as planned.

Let the protagonist balk: Not acting at the right moment can ripple problems down the line. Look for fears or flaws that might come into play and cause hesitation at the worst possible moment.

Blow the protagonist's mind: Discovering something shocking that changes the protagonist's worldview can send her into a tailspin. Having her world turned upside down will affect her judgment, her belief system, her self-image. When everything is off kilter, *anything* can happen. What revelation might make the protagonist question or doubt what she's doing or believes in?

Let the protagonist be wrong: If the protagonist is so sure she needs to act in a certain way, she'll ignore good advice and even warning signs she's wrong. Is there anything in the scene she's wrong about? Can there be?

Let the protagonist be right: Have you ever lied to someone and they called your bluff? Protagonists can call bluffs too, and then cause worse trouble than if they just let it go. Embarrassing someone they'll later need help from will cause trouble for sure. Is there anyone hiding something the protagonist might expose, or information she can reveal at the worst time?

External conflicts help create the problems the protagonist will solve during the novel, but those obstacles aren't the only things getting in the protagonist's way.

Step Two: Strengthen the Internal Conflicts

The heart-wrenching conflicts that keep readers glued to the pages are more often than not the internal conflicts. You don't know what a character might do when faced with an impossible choice, but you can see that choice is going to have a strong consequence.

Look for ways to force your protagonist to do what she *doesn't* want to do:

Make the protagonist go against her morals or belief system: Sometimes you have to do the wrong thing for the right reason, and those can be the toughest acts to reconcile.

Force the protagonist to make a choice she doesn't want to make: Deep down, you usually know what you have to do, even if you don't want to do it. Are there any choices the protagonist has been dreading?

Force the protagonist to make a bad choice: Mistakes are strong fodder for plot. Protagonists can mess up, and their actions cause more trouble than they were trying to prevent in the first place. This works even better if they make the wrong choice because they're trying to avoid violating one of their belief systems.

Make the protagonist fail: This one can be dangerous, so be wary of putting the characters in situations that stop the story, but sometimes failing is an unexpected and compelling path to take. It's not a setback, it's real failure with real consequences. If those consequences play off an inner conflict, so much the better.

Make the protagonist do something she'll regret: This works well if what the protagonist does early on affects the plot later. For example, a choice she makes trying to avoid one problem directly makes her obstacles tougher to overcome down the road. Maybe she can see this coming and has no choice but to do it anyway. Maybe she has no clue what problems she's about to bring down on herself, but the *readers* do.

It's easy to throw more "stuff" in the way of the protagonist, but also look at your scenes and see what mental obstacles you can toss onto the path. That can not only help deepen your plot, but deepen your characterization and themes as well.

Revision Option: Ways Characters Can Screw Up Their Decisions

As a good person, you want to make the right choice, so it's only natural that those choices come to you first as you write. But doing the right thing doesn't always cause wonderful conflict (though when it does it's writing gold). Characters shouldn't act like people who've had three weeks to consider their options because the author took that long to write the scene. A decision made in the heat of the moment isn't the same as one made with weeks to consider.

Here are some ways your protagonist can make the wrong choice next time she's faced with an all-important decision:

Let the protagonist be impulsive: This is a helpful flaw for protagonists who need to learn patience, or who don't always consider how their actions affect others. For example, they might make snap judgments, quick decisions, or charge full-speed ahead without thinking beyond the now. If you need to get your protagonist in over her head fast, consider this mistake.

Let the protagonist make decisions under pressure: A ticking clock is a reliable way to raise stakes and increase tension in a story. Small pressures build to big explosions, so if you need your protagonist to blow her top, try looking for small ways to eat at her leading up to that explosion.

Let the protagonist over-analyze everything: If the protagonist is so busy deciding what the right thing to do is, she might totally miss the opportunity to act at all. Lost chances that lead to regrets make wonderful seeds to plant early on in a story, and can cause huge emotional trauma during that Dark Moment of the Soul at the end of Act Two. Over-analyzing can also work to sneak in possible dangers and outcomes, helping to raise tensions and keep the plot unpredictable.

Let the protagonist assume she knows it all: Perfect for the protagonist who needs to learn a valuable lesson about working with others. Let her be convinced she's always right, doesn't need advice from anyone else, and has no problem stating that fact to anyone who will listen. The fall here when reality strikes will be devastating, and all the more satisfying.

Don't let the protagonist consider all the options: An informed protagonist is a boring protagonist. Choices made without the benefit of a solid foundation of knowledge can lead to a myriad of delightful screw-ups. Maybe there's no time for research, or there's something she doesn't want to think about (denial, much?). Missing key information can send a character into a mess of her own making.

Don't let the protagonist ask for advice: Who needs a long-winded story from some old geezer about how he did it when he was younger? Times change, and what worked then surely won't work now. This is a flaw for the protagonist who doesn't respect tradition or the consul of others. The more people she pisses off, the fewer there will be when she needs them at the climax.

Don't let the protagonist make alternative plans: Plan B is overrated. An overconfident protagonist might never see the need for backup plans, because everything is going to go as she expects. So when the plan starts falling to pieces, she's incapable of wise action to correct her mistake, which causes events to snowball, getting her into more and more delicious trouble.

Making smart choices is vital in the real world, but making conflict-creating *bad* choices is a must for the fictional world. While you don't want your characters to be stupid (unless it's by design), mistakes lead to growth, and a good character grows by the end of the tale. This is especially useful for weak character arcs that need a little help.

REVISION RED FLAG: It's a fine line between likable characters who make mistakes and too-stupid-to-live characters who make the same mistakes and never learn. Make sure you don't accidentally turn a character into an unlikable screw-up who annoys or angers readers.

Revision Option: Ways to Make the Decisions Harder

You know what your protagonist wants, and you know why she wants it. Now, make it as hard as possible to get it.

Mix the external challenges with the internal ones: Look for ways to play the internal and external conflicts against each other. This works well because the outcomes aren't obvious, so it keeps readers guessing what will happen.

Put the character between a rock and hard place: Force characters to make impossible choices—neither option is good, but they have to do *something*.

Give each option risks or consequences: Stakes grab readers, so look for ways in which the choice has consequences and ramifications after that decision is made. Give all the options downsides—even if the protagonist doesn't see them.

Demand a sacrifice: Give the decision a cost and make it harder for the protagonist to win. Early on in a story, she probably won't be willing to make that sacrifice, but later, she'll have little choice. Offering the same sacrifice at the beginning and end of a story can be an effective technique as well. What is she willing to give up now that she wasn't before, and why?

Let the action mirror something critical that will come later: Just like a sacrifice, if there's a theme or aspect of character growth that needs to occur, try starting the groundwork for it early. If the protagonist is faced with a similar choice later, perhaps show her making the *wrong* choice early to show growth (or foreshadow failure) for that later moment.

Exploit a fear, flaw, or weakness: Is there anything the character is afraid of that you can take advantage of? Maybe it's a flaw you can show in action so readers can see how that character overcomes that flaw (and probably wins despite it).

⚑ **REVISION RED FLAG:** Be careful not to mistake a tough choice with one that looks tough, but really isn't. Look at the options. If the "right" choice is obvious, even though that choice is something that will be hard to do (or hard to deal with), it isn't really a choice. It's just something hard the protagonist has to do.

Revision Option: Adding Quiet Conflicts

Smaller moments can add conflict and tension to a scene without turning it into a melodramatic mess. They're great for character-driven novels where the focus is more internal than external, but also good for internal goals and character arcs.

If you have scene with weak conflicts, you might add:

Conflicts over emotions: Some conflicts are out of love. The protagonist wants to go to a party, but her best friend wasn't invited. If she goes, it'll hurt her friend's feelings. Sparing (or hurting) someone's feelings might have huge repercussions later on. Since these conflicts are personal, the stakes are naturally higher even if the conflict is mundane. No one wants to hurt someone they care about.

Conflicts over friendships: Rivalries and friendly competitions can cause conflicts, especially if they start out friendly then turn more serious. Even a constant one-upmanship can still be fun and make readers curious how the situation will turn out. Who will get the upper hand this time? Will there be a moment when that upper hand matters? They're even handy to show a skill the character might need later on without making it obvious.

Conflicts on the lighter side: Some conflicts can focus on the funny, such as a mom trying to put a diaper on a kid who's running around laughing. Their goals are in opposition (mom wants a diapered baby, baby wants to be naked and free) but there's nothing adversarial here.

While funny conflicts won't work all the time (there's often little to no stakes in this type) they can add enjoyable levity that can work well with more serious moments—a light scene right after a dark one, the calm before everything breaks loose. It can give your character something to do if the scene is mostly dialogue and feels static.

Try looking at any weak scenes to see if a quiet conflict will improve it:

- Can you make two people disagree?
- Can you make anyone else want something different from what the protagonist wants?
- Can someone try to talk the protagonist out of something? Into something? Change her mind?
- Can one person be trying to spare another's feelings?
- Can one person be trying to keep another from finding out something?
- Can someone be trapped between two others and be torn about who to side with?
- Is there a friendly rivalry?
- Does anyone want the same thing the protagonist wants? (in an "only one can get it" scenario)
- Can anyone have/get what the protagonist wanted?
- Can the conflict be played for laughs?
- Is there humor in the situation if two people disagree or have different approaches?

Step Three: Fix Low or Missing Stakes

Low stakes is the most common problem with scenes that are doing everything right, but still aren't quite working.

A handy test for low stakes is to ask these two questions:

If the protagonist walked away, what would change? This can help spot stakes that seem high, but aren't really. For example, "they could die" should be the highest stake of all, but if the protagonist walks away she'll live. Problem solved. Sure, others might die, but do readers *really* care about a faceless mass of unnamed people? Nah.

If you put the second-most important character in the protagonist's slot, what would change? Those close to the protagonist often have similar things at risk. If the story would unfold pretty much the same way, the stakes aren't personal enough. "The bad guys invade her town" is a good start, but again, so what? Anyone who lives there has that same thing at stake.

Common problems with stakes:

Stakes are too low: The consequences are either missing, or not something that would cause anyone any lasting harm. It's also common to see stakes so high they feel low because readers know they won't happen. Stakes without real bite are no stakes at all.

Stakes aren't personal enough: If the protagonist can stop at any time with no personal repercussions, why put herself at risk? Impersonal risks often indicate a lack of motivation, since there's no reason for the protagonist to act other than "plot said so."

Stakes are raised too high, too fast: Starting the stakes too high can hurt a story because tensions can't rise if the stakes can't get any higher.

Mix up the types of stakes so situations keep getting worse and worse until the end. Save the biggest risk for the climax, and build up to that. Create waves of low to high stakes, peaks and valleys like a roller coaster.

Stakes turn into melodrama: Constantly high stakes can start to feel melodramatic after a while. If *everything* is always life or death and the end of the world, then nothing matters because readers know the protagonist isn't going to die and the world won't end. Create stakes where the protagonist *can* lose.

What makes something high or low stakes is how it affects the protagonist on an emotional level. The smallest, most mundane event can be devastating to the right person in the right circumstance. The largest, most horrendous event can be just another day at the office to someone who commonly makes those choices.

Refer to your scene analysis and look for notes on low or missing stakes, or scenes where the protagonist's actions didn't affect anything, or didn't seem important enough to make readers care about the outcome.

Look for ways to:

Change or affect the protagonist's life if she fails to achieve the goal: Even if the change is small, every scene should affect the protagonist. What consequences can you add to this scene? What existing consequence can be made more dire? How might you make it impossible for the protagonist to walk away from this problem? If there *are* good stakes, can you make the risks or consequences more clear?

Have the stakes affect the protagonist personally: How might you make the stakes more personal for the protagonist? How might you narrow the focus so it affects people closest to the protagonist? How might the stakes trigger a memory or personal issue the protagonist has that makes the goal harder? How might the consequences of the action cause a personal problem?

Give the protagonist something to lose if she walks away from this problem: Failing isn't that dire a threat if there's no price to pay for it. What can the cost of failure be in the scene? What will the protagonist lose is she doesn't get the goal or fix the problem?

Escalate the stakes: If the stakes at the end of a scene match the beginning, that could indicate nothing has changed or gotten worse (stakes don't need to increase every scene, but if something's wrong with the scene and everything else checks out, this could be the reason). Where can you escalate the stakes? Where can plans go wrong? Are there any places where the protagonist wins that would be better if she lost instead?

Make the stakes clear from the beginning of the scene: Inform readers what's at stake. Sometimes it's not obvious, and the reasons behind a character's actions don't make sense. Look for places where your characters can discuss or consider the risks—even if you never plan to have them happen. It's the fear of what *could* happen that helps raise the stakes.

Just having stakes isn't enough if the stakes are minor or inconsequential. Make sure the stakes change the protagonist's life in meaningful ways.

Revision Option: Ways to Raise the Stakes

Stakes are the emotional fuel of your story and drive your protagonist to act. The more compelling your stakes, the more compelled your reader will be to see what choice your protagonist will make—and how it'll all turn out.

Look for low-stakes scenes and:

Have something go wrong: Protagonists assume their plan will unfold in a certain way, and when it doesn't go as expected, the dangers—and the risks—get higher. Look for places where mistakes can be made and plans can fail.

Make it personal: Bad things happening to faceless people don't tug at the heartstrings the same as something bad happening to someone we care about. This is why the hometown football hero who dies in a car accident hits us harder than the thousands of teens who die in car accidents every year. We know the local boy, but the others are strangers. Let the characters readers know and care about suffer.

Demand a sacrifice: Giving up something that matters a great deal shows how much is at stake for the protagonist and what she's willing to risk to succeed. Take away what matters most and force her to go get it back (or find a way to live without it).

Create cascade failure: Bad choices made early on can trigger catastrophic problems later in the story. Knowing that events might have turned out differently makes every action mean more, and seeing how the story ties together makes readers worry about even the smallest actions or choices.

Start small, get bigger: Start off with small stakes that can be escalated throughout the novel, so problems constantly get worse. Even better, look for problems that will snowball, so the small stake in the opening scene eventually turns into the dire stake at the end of the book.

Revision Option: When to Raise the Stakes

You don't need to raise the stakes every chapter, but aim for at least an escalation of stakes at major plot turning points where the protagonist is faced with a decision that will send the story in a specific direction. Moments such as:

The Inciting Event: This is usually the first time the stakes are introduced. Something goes wrong and it matters enough to the protagonist to fix it so the consequences won't affect her.

End of Act One: This is the moment when the protagonist realizes the problem isn't so little, and her first attempt to fix it failed or had unexpected consequences.

Midpoint Reversal: Often, this is the first indication that the problem affects more than just the protagonist, with glimpses of the bigger picture. Or, if the stakes have always been big picture, then this moment might be when issues become personal for the protagonist.

End of Act Two: The full scope of the problem and what it means hits the protagonist. Frequently, a sacrifice is required at this time.

End of Act Three: This is the climax, with the highest and most personal stakes of the novel. It's all or nothing, do or die. Failure is not an option.

Of course, these aren't the only places to raise the stakes. Also look for moments where:

- Choices must be made.
- Beliefs are questioned, and the protagonist must act in a way that goes against those beliefs.
- The internal conflict is at odds with the external goal. Success in one means failure in the other.
- Choices or acts are questioned, and the protagonist is second-guessing what she's done and what it means.

Novels with strong conflicts and high stakes are hard to put down. Make the most of your scenes by tightening every conflict and raising every stake you can.

Next, let's develop how the subplots are taking advantage of all these goals, conflicts, and stakes.

Developing the Subplots

Sometimes a subplot leads you to a wonderful place you never would have found otherwise, but it can also lead you off to die alone in the woods. As long as you pay attention to the path you're on and where you're going, you'll be better equipped to tell the difference.

In this session, the goal is to cut unnecessary subplots, develop any weak subplots so they're working as intended to enhance the story, or add a subplot to flesh out the story.

Step One: Cut Unnecessary Subplots

If you did the subplot analysis in Analyze the Plots and Subplots, you should have already identified subplots that aren't working. Start by eliminating those.

Don't forget to track down any information, characters, or details associated with this subplot in other areas of the manuscript. It's common to find revision smudge—leftover bits of story—after cutting a large chunk of the novel. Searching for names or unique words associated with the subplot can help find any leftovers.

Step Two: Strengthen Weak Subplots

Subplots enhance the story by deepening something in the plot, theme, character, character arc or other aspect of the novel. Look at any weak subplots and pinpoint how and where they connect to one of these elements. These are also good things to consider if you want to add subplot.

Look at the existing subplot and consider what the focus of the subplot is:

To show an aspect of the protagonist: Subplots focusing on the protagonist typically allow her to display skills needed for the core conflict, teach her a lesson that will be needed later, give her greater understanding of herself or what she faces, etc. They're commonly connected to the character arc, helping the protagonist grow into the person she needs to be, while at the same time making her quest for the core conflict harder to accomplish.

- What about the protagonist will this subplot explore?
- Is this aspect something readers are going to want to know?
- How does this aspect aid the protagonist in the core conflict or character arc?

To show an aspect of the core conflict or story: Subplots focusing on the core conflict typically make the main story problem harder, provide avenues toward solving that problem, show a larger connection to the world, etc. They're often more plot-focused than character-focused, adding complexity to the main storyline.

- What about the story problem will this subplot enhance?
- Will it shed additional light on what it all means?
- Does it add dramatic irony to raise tensions or up the stakes?
- Does it send the protagonist toward a discovery she couldn't otherwise make?

To show an aspect of the theme: Subplots focusing on the theme are often also strongly connected to another aspect, using the theme to give greater meaning to that aspect. It might show why the fight is so vital, or what larger concepts the fight represents. It could show how the fight will affect the protagonist or what she's risking by trying to resolve the issues. Overall, a theme-focused subplot usually makes the novel deeper and richer on some level.

- What about the theme resonates in the subplot?
- How does the theme affect the other aspects of the story, such as plot and character?
- Will it create a greater understanding of the story as a whole?
- Does it shed light on the protagonist or another major character?

If a subplot isn't enhancing some aspect of the novel, odds are the story doesn't need it.

Revision Option: Evaluating the Benefits of a Subplot

Occasionally, you'll have a subplot that works as a subplot should, but you're not sure if it's doing all that much for the novel. This is especially true for novels you want to trim. It works, you like it, but is it *vital*?

Look at the subplot and consider:

Does the subplot use an existing character, or a new one? Subplots with new characters are likely less connected to the rest of the novel, so they're good candidates for deletion. They can also indicate a story tangent that's on the edge of the main story.

Does the subplot make the story better? Better can be subjective, so be ruthless here. Would the novel as a whole be worse off if you cut this subplot? What exactly does having it gain you? If it's not adding multiple layers of benefit, it might be worth getting rid of.

Evaluate the time spent vs. story gained: If a subplot only needs a few scenes to unfold, and it adds good value to the story, it's probably worth keeping. But if it requires a lot of page time for not a lot of gain, it's a good subplot to cut or cut down.

How many steps are needed to complete the subplot? Some subplots are so large they're almost novels by themselves. Is this a subplot that's close to taking over the focus of the novel? It could indicate a problem—especially if you wind up with two major conflicts to resolve by the end.

Revision Option: Ways to Add Subplots

If you think your plot is a little light and needs a subplot to enrich it, start by examining common places for subplots to flourish. Perhaps you can:

Explore a relationship: Look at the protagonist's relationships and what issues these characters deal with over the course of the novel. Consider how the relationships might change the protagonist or situation and ripple through the novel. For example, what happens if the protagonist has a fight with a jealous classmate right before she must make the hardest decision of her life? That's bound to affect her decision—and might even cause her to make a bad one.

Explore a character: Look at both the protagonist and the other major characters. Are there juicy conflicts brewing? Don't just look at conflict between them and the protagonist, but other characters and other people in the story as well. These might make excellent subplots, so see if they also develop or benefit some other aspect of the character or plot. Maybe there's a lesson to be learned in a subplot surrounding the best friend, or maybe how the love interest deals with something is a beautiful mirror for the theme.

Illustrate a theme: Look for characters who can represent your theme or a facet of that theme. What problems do they face? What are they trying to do in the novel that can touch your protagonist? Who might be a good candidate to foreshadow a choice or consequence the protagonist will face later?

Give a secondary character a small plot arc: Think about how the other characters in the novel might affect the outcome of the main plotline. Does anyone influence the protagonist at a key moment? Are there choices made that would have turned out differently if this character had not been involved? Is there an important element you want to explore but suspect it's not strong enough to be a subplot?

When developing subplots, don't forget the "arc" part of the story arc. Three points make an arc, so you'll want to have a beginning, middle, and ending for your subplot. It can have more than three scenes of course, but an arc is something readers can follow and anticipate.

If you want to add a few surprises, a plot twist might be what the scene needs instead. Let's look at those next.

Developing Plot Twists and Twist Novels

There's no formula for devising a compelling plot twist, because every plot is different and any number of things can work in a novel. But one trick for twisting a plot is pretty simple: Defy reader expectations.

In this session, examine any plot twists and make sure they're grounded in the story and not appearing out of the blue, and look for a good place to add a twist if you think you need one.

Step One: Fix Weak Plot Twists

The trick to a good plot twist is to give readers what they expect, but not in the way they expect it. Twists work when they shock readers, but then they realize they should have known all along. It's a surprise, but it feels inevitable once the secret is out.

If you think your twist is looking a little murky you might want to (and don't worry if you're not sure how to fix the issue yet—you'll explore that further in the Revision Options):

Pinpoint the clues leading up to the twist: Identify where and when clues to the plot twist are dropped. Make sure they feel natural to the scene and aren't telegraphing something to come.

Add or cut clues as needed: If you think you need more (or fewer) clues, add and cut as necessary. Look for places where the clue would most likely slide right by readers, but still linger in their subconscious.

Determine the right spot for readers to start suspecting the truth: Sometimes you'll want the twist to be a huge surprise; other times you'll want the anticipation of trying to figure it out to help pull your story along.

Determine the right spot for the characters to start figuring it out: Readers often spot details long before characters, but if it's *too* obvious, then your characters look dumb if they haven't figured it out yet. Make sure you have a good balance between reader hints and character hints.

Use twist clues to fix any slow or weak scenes: Weak scenes in need of help could be opportunities to foreshadow the twist. Would adding a layer of mystery to a slow scene help it?

Let characters encounter things thematically or metaphorically linked to the twist: Sometimes someone says something and makes you think of something different. Your brain picks up on it because there's some link between the two details that combine in just the right way. Let the characters hear or experience the perfect trigger for a memory or realization in a later scene.

A twist doesn't have to be a full-blown mind blower to work. Sometimes, smaller, more frequent twists can keep a plot unpredictable and compelling.

Revision Option: Ways to Add a Plot Twist

If you think a plot twist will fix a problem scene, look at your plot and pinpoint the obvious outcomes—even if they're exciting and wonderful and do what a good plot should do.

Once you have some candidates:

Brainstorm for the unexpected: What is the most obvious thing to do in that scene? Scrap that idea. Now what's the *least* likely thing to happen? Most times, you can scrap that idea, too, because it's so far off in left field it won't work for the book. But it usually loosens your brain enough that you start thinking about ideas that *are* unexpected, but not so far off.

Don't think about practicality at this point. When something grabs you, test how it fits into your scene and plot. Don't discard an idea because it doesn't fit or would require a lot more revision—let it simmer and see if a great twist develops from it. A twist is a surprise, and if it was an obvious fit, it wouldn't be a twist.

Reveal a secret: You can also surprise readers by revealing information that ties into the problem. You may have your protagonist resolve this issue exactly as readers expect, but then you slip in a *major* secret or detail that blows their minds and changes the meaning of the events they just saw. What they expected isn't at *all* what's really going on.

Make it worse: Ask the delightful, "What's the worst than can happen?" question on a variety of levels. What's the worst thing for the scene? For the current goal? For the protagonist's inner goal? For the protagonist's flaw or weakness? For a *secondary* character that's important to the protagonist? For the antagonist? The "worst thing" isn't always an external physical thing about to hurt the protagonist—it might be something that tears her world view apart, or shatters her beliefs, or makes her doubt something she's always trusted. It might be choosing between her, a friend, or a loved one.

Expose a liar: An unexpected betrayal can surprise readers and change expectations. So can someone who's been lying about information the protagonist thought was reliable. Or maybe the protagonist has been lying and is finally forced to fess up. Lies don't have to be for nefarious reasons either—a lie told with good intentions can be just as effective.

Let the protagonist lose: Do the unthinkable and let the protagonist lose and the antagonist win. Everything she's been fighting for is gone and now she has to regroup and find a way to go on. This is an extra sticky one though, because it can be easy to make your readers think everything they just read was pointless. Make sure that even if your protagonist loses, what she went through to get there still has meaning and wasn't a waste of your readers' time.

Ask beta readers what they think will happen, then do something else: Have your critique partners or beta readers write what they think will happen at the end of each scene and see if they guess correctly. Change as much as you can without adversely affecting your story or plot.

Revision Option: Is the Twist the Whole Book?

The problem with these types of twists is that since the reveal is secret, the protagonist usually doesn't seem to be driving the story, so the plot often reads as though the characters are wandering around aimlessly. Or worse—that the author is intentionally keeping critical plot secrets from the readers.

If you're revising a twist novel that's giving you problems, it's worth asking, "Does the plot work if readers know the twist, or is the plot all about the big reveal?"

If the novel is one long setup to, "Surprise!" there's a good chance there's not enough plot to hold a reader's attention.

The plot must stand on its own and be exciting, even if readers figure out the twist. It has to have suspense and wonder and hooks, and leave behind all those wonderful little clues that even readers who know the twist will see and delight in—and provide re-read value to go back and see what they missed.

If you're worried your novel is all about the twist, ask:

If you take out the twist, does the plot still work? Use something vague to describe the plot. For example, if the twist is that the protagonist is an alien, make it "protagonist with a big secret." If all the major plot points revolve around discovery of that secret, that's a good clue something is wrong. The protagonist should be doing what matters to her, and *in the process of that*, she discovers that big secret. Subtle difference, but it puts the narrative drive back in the protagonist's hands.

An exception here is for plots that truly are all about discovery of the secret, such as finding a killer, or uncovering a sinister plan. Readers can clearly see what's driving the plot and the effects of the secret, but the point is to work hard to uncover what it is. Uncovering the truth kinda defines those.

Is this idea to show how cool it is that you fooled the reader? This one's a toughie, and you'll have to be honest with yourself. As writers, we want to keep our readers off balance and make our stories unpredictable, but we've all read novels where the author came across as trying to pull a fast one. Key clues were held back, truths were purposely misdirected, everything was done so the author could trick the reader and by the end say "Ha ha, I so fooled you. It was X all along." If readers can't figure it out by they're paying close attention to the clues, you're not playing fair.

Are there subplots that aren't about the twist? With a well-rounded protagonist and solid goals and stakes, there will be subplots and other problems that enhance the core conflict. But if all the subplots are more ways to distract readers (or the protagonist) from the truth, then it might be a red flag the twist has taken control of the story.

Twist stories can be a lot of fun to read *and* write. Discovering the situation wasn't what you thought, and seeing the story in a new light that deepens both plot and character makes for an awesome book. But they can sometimes be a one-trick pony if you aren't careful about developing the *whole* story and are just setting up the big twist.

Finally, let's take a look at dealing with an over-plotted novel.

Fixing an Over-Plotted Novel

Often it's hard to come up with a *single* plot, but some writers can spin a tale like they have an unlimited supply. Trouble is, too many plots in the same novel can spoil a story, and knowing where the line is between complex and complicated can be hard.

In this session, prune out any unnecessary plots and refocus the novel's core story.

Common Problems for an Over-Plotted Novel

Complexity of plot varies by genre and market, and what works for a middle-grade mystery won't fly for an adult political thriller. It's a good idea to study your genre and market to see what's typical for those types of books, and develop guidelines on how much plot works for that type of story.

Common areas for over-plotting include:

Too many people: You most often see too much plot in multiple point of view novels. This structure lends itself to every point-of-view character having a story and plot of their own, and those plots often have several subplots as well.

You might be over-plotting if:

- Each point-of-view character's problem requires its own resolution.
- Each point-of-view character's problem has subplots of its own that are not connected to the core conflict.
- Each point-of-view character's problem is unique and not connected to the core conflict.
- You can't say which point-of-view character is your protagonist.

Same event, with different characters and problems: Having different characters take different elements away from an event is good, but be wary when it starts to feel like different books about a similar subject. You might be over-plotting if:

- One event creates several storylines that unfold in separate directions, while at the same time bringing nothing new to the core conflict of the novel.

- The event triggers issues or problems unrelated to each other.

- Each problem has enough meat on it to become a full book on its own.

It shows all sides, but still needs more to "get it": Adding plots to show another side or perspective because you think, "Readers won't get it if I don't," should make you pause. Your instincts are in the right place—you know you need more to make the story work—but you're looking wider, not deeper, and adding information that won't serve the story. Are you:

- Focusing only on the premise aspect of the story and ignoring the characters and their problems?

- Adding characters whose sole job it is to get one point across?

- Getting caught up in cool backstory for one (or more) of your secondary characters or antagonist and thinking they deserve their own character arc?

- Trying to tell everyone's stories?

- Pulling your protagonist in so many directions you lose the narrative drive, because it's hard to tell what the story is about anymore?

You can't easily say what the novel's about: Try writing a query letter. It doesn't have to be good, but you should be able to say in one or two paragraphs what the novel is about. If you can't, you might have too much plot going on.

- Do you need a paragraph per major character to say what the novel is about?

- Is it impossible to say what the ending is, or what constitutes a win?

- Can you pinpoint a core conflict?
- Can you pinpoint the inciting event?
- Can you write a query at all?

An over-plotted first draft isn't the end of the world, so don't worry if yours is a little bloated. Grab your editorial map and start looking for ways to trim down and get the plot back on track.

Step One: Get Your Plot Back Under Control

An over-plotted novel usually goes in too many directions, so first, decide what the story is about and what plots serve *that* story.

Ask yourself:

Who is the protagonist? This will help pinpoint who is driving the story and who has the most at stake in the problem.

What is the protagonist's problem? This will help pinpoint what the core conflict is, and allow you to cut away all the plots that don't connect to or support this.

What does the protagonist need to do to solve that problem? This will help pinpoint what aspects of the plot and subplots go with this character and this problem.

What internal struggle is the protagonist facing that connect to this problem or need? This will help pinpoint what the character arc is, and what aspects of the plot relate to this growth.

Who is the antagonist? This will help pinpoint where the conflict lies.

What does the antagonist want? This will help pinpoint what the antagonist's goals are, and how that might affect the protagonist and her goals.

How is that conflicting with what the protagonist wants? This will help pinpoint what the core conflict of the novel is and how these two sides interact.

What existing plots are critical to resolving the protagonist's goal? This will help pinpoint which plot elements are necessary to drive the plot.

What characters are critical? This will help pinpoint which characters to keep, and which to cut.

What's your overall theme? This will help pinpoint what scenes or story elements connect to the overall plot, and help you shape remaining elements to better fit the story.

If a plot doesn't connect to the protagonist and core conflict, save it for another book. It's fine for subplots to weave in and out, for other characters to share the spotlight a little, and for multiple events to be going on, but everything should serve the story and drive it toward the same resolution. That resolution may mean something different for every character, but each one will still work within the framework of that story.

Over-plotting usually occurs when you lose sight of what the story is about—a person with a problem. Put the attention back on that person trying to solve that problem and you'll find your way.

Now that the plot is all worked out, let's take a closer look at the individual scenes.

If You Want to Develop the Scenes

Scenes are the pieces that make up the plot. They connect like stepping stones, getting the protagonist from the opening scene to the final scene of the novel. From a structural standpoint, they help you focus the plot and manipulate your readers' emotions. Strong scenes make for strong plots, and thus a strong novel.

In this session, the goal is to fix any scene issues found in your analysis, and strengthen any weak scenes.

Step One: Fix Scenes That Aren't Working

Most times, if a scene isn't working it's because there's no personal goal or stakes driving it. Things are happening *to* the protagonist, not *because of* the protagonist, and she's just along for the ride.

If you have a scene that's not working, first:

Check that you have a proactive protagonist: Make sure the protagonist is actively trying to do something to solve the big story problem.

Then, look for ways to:

Clarify the goal of the scene: Pinpoint what's driving the scene and where the scene needs to go to advance the plot. You might have both external and internal goals here as well, so check to see if those goals support each other or if they conflict (both can work depending on the scene).

Clarify the conflict of the scene: What's the conflict in this scene? Something or someone should be keeping the protagonist from the goal, and it must be circumvented, overcome, or endured. What can you do to add conflict back into the scene? Who or what can be between the protagonist and her goal?

Clarify the stakes of the scene: If the stakes aren't going up even though things are going wrong, that's a red flag that it's just extra trouble and not a real plot obstacle. How can this problem make the risk higher? Personal risks to the protagonist are usually best, but you can also make problems worse for other characters important to the protagonist. Look at internal and external goals, and think about how they will affect the conflict and story down the line as well as the immediate problem in that scene.

Clarify how vital this scene is to the plot: Is this a key moment or one more tiny step in the plot? Steps are good, but too many can send the story off track if the steps aren't advancing the plot. You might have a goal driving the scene, but achieving it doesn't matter to the bigger story, so the scene flounders. If nothing will change if you took the scene out, you probably don't need the scene (or you need to make it matter).

Clarify any reveals in the scene: While not every scene has to have a gasp-worthy, plot-centric reveal, a discovery of some kind is a good way to maintain momentum. It can be new information about the world, a discovery about a character, or a clue that hasn't been solved yet.

Clarify the hand-off in the scene: Maybe the scene is working fine, but it's not doing anything to move the plot to the *next* scene. Look at the results of the protagonist's or point-of-view character's actions. Why will readers want to read the next scene, and what is the likely goal for the next scene?

🚩 **REVISION RED FLAG:** If the attempt to accomplish a goal doesn't have a consequence or trigger a reaction, that indicates the scene might be part of a series of events happening with no narrative drive. Episodic scenes often lack conflict, because there's nothing in them that moves the plot forward. Protagonist does X...and stops, then she does Y...and stops. Add a conflict or obstacle and force the protagonist to make a decision, or reveal information that will give the next scene its goal.

Is the Scene *Still* Not Working?

Sometimes, no matter what you do, a scene doesn't want to work and play well with the rest of the novel. Look at the words you use to *describe* the scene (trust me on this). You might be inadvertently focusing on the wrong narrative aspects and that's leading you astray.

How are you describing the scene? Pay attention to the verbs you use in your summary. Are your characters running, chasing, searching, crying (all active, external verbs), or are they thinking, pondering, considering, debating (all internal verbs)? If your verbs all mean "being inside a character's head," nothing is physically happening in the scene to move the plot. Revise to get the characters out of their heads and into action regarding whatever internal thing is going on.

What will readers learn or discover in this scene? Pay attention to the types of details discovered in your summary. Are they all traits or information about the character and her past, or information that moves the plot forward? If the discoveries are heavy in the character area, that could indicate there's too much backstory, infodumping, or exposition.

Aim for a mixture of discoveries, with character traits, potential problems, and plot elements. There's no perfect mix here, but try to add at least one plot detail to help move the story forward. Add in other details depending on the type of scene it is: a character-developing scene, a plot-moving scene, a set-up-scene, etc. Revise your discoveries as needed.

What will readers worry or wonder about in this scene? Pay attention to how specific the details are in your summary. Vague responses suggest vague conflict or stakes, which can make the scene feel like it's not going anywhere. If there's nothing for readers to worry about, that could indicate low or missing stakes and consequences facing the protagonist. There's a good chance there's no dangling carrot (a story question) to entice readers to keep reading. Raise the conflict and/or stakes or leave the outcome more uncertain to keep the tension high.

This will probably be one of the harder questions to answer, because a lack of conflict is a common problem in early drafts. Often, there *is* nothing to worry about because you (as the author) know the protagonist gets through the scene unscathed. Try letting the protagonist's uncertainty shine through, and making it *look* like things could go wrong, even if you know they won't.

What will make readers want to read the *next* scene? Pay attention to the story questions left unanswered and the consequences of actions taken in the scene. Vague responses here can indicate there's not enough mystery to keep readers hooked.

Also consider predictable outcomes vs. unpredictable ones. "To see if the protagonist makes it out of the hotel alive" probably won't entice readers read on, as the protagonist isn't likely to die. But "To see if the protagonist makes it out of the hotel with the information that will get her inside the secret lab" creates a scene-moving element that also advances the plot. Will she get the information? That answer *could* be no, so readers will want to read on and find out what happens.

🚩 **REVISION RED FLAG:** If you think you *have* to keep a scene even though everything says you should cut it, then odds are there's something about that scene that matters to the story and can't be moved to any other place. This scene is a good candidate to combine with another weak scene.

Step Two: Cut Scenes That Aren't Working

One of the harder things to do during revisions is to cut a well-loved scene, but not every scene is right for every plot.

If you're not sure if you *should* cut the scene, try pinpointing *why* this scene would be missed. Often, there's something in there that you don't want to give up.

Make a list of everything that has to stay and consider why you want it there. Is it because:

It lets you keep a well-written line you love: You'll probably have to cut the scene. Many a writer has forced an entire scene just to get one kick-ass line in there. You know those movies and TV shows where there's a big buildup to a joke, and you think, "Wow, they worked hard for that one." And then the joke isn't nearly as funny as all the work it took to get there. This is the writer's equivalent. If the single line will work elsewhere, move it, but don't force an entire scene into the novel for one good line.

It lets you show a bit of cool history or motivation: You might be able to keep the information if the information can be moved. Look for scenes with similar context. If the history is about your protagonist's childhood, where else does she think about children or growing up? If it's a bad memory, are there any scenes where remembering this would make it harder for her to deal with what's happening? For motivation, where else is she acting based on this same motivation? Are there any spots that could be deepened if this bit was the motivating factor?

It lets you show something that was once important: You can probably cut it. Ideas change as you write and remnants of those ideas can linger. Maybe you had an idea you explored for a while, but a better idea occurred to you three chapters later and you built the rest of the plot on it. Can this idea be woven into something else? Are there any other places where this idea would deepen the conflict or stakes? And the hard one: Is this an idea you like, but which no longer fits the story?

It lets you show description or world building: If that's *all* it does, cut it, or find another scene to add those details in. Does the description evoke a mood you can use to enhance another scene? Is there a perfect spot where the world-building information can be illustrated and not explained?

Some items might need tweaking to fit elsewhere and that's okay, but often, getting it *out* of the story makes you realize you don't need it at all.

Revision Option: Combining Scenes

If you find yourself with several scenes with aspects you want to keep, try merging them into another scene. Look for:

Events with similar stakes: Multiple things going wrong at once can make for some gripping scenes, and allow you to layer the plot and add depth through inner conflict. One external problem might work well with an internal problem and turn a so-so scene into a *wow* scene.

Events that can be made harder if you combine them: Find scenes with similar goals, or scenes that happen around the same time that might work together. Maybe the goal of one scene will cause more trouble or increase the difficulty of another if you introduce that second problem at the same time. For example, the protagonist finds out her husband cheated on her during a scene when she has to give a career-making speech.

Ways to raise the tension in each act: From a more macro-level approach, find story arcs that can be deepened if you combine scenes in that act. Give your protagonist more choices, and make the choices themselves tougher. If both choices have consequences and outcomes, what happens if the protagonist *has* to pick one over the other? What changes?

Places where you can deepen the emotional conflicts: For the micro-level approach, find situations that tweak the emotions, not just the external goal-focused plots. If the protagonist faces an internal struggle in scene A, and an external struggle in scene B, what happens if she faces both at the same time?

Places where you can raise the personal stakes: Bad things happening can be exciting, but it's the personal that gets readers. Find scenes that are big and exciting, yet impersonal, and determine how you might add a personal moment to them from elsewhere in the novel. For example, maybe one of those, "I need this but I'm worried it's a boring scene" types. Themes can be helpful here, as a larger-than-life moment can mirror or symbolize a deeper internal issue.

Don't mix scenes willy-nilly. You want them to work together and build toward a strong plot.

Revision Option: Making Similar Scenes Seem Different

Books often have scenes common to that genre in the plot. If it's a pulse-racing thriller, it'll have lots of action or chase scenes. Romance will have lots of relationship scenes. Mysteries show lots of sleuths looking for clues. After a while, these similar scenes seem repetitive and even predictable.

If you have a lot of chase scenes where the protagonist is never caught, readers might assume she won't be and stop worrying. If you have lovers who *almost* kiss over and over—they won't be the only ones frustrated. But these core scenes are central to these novels, and are even expected by readers.

Here are some ways to make similar scenes seem different:

Change the focus: Look at any similar scenes and determine what the main focus is for each one. How might you shift that focus to achieve the same story goal, but make the scene different? Can any of the scenes end with the current goal being the *result* of something else happening? Can a larger issue drag the characters away from what they were focused on? Can a smaller annoyance become the main problem and the main problem shift to a smaller annoyance?

Change the goal: The core conflict should tie into everything, but if every scene is "let's save the girl!" then the novel can seem stagnant— they're *always* trying to save the girl. Maybe in one scene, show why saving the girl matters, or make it the result of a previous plan gone wrong. Maybe the goal is indirectly tied to saving the girl, but connects more to a subplot. If the goals are always about "getting something," then maybe have a scene that deals with losing it, or keeping it.

Change the stakes: If every stake is death or capture, the tension levels drop right to the floor. Look for problems or decisions that can have consequences and create stakes. Think of them as lynchpins—they might seem small at first glance, but pull one and the entire plan comes crashing down.

Also look for ways to narrow the stakes to an immediate problem or action. If "losing the guy" is the risk, maybe have the scene be something that would *lead* to losing that guy. On its own it's not a horrible consequence, but under the right conditions—catastrophic.

Change the location: Are there too many scenes around a table? In a car? In someone's room? Kick the characters out! A setting change can add all kinds of different (and unexpected) layers to a scene by working thematically with it, or contrasting it. It can add extra dangers, extra problems, and the unexpected. Think outside the box and look at places that—at first glance—look like the worst places for that type of scene to happen.

Change the emotion: Horror might be about the fear, but if the characters are *always* scared, there's nothing to contrast it against. Look at the most emotionally redundant scenes. What would happen if you used the opposite emotion instead? If the protagonist is happy, make her miserable. Terrified? Make her amused or angry. What unexpected emotions might you play with and how might that change the scene?

Change the mood: Think about how movies use mood. Someone breaking into a house in a thriller feels dark and foreboding, but a cat burglar sneaking in to steal a priceless jewel can be sexy and playful. A heist is almost always fun if the thieves are the good guys, yet sinister if they're the bad guys.

Some plots need to have similar situations in multiple scenes, but the scenes don't all have to feel the same. Mix it up and even the same scene done three times can offer something new.

Getting the scenes in order and flowing smoothly from one to the next will go a long way toward creating a strong narrative drive.

Let's tighten that up next.

If You Want to Strengthen the Narrative Drive

Narrative drive is the engine that keeps the story and plot moving forward, giving the novel the momentum it needs to keep readers hooked.

In this session, the goal is to address any narrative drive issues discovered during the analysis.

Step One: Ensure the Protagonist is Driving the Plot

The most common narrative drive problem is a reactive protagonist who does nothing to drive the plot.

Make sure your protagonist is making the plot happen (you should have already fixed any goal issues in Developing Goals and Motivations, but if not, review that next). She has an opinion on what's going on, ideas for what to do, and thoughts that might even go against what others are saying. She should effect change by her choices, and act to accomplish a goal instead of watching it come to fruition.

Your protagonist might not be in the driver's seat in a first draft (it can happen as you work out the story), but by the final draft, she needs both hands tight on the wheel. Make sure she's advancing the plot and character arc so readers always know whose story it is and why that story matters.

REVISION RED FLAG: Be wary if other characters talk more than the protagonist. A protagonist along for the ride often comes across as an observer while other characters talk, plan or even act. Long stretches of dialogue go by where she barely says a word or has a thought. There's no internalization to show how she feels about what's being said, so you could effectively yank her from the scene and readers wouldn't notice she was gone.

Step Two: Identify What Changes in the Scene

Scenes move the plot forward through goals and conflicts. Trying to achieve a goal causes action, and action causes change, so if nothing changes, that's a good indication that the scene lacks the drive to keep the plot moving.

While not every aspect of a scene needs to change every time, if nothing does, the scene is probably missing something important, or it's not needed and is a good candidate to cut.

Examine any stalled scenes and ask:

What changes in the goal? Changes in the goal alter the plot and either push the protagonist farther away from it, or move her closer to it. If the goal changes completely, there's a good chance it also changed the conflict, stakes, or both.

What changes in the conflict? Changes in the conflict are often the result of discovering new information (such as, who is *really* after the protagonist) or changing settings. As tension comes from conflict, this is an area where changes can have a major impact on the narrative drive.

What changes in the stakes? Changes in the stakes usually mean the problem became more personal. It's common to see a reveal or discovery around the same time.

What changes in the motivations? Changes in motivations often come after major setbacks or shocking reveals. Characters who start out with good intentions might sink into more selfish wants as the scene unfolds. The good guy might get sick of always playing by the rules and decide to cut loose, or the character with ambiguous allegiances might finally pick a side.

What changes in the plot? Changes in the plot are typically on a macro level, as the protagonist tries to accomplish the goal in a variety of ways. For example, three chase scenes in a row with the same resolution will feel repetitious and make the story feel stagnant, but three chase scenes with different resolutions that change what the protagonist does, learns, and feels are compelling even if they're similar.

What changes in the setting? Changes in the setting often accompany goal or plot changes, as characters move to a new location to put the plan into action.

It's worth looking at each of these potential changes to see if a change would strengthen the scene. It can also help to consider the point of the scene, both from the author's standpoint (what you want to show by having this scene there) and the character's standpoint (how she sees the scene and what she wants from it). If the point is to explain something, odds are there's not enough change going on to drive it.

Revision Option: Kickstarting Stalled Scenes

If you have a stalled scene, it's usually a lack of one of the core, scene-driving aspects—the goal, conflict, or stakes.

Review the scene and ask:

Are there plausible and strong motivations for the protagonist to be doing what the plot requires? If not, look for ways to motivate the protagonist. This might require going back a few scenes, but somewhere you probably lost the reason the protagonist is on this story path in the first place. At some point, solving the plot problem stopped being the most important thing in her life. More than likely it's because the stakes vanished.

Did the stakes decrease or disappear? When the protagonist stops caring it's usually because there's no longer anything at stake if she fails. Maybe the big bad is still out there, but there's nothing at risk for her *right now*. She feels safe, even if she's still technically in trouble or on the run. Look for ways to put the protagonist back in danger.

🚩 **REVISION RED FLAG:** Don't just throw random danger at the protagonist. That's equally boring because the danger doesn't matter. Look for places where failure matters to the character, character arc, or the plot.

Did the scene lose its conflict? If the protagonist is merely going through the steps to get from point A to point B, and nothing is in the way (as in, something working to prevent her from obtaining what she wants) the scene can feel lifeless and stall. Look at the internal and external goals and issues. How might you crash those two together so they're at odds with one another? Maybe have your characters disagree over what needs to be done, or have the only way to succeed require a sacrifice the protagonist isn't willing to make. Find ways to make the protagonist face a tough *choice* instead of a tough situation everyone knows she'll get through.

Has a subplot taken over? Sometimes a subplot becomes more interesting and leads the protagonist off on a wild tangent. Then it reaches a point where you don't know what to do or where to go, but you can't get the plot back on track. Look for where you left the plot highway. It might be a plot event or you might have changed the goal or motivation of your protagonist. Did she suddenly change her mind about what she wanted or why she wanted it? Sometimes an exciting subplot idea can push aside the core conflict and you'll find your protagonist has shifted goals with no strong reason to do so.

If a stalled scene won't re-start, that could indicate it's not needed. Consider how cutting it affects the novel. If it won't change anything (or change so little that it's easy to adjust), it might be best to shove it to the curb.

Another way to strengthen the narrative drive is to increase the tension and hooks, so let's explore those next.

If You Want to Increase the Tension and Develop the Hooks

The hook catches your readers' attention and the tension makes them anticipate the outcome. If readers have nothing to anticipate (good or bad), the scene feels weak and slow. That's the key with hooks and tension—it's all about the *reader*, not the character. The protagonist might have no idea a problem is barreling down on her, but if readers can see it coming, and they know it's going to affect the protagonist in a way they worry about, then the tension will be high and they'll stay hooked in the story.

In this session, the goal is to increase any low tension and sharpen any dull hooks.

Step One: Raise the General Tension

Tension is vital to your story, but let's face it—you don't always have it in every scene. A lot of first draft scenes lack tension because the focus is often on the story, the setting, or the characters (or any combination of those). Check out your scenes and:

Eliminate moments where the characters are relaxed: Any time the characters relax, that signals readers there's nothing to worry about. If no other indicators of a potential problem exist, that could result in a lack of tension in the scene. If the scene focuses on relaxing or reflecting characters, try slipping in ways to make them nervous or anxious.

On a scene-by-scene basis try adding:

Something for readers to anticipate (good or bad): It doesn't have to be big to work. A small suggestion that something isn't right can work just as well as a large declaration of plot.

Something for readers to worry about: Conflicts can come into play here. Perhaps drop hints that something will go wrong, or show that situations are not what they seem.

A bit of foreshadowing to an upcoming problem: Show that the characters are headed toward doom. This also works if they're headed toward something positive (like the first kiss in a romance).

A hint of a possible problem, even if it doesn't happen: Problems don't have to come true to be tense. It's the feeling that any second, something might come out of nowhere and surprise them that keeps readers invested.

A ticking clock: The problem that can be solved "whenever" isn't as dire as the one that needs to be solved in the next two hours or else. Even better—if the protagonist is rushing, she'll likely make mistakes, which allows you to craft tougher obstacles and cause her more trouble. Create a nasty consequence for missing a deadline. Raise the stakes. Put that "or else" in there so there's a price for failing.

It doesn't take much to raise the tension in small ways, and it adds a lot of drive to the narrative.

Step Two: Add Tension Between Characters

After you've done a general tension touch up, look at the characters in your scene. If everyone is working as one, you could be missing out on potential areas for tension.

Can anyone be actively trying to prevent the protagonist from getting or doing what she wants? Look for people with reasons not to help the protagonist. A clerk who isn't being helpful. A guard she has to sneak past. A minion of the antagonist with a full-on plan to stop her.

Can anyone disagree with the protagonist? Even if two people want the same thing, they might have different ideas on how to get it. Look for characters who might have other ideas about what the protagonist is doing. Maybe they think she's wrong, or they agree but think she's going about it the wrong way. These opposite opinions can make readers wonder if the protagonist's view is right or not, adding more uncertainty.

Can anyone have an agenda that interferes with the protagonist's plan? If two guys are after the same girl, one might try to sabotage the other. Or maybe a secondary character thinks she's protecting the hero by making sure he fails. Even good intentions can create trouble.

Can anyone be keeping secrets from the protagonist? Secrets add uncertainty and keep readers guessing, especially if they suspect that secret could affect the protagonist or her plan. Even something minor that does little more than embarrass a character if revealed could keep things interesting.

Unpredictability increases not only the tension of the scene, but strengthens the characters as well by turning them into three-dimensional people with wants, needs, and views all their own.

Step Three: Add Tension With the Setting

Life doesn't always play along. It rains when you want to go on a picnic, the restaurant that was supposed to be romantic has a busload of rowdy school kids on a field trip, or the power goes out when you need that computer. Murphy's Law happens, and the environment you put your characters into could add some conflict and raise the tension in that scene.

Can weather be a factor? Someone who's cold and miserable might say things she ordinarily wouldn't. A trip that might be easy in clear weather could be dangerous in bad weather.

Will changing location make the goals harder? Sneaking through a park you grew up next to feels different than sneaking through an area you've never seen before. A new location can add a layer of uncertainty and make the protagonist second guess herself.

Is there a setting or location that causes the protagonist stress or discomfort? If the protagonist is terrified of heights, forcing her into the air will affect how she'll act.

Don't underestimate the value of the right setting to raise the tension. Do the unexpected to keep readers off balance and guessing.

Step Four: Add Internal Tension

Sometimes a problem isn't caused by external forces, but by the protagonist's internal conflict. A personal struggle can be even more powerful because it's so emotional. Making readers wonder what a character might do in a rough situation is a surefire way to keep tensions high.

Can the protagonist face a moral dilemma? Maybe she can get what she needs, but she doesn't approve of what she'll have to do. Or she must make a personal sacrifice and she's not prepared or ready to do so. Maybe the cost of that action has far-reaching consequences. Do the ends *really* justify the means?

Can the *right* choice require going against personal beliefs? What if the "right" course of action is clearly, absolutely in conflict with everything the protagonist knows is right and true, such as doing a bad thing for a good cause?

Can the protagonist face something that forces her to address an issue she's been avoiding? This is a good tension builder for that protagonist who needs to learn a lesson and grow. People don't always want to face their demons, but if they're forced to, the fallout can be devastating.

Can the protagonist face an impossible choice? Impossible choices have no clear answer, which means readers won't see the answer coming. Maybe the only way to save the child is to let the mother die. Or something horrible will happen no matter what the protagonist does. If you get your readers thinking, "I have no idea how this is going to turn out," you'll keep them hooked.

Small changes can effect big results, so look for ways to build tension on a smaller scale, with simple changes to a character's dialogue, or re-action. You *can* raise the tension without changing how a scene unfolds.

Step Five: Add Hooks and Discoveries

Keeping readers hooked is about making them want answers to their story questions. What happens next? What else will these characters do? How will they get out of this? What's the deal with X? Why is Y do-ing that? Learning new information keeps readers interested and want-ing to know more.

If you added reveals and discoveries to your editorial map, start there and look for any holes or weak areas that would benefit from additional hooks or discoveries. Try to:

Leave an unanswered question in every scene: What is left hanging in the scene? What don't the characters know that will hook readers and give them a reason to move on to the next scene or chapter?

Space out the plot-related reveals: Check to see if the plot reveals are nicely spaced throughout the entire novel and not all clumped together. Your major plot turning points will help ensure they're spaced to help keep the story moving.

Add backstory and character-related reveals: Is there something new to learn about the characters over the course of the novel? Look to see where and when character secrets are discovered. Aim for a mix of char-acters actively working to discover secrets, exhibiting a trait, or sug-gesting a secret.

Add world-building-related reveals: Setting and world building often fade as the novel unfolds, so look for places to keep adding new aspects of the world to show what it's like to live there.

New information creates momentum, even when the plot hits a slow spot.

Step Six: Use Secrets to Add Tension

People don't tell each other everything, and even best friends hold in-formation back. Sometimes that information is important; other times it's just embarrassing. It's common in an early draft to have characters be a little *too* forthcoming as you work out the details, but once the story is solid, see who might not be so eager to share what they know.

In every scene, ask:

What doesn't the protagonist know? The simple act of asking this can get you thinking about possibilities. What backstories or potential complications could the secondary characters be hiding? What basic, totally predictable events in the scene can be changed to add a surprise that might deepen the plot? What character arcs for secondary characters might be created if the protagonist learns something unexpected during something mundane? What might happen that would cause a reader to say, "Wow, I never saw that coming!"

What secrets are the characters keeping? This could change how they act or how they'd influence others to act. If someone avoids a certain topic, both readers and the other characters might wonder why.

What don't the characters *want* the other characters to know? This could suggest secrets to reveal that change the scene and surprise readers, and a once-simple act could have huge consequences. For example, if the protagonist goes into his girlfriend's backpack and finds something she said she'd lost, readers suddenly wonder why she lied and what the protagonist is going to do about it.

Revision Option: Making Information-Heavy Scenes Tense

We've all written scenes where we have to convey a lot of information and there's no action to keep tension high. You can't just flop the information out there and get away with it—you have to convey all that information and *still* keep the scene tense.

Even in a scene that has no action, there are plenty of places you can tweak to keep it interesting. Consider:

How the information affects the goals: The protagonist is either telling the information or hearing it. If she's telling it, it's for a reason. What is that reason? It should be more than just "it needs to be conveyed to the reader now."

Is there a way you can make the information or the reason for telling it now adversely affect the scene goals? Is there a chance the person hearing it won't like it, or won't do what the protagonist needs them to do? Is there anything about the scene that can cause the protagonist to fail at their goal if they reveal that information now? If they're the one hearing the information, does that information affect their goal? Does it make it harder?

Think about why the information is being revealed now instead of later, and what that gains you from a storytelling perspective.

How the information affects the stakes: Something is at stake in the scene, and if that information can raise those stakes, so much the better. Even if it just adds a new layer, risk, or consequence, that's still a win. Is the protagonist risking anything by hearing or telling this information? Are the people in the scene at odds with each other over anything? Does the information raise the stakes at all? If it doesn't, can it?

If the information being revealed doesn't change the situation at all, that could indicate it's infodump or backstory you might not need.

How the information affects the conflict: If it helps solve the problem, then you might look for something to counterbalance that so there's tension again. For example, the protagonist gets the information she needs, and then has to act on it and that will cause trouble. How does this information cause trouble for the protagonist? Does the information affect her personal relationships? Does it change what she thought she knew and cause inner conflict or turmoil?

The conflict can be big or small, as long as it makes *something* a little tougher now.

How the information affects the setting: Sometimes the information *is* just details that have to be conveyed. If so, perhaps look for ways to put the characters in a "dangerous" setting when they have this conversation. Can they be in a place that has inherent conflict even if the characters themselves aren't in conflict? Could something interrupt them so they don't hear the information they need? Could it be a bad time to have this conversation, but there's no other time to do it?

If there's absolutely no tension in the information itself, then look for external factors to keep the scene tense.

How the information affects the dialogue: Even information shared between friends and allies can be tense if those friends are at odds over what to do with the information. If everyone is on the same page, try looking for ways to have them disagree. Does the other person *want* to hear or tell this information? If the protagonist is trying to get someone else to talk, is there a chance she won't be able to draw out that information? Maybe the protagonist has the information and she's trying hard *not* to talk? Is she *afraid* to talk?

REVISION RED FLAG: Check how much people are saying when they speak—short back-and-forth sentences, or long, heavy paragraphs? Speeches often indicate infodumps through dialogue, and are prime suspects for sapping tension.

How the information affects the internalization: How a character reacts to what she's hearing or saying goes a long way to getting readers to feel the same thing. Consider how the internalization can help the scene. Where is the protagonist emotionally when she hears this information? Is she worried about the information? How? Can any of her fears come true in that scene? Can something *worse* than she feared occur? What does she expect to happen? How can you thwart those expectations?

A character who's tense will make readers tense, even if there's no "action" going on in the scene. If she's worried about what she's about to find out, and she's thinking about what it all means, readers will feel it along with her.

Information-heavy scenes don't have to kill the tension if you look for ways to add excitement (even if that excitement is quiet terror or subtle longing). Layer in conflict and emotion and you'll build the tension so the characters—and readers—never get a chance to relax.

You've done a lot of plot work this workshop, so let's shift gears again and return to something more character-focused—point of view.

Workshop Four:
Point of View Work

The Goal of This Workshop: To strengthen the point of view and internalization of your manuscript.

What We'll Discuss in This Workshop: How to analyze your manuscript for common point of view and narrator errors, and find ways to strengthen the point of view and internalization.

Welcome to Workshop Four:
Point of View Work

Readers will experience your novel by seeing the story through the point-of-view character's eyes. Your point-of-view characters are their guides to what happens, conveying the information readers need to know (and hiding it when necessary) so they feel part of the story. It's the most powerful tool in your writer toolbox, allowing you to show how your characters feel, think, see, and judge the situations you put them in.

A strong point of view also guides you as a writer and helps you determine the right details for your story, and the right way to add those details to the scene.

Analyze the Point of View

Weak points of view hurt a novel, because readers have no sense of who's telling the story. Scenes can seem detached, aimless, even dry with nothing but generic descriptions and explanations that "tell" a story, but don't allow a reader to experience that story.

In this session, the goal is to examine your point of view for common problems.

Point of view and internalization are closely linked, so you'll examine how that's working next.

Step One: Determine if the Narrator is Working

The narrator tells the story, whether she's a character in the novel with a tight first person point of view, or a distant omniscient third-person point of view outside the story.

Go through the following questions to clarify who your narrator is and how she's working with your novel:

▶ **Is it clear who the narrator is?** Even in a first-person point of view, reminding yourself who is telling the tale can be a good thing. It's a nudge to remember to put the narrative in *her* voice, use *her* judgment, *her* worldview, and not yours.

▶ **Is the narrator's voice consistent with the novel's tone?** Maybe the narrator is flippant and sarcastic, or reverent and respectful. Whatever she is, this voice will permeate the entire novel, so you'll want it to fit the story's tone.

▶ **Is the narrator getting in the way of the story?** Some narrators simply narrate, but others play a role and influence events. Where does your narrator fall on that scale?

▶ **Is the narrator revealing too much? Not enough?** Fully omniscient narrators know and see all, but the less all-knowing narrator might not be privy to everything that happens in a novel. A retrospective narrator might only know what was told to her or what she personally witnessed.

No matter what story you're telling, *somebody* is behind it. Understanding who that person is can help you create a richer novel that better illustrates the story you want to share.

Step Two: Determine if the Point of View is Working

Point-of-view errors can make a novel seem distant, confusing, or even awkward. Go through the following questions and determine if there are any point-of-view issues:

▶ **Are there any point-of-view shifts?** Look for places where the point of view is suddenly out of a non-point-of-view character's eyes, or revealing information the point-of-view character couldn't know.

▶ **Is the point of view consistent?** Are there any scenes in a point-of-view style that differs from the rest of the manuscript? This could indicate a scene that's there to dump information or explain something about the story.

▶ **Is there too much filtering?** Filter words distance readers from the point-of-view character, remind them they're reading, explain details that are obvious, and often lead you into telling or crafting passive sentences. Look for words such as heard, felt, thought, saw, etc.

▶ **Do characters know details they couldn't possibly know?** Look for places where characters sound like mind readers and know what the other characters are thinking, and places where characters make huge leaps in logic without any groundwork for it.

▶ **Are any point-of-view characters oddly self-aware?** People don't typically self-analyze their motives and reasons for acting. Be wary of characters who know why (and state why) they're feeling or acting during a highly emotional state.

▶ **Are there any inconsistent or out-of-the-blue emotional responses?** Look for reactions where characters overreact, suggesting they know more than what made it to the page.

▶ **Are any point-of-view characters stating the obvious?** Look for places where the characters are explaining what is clear by how they're acting.

▶ **Are any point-of-view characters reacting before something happens?** This could indicate that the stimulus/response structure is off, which could confuse readers.

▶ **Are there any point-of-view scenes that are there only to show information the main characters can't witness?** If so, you're better off finding another way for your characters to discover that information.

▶ **Do you use one point of view per scene (if it's not an omniscient point of view)?** If not, you might be shifting points of view within a scene.

▶ **Is it clear when you've switched points of view?** Make sure you give readers a clue when you change point-of-view characters. Use a name in the opening paragraph, or some other indicator of whose head you're in.

REVISION RED FLAG: It's not uncommon to have a lot of unnecessary points of view in a first draft as you explore the story and determine the best way to tell it. Watch out for characters with only one or two scenes—they might be there just to dump information. Another common issue to watch out for is a single-point-of-view character who relays every aspect of their day.

Problems Found?

If you find any point-of-view issues, spend some time doing the exercises in If You Want to Strengthen Your Point of View on page 208.

Analyze the Internalization

Internalization is the window into the minds of your point-of-view characters. It lets you know what they think and how they feel, which helps you craft a compelling narrative flow that hooks readers and makes them care about the characters.

In this session, the goal is to examine your internalization for potential problems.

Determine if the Internalization is Working

It can be challenging to find the right balance of internalization and action, and many first drafts go too far in one direction or the other (too much or too little).

▶ **Is there too much internalization?** Too much thinking is often seen in slow areas, or places when the pacing drags. It could also indicate a protagonist who's thinking more than acting.

▶ **Is there too little internalization?** Not enough thinking can indicate a lack of motivation or goals, or the understanding of those goals. Readers don't know why characters are acting or what it means. Sometimes, you don't know either, which is why the internalization is light.

▶ **Does the internal thought clarify the dialogue or action?** Good internalization works with dialogue and action to show why and how a character is acting. Look for any places where the thoughts muddy or confuse what's going on.

▶ **Does the internal thought show the point-of-view character's opinion on the situation?** Who the character is shows in how she thinks and what she thinks about. Look for places where the thoughts are flat and devoid of personality.

▶ **Does the internal thought provide necessary information without infodumping?** Characters think about what matters to them; they don't dump unnecessary details into the story. Look for scenes where characters explain a lot of information or the text reads more like the author making notes. Keep an eye out for details you think are "necessary" that are infodumps in disguise.

▶ **Does the internal thought convey background information without telling**? Internal thoughts should imply details of the character's backstory, not stop the story to explain those details or why they matter. Look for places where characters suddenly sound like they're reading from someone's dossier, a travel guide, or a textbook.

▶ **Are there internal thoughts in *every* line of dialogue?** Too much thinking bogs a story down. Be wary of scenes where the character mentally debates something every time she speaks.

▶ **Are the internal thoughts often paragraphs long, and do they happen every time the point-of-view character thinks?** This is a red flag for protagonists who think too much, and often act too little.

▶ **Does the internal thought summarize a scene or idea at the end (or describe it at the start before you show that scene or idea)?** Be wary of thoughts that summarize the action of the scene. Often, the thoughts tell readers what's about to happen and lessen the tension.

▶ **Are you repeating the same idea in multiple ways?** Sometimes you show the same thing through thought and action, such as having the character slam the door, scream, "I hate him!" and then think, *She was so pissed.* The screaming and dialogue make it clear how the character feels.

REVISION RED FLAG: Internalization is a common area to find infodumps (both description and backstory) and told prose. If you've gotten feedback about those issues, try checking your internalization for trouble.

Problems Found?

If you find any internalization issues, spend some time doing the exercises in If You Want to Streamline the Internalization on page 212.

If You Want to Strengthen the Point of View

A strong point of view leads to a strong novel. It helps you decide what details to use when describing, allows you to show how the world works and what the rules of the world are, and it lets your characters show your readers that world.

In this session, the goal is to fix common point-of-view problems.

Step One: Revise Any Unnecessary Filtering

A point-of-view character, by definition, is relaying (and thus filtering) everything she sees, hears, feels, touches, smells, thinks. If it's described, readers know she experienced it.

Depending on your narrative distance, different degrees of filtering are acceptable and even expected. Sometimes this filter is invisible and readers don't feel any distance between them and the point-of-view character. Other times the filters are obvious and readers feel the wall between them and the characters. One looks *through* the eyes of the point-of-view character, the other looks *at* the point-of-view character.

General rule of thumb: The tighter the point of view, the less filtering you usually see.

Filter words typically show up in told prose, passive prose, or weak writing. You'll also find them in unintentionally distant points of view.

Common red flag filter words: Saw, heard, felt, knew, watched, decided, noticed, realized, wondered, thought, looked.

Common filter words found with passive, telling cousins: to see, to hear, could tell, to watch, to decide, to notice, to realize, to wonder, to think, to look.

You don't have to cut every instance of these words, but they are good words to check (and maybe change) if the scene feels told or readers aren't connecting to it.

Step Two: Fix Any Head Hopping or Point of View Shifts

Unless you're writing full third-person omniscient, the rule is one point-of-view character per scene. Check your scenes for any instances where someone other than the point-of-view character has a thought, or expresses (internally) a motive, judgment, or opinion, and thus "shifts" the narrative out of the point-of-view character's head. All the information in that scene should be what the point-of-view character can realistically experience.

This doesn't apply just to third person—first-person writers, watch out for places where the point-of-view character explains another character's motive when it's not logical to have known that motive. If the point-of-view character has no idea a character is going to go to the car "to get his phone" she can't describe his movements that way.

Spotting Point of View Shifts

"To verb" is easy to search for and you'll eliminate a lot of smaller point of view shifts by using "and" instead of "to." For example, "she reached over to pick up the cup" implies motive (how does the narrator *know* she intended to pick up the cup until she did it?). "To verb" often has a non-point-of-view character explaining the motive of another character's action before they physically do it in the scene. Until the character sees it, she can't know why another character is acting.

Other things you can look for:

Any judgment or opinion statements of non-point-of-view characters that aren't in dialogue: A non-point-of-view character will only convey information by what they say and how they act. That's all the point-of-view character can observe.

Places where the point-of-view character states motive or opinion of a non-point-of-view character: If the point-of-view character is guessing or basing her thoughts on what she can observe, then it's probably okay. But if the point-of-view character is attributing a motive as if it's a fact and it's not clear how she'd know, you might be shifting.

The point-of-view character referring to how she looks as if she could see: For example, "my face turned bright pink." Unless she can see it, she can't know what it looks like.

Step Three: Fix Any Inconsistent Points of View

If you use multiple points of view, check for places where your point of view (especially your narrative distance) varies. If you've been in a tight third person for most of the book, but have a few scenes in a distant third, those scenes will jump out at readers and feel out of place (unless there's a good and clear reason for the switch).

Maintain the same point-of-view style throughout the book, and if you need to switch styles or narrative distances, make sure the rules of that switch are clear and consistent.

Step Four: Fix Any Characters Who Know Details They Can't Know

With everything you have to keep track of in a novel, it's understandable that sometimes, you'll accidentally have a character remark on something you forgot to put *into* the novel. Or you'll have characters make huge leaps in logic without having enough groundwork for those leaps to feel credible.

Check your scenes and look for moments (especially big "I figured it out!" moments) to ensure no one has information or is making leaps they couldn't possibly know or make.

Step Five: Fix Any Oddly Self-Aware Character Moments

While some people are good at knowing their motives and analyzing their feelings, most of us aren't that self-aware. We get mad at spouses when we're angry about work, yell at the cat because we did something we're ashamed of, and let past traumas influence our behaviors—we don't realize our bad behavior is due to our fears of abandonment.

Check your scenes for any moments where the character feels too aware of her motives or why she's behaving as she is. Instead, show hints as to the real reason.

Common self-aware red flag words: She knew, she realized, she felt, she thought. Not every instance will be a problem, but it's a good place to start the search.

Step Six: Fix Any Unsubstantiated Emotional Responses

Sometimes a character needs to feel a certain way for the scene, but the groundwork to support that emotion isn't there.

Look for places where your point-of-view character has a strong emotional reaction or feelings about something or someone. If the protagonist can't stand another character, is it clear why? Have there been signs or clues that support why characters feel the way they do? Clarify any responses that feel out of whack.

Step Seven: Fix Any Places Where Characters Are Stating the Obvious

If a character runs into her room, throws herself onto the bed and starts crying, it's a pretty good indication that she's upset. Adding, "She was so upset she thought she'd die" is unnecessary. Since these little phrases tend to slip in when you aren't looking, it's not a bad idea to scan the scenes and look for places where your characters are being a little *too* on the nose.

Step Eight: Fix Any Faulty Character Reactions

This is all about stimulus/response. A character can't respond to something that hasn't happened yet. "Jane dodged out of the way when the zombie lunged at her." Until readers see the zombie lunge, they have no clue why Jane is dodging. Make sure the chronology of the actions unfolds in a logical and clear fashion.

Common stimulus/response red flag words: when, as, before. Revise as needed so the stimulus comes first, *then* the character reaction.

Now that you've caught and fixed any point-of-view and narrator issues, let's get closer and look at any internalization issues.

If You Want to Streamline the Internalization

Internalization is where your characters think and reflect on what's happening to them. It's strong vehicle to show their voices and how their minds work, which helps turn them into real and solid people. Readers get to see the world through the characters' eyes and hear their thoughts about that world.

In this session, the goal is to eliminate any internalization that isn't working, and make sure your characters' thoughts are clear.

Step One: Adjust Any Out-of-Balance Thinking

How much (or how little) thinking a character does in a scene can be a red flag for other issues. It's a good place to start when reviewing your internalization. Be wary if:

The protagonist thinks too much: A thinking-too-much protagonist needs a boot to the butt to get her moving. This type of draft often feels like nothing is happening and readers are waiting for you to get to a point.

Look for scenes where there's a lot of deliberating about what to do. The characters might be talking about the action the protagonist needs to take, and either showing it afterward (making the story repetitious) or skimming through the action itself because it feels like you've already written it. You might even find yourself summarizing the action in a "so we did this" or "after we did this" type fashion.

Take those internal planning sessions and turn them into active scenes. You know what happens, so either skip the planning altogether (often you can) or trim that planning scene down to the bare minimum and let the scene play out in real time.

The protagonist thinks too little: A thinking-too-little protagonist is one who's there to act out plot, but has no feelings about what she's doing. This usually results in a plot that feels aimless, since nothing matters, and there's no sense of stakes to carry the story forward.

Now that you know what happens in your plot, it's time to dig in and let your protagonist say *why* it's important. Look for scenes where:

Choices are made: Choices send the plot in new directions, but without understanding why those choices are made, readers might start wondering why they're following along. Before long, plot events starts to blur and it's hard to remember what's happened since none of it carried enough meaning to sink in. Readers feel lost and ungrounded, and they don't get it.

Make sure your protagonist thinks about what she's doing, weighs the pros and cons, and makes a choice that seems logical to her, *and* keeps readers interested. Provide a sense that the protagonist is acting on her own feelings and needs, driving the story forward toward a personal goal.

Stakes are mentioned: You might say why something is bad, but without context from the protagonist to put it into perspective, readers might not get exactly what "bad" means. Or worse, they might not realize the stakes have escalated at all if the protagonist isn't concerned or does little to say why this is a bad thing. This leads to flat stories that are easy to put down and never pick back up.

Make sure the stakes and how those stakes affect the characters are clear. This is personal for your protagonist, so get into her head and show the how and why. Show the consequences so readers can worry right along with her.

The protagonist is over-thinking everything: Thinking about the past, making witty observations, and chatting with the reader are all ways in which your protagonist might be delaying *doing* something. While it's good to know the reasons behind an action, over-explaining why it matters at every step can indicate you're not sure what action you want the protagonist to take. So you brainstorm on the page by going over it all in her head.

Look for reasons for your protagonist to be thinking those thoughts. Perhaps put her in a scene where getting out of a jam depends on what she's done in the past, allowing you to keep the action moving and still show those deep thoughts. You can also give her a friend (or even an enemy) to talk to and make the conversation part of a larger and more active scene.

Step Two: Check for Judgment and Reactions

Internalization is where the character does her thinking, which usually means she's reacting to something that happened in the story, judging or considering it (or reacting without thinking), and then acting on that information and assumptions made from that information.

While it's unrealistic to go through every line of internalization (unless you're doing a deep edit), there are some red flags you can look for to spot potential problems:

An abundance of pronouns: Excessive pronouns can indicate filtering, especially when combined with filtering red flag words, such as "she felt, I realized, he knew."

An abundance of questions: A litany of internal questions could indicate the character is telling readers what *they* ought to be thinking about instead of showing the character thinking and reacting to it. Often, these questions are unnecessary, and having too many of them will distance readers from the character. A lot of internal questions could also indicate an opportunity to flesh out a character's emotional state so those questions are implied, not stated.

Reasons to Use Internal Questions

When it's something the character would believably ask in that situation: Sometimes people do ask internal questions, especially if angry or upset. "How could he do this to me?" is a good (if clichéd) example. "Is he serious?" is another. Thoughts that could be spoken aloud often work just fine as internal questions, though it's fun to consider how the scene *would* go if the character *did* say them out loud.

When you want to remind readers of the goal: An internal question can work as a scene goal statement: "Where was the murder weapon?" This shows the character is probably going to be looking for this item. "What if she *wasn't* at the bar?" suggests figuring this out is important. It can also tell readers what the overall story question is, and what the plot is trying to resolve: "So what *really* happened to Mario?"

When it would create more mystery, tension, or a dramatic pause: Questions can work as those "dum-dum-DUM!" cliffhanger moments to raise tensions or hook readers. It might be a revelation: "Did that mean John was alive?" Or it could be an internal conflict the character will be struggling with: "Could she trust him?"

When it would show a different attitude or opinion from what the narrator is displaying: Sometimes a character feels one way internally, but is forced (or wants) to show a different attitude or emotion externally. An internal question is one way to show this dichotomy: "You make a good point." She nodded. What kind of moron was he?

When a character is debating with herself: Although you have to be careful here (it's easy to go too far), questions can be a handy way to show a character having an internal debate. This can be especially helpful if you need to show how a character made a connection or a leap in logic that might seem contrived without the explanation.

Reasons *Not* to Use Internal Questions

When they're there solely to lead readers to the conclusion you want them to make: If readers can't get to that question on their own by what they see in the text, and there's no reason (or a weak reason) for the character to ask it, there's a good chance it's going to read awkwardly.

When they're repetitive: Lots of questions in a row can read as if you're badgering readers, especially if they all basically say the same thing. Try showing internal thoughts or actions that suggest those questions (or answers to those questions) instead.

When they don't convey any real information to move the story: Empty internal questions can feel like empty dialogue. They're not necessary to understand anything in the scene, but they feel like they ought to be said. Try cutting them and seeing which versions read better.

When they're redundant: If the internal question is followed up by thoughts, action, or dialogue that implies the same question, there's no need to shine a light on it. For example, if the character is staring at a crime scene and describing it in detail, starting or ending with, "What happened here?" isn't necessary.

If you're not sure if the question should stay or go, ask:

- Does the scene read well without the question?
- Is it shoving the idea/thought/mystery in the reader's face?
- Would the reader ask the same question from seeing what's in the scene?
- Does it feel awkward?

If you answered yes to any of these, odds are you can cut it.

Internal questions show what a character is struggling with and what she's trying to do, but they can be overused if you aren't careful. Trust your instincts—if it feels awkward or melodramatic, it probably is and cutting it would strengthen the scene (reading it out loud is a good test for melodrama).

Step Three: Examine Italicized Text

Immediate thoughts are often italicized, so a search for italicized text could help spot any internal dialogue that isn't working, or which could be stronger as internalization. Often, a simple tense change can turn internal dialogue into internalization, such as *Is he asking me out?* vs. Was he asking her out?

🚩 **REVISION RED FLAG:** Italicized thoughts should be used sparingly (some advise not doing it at all, but this is a personal taste issue). If you find a high percentage of italicized thoughts, or most of the internalization is in italics, there's a problem or a misuse of internal dialogue. Look for ways to shift those thoughts into the narrative and eliminate all but the most critical italicized thoughts.

Revision Option: Internalization and Voice

How characters think and what they notice, from their internal thoughts to the narrative itself, is where voice thrives. The always-distracted scatterbrain is going to see the world differently from the detail-oriented observer, and their voices will reflect that.

You'll cover voice in more depth in Workshop Seven: Dialogue and Voice, but here are some things to keep in mind as you revise your internalization:

What does the point-of-view character typically think about? This can show how her thought process works, what she worries about, or what distracts her.

What types of words best fit or exemplify the point-of-view character's personality? A sports fanatic might use a lot of sports terms or metaphors, or a quiet, shy type might have a cutting wit hiding behind the shyness. Look for language that shows who that character is.

What type of sentence structure best fits the point-of-view character? The person who thinks in short, choppy sentences is different from the one who waxes poetically about her emotions.

What does the character's dialogue sound like? This is a good way to show someone whose inner self differs from the person she shows the world.

Some elements of who you are as a writer will naturally seep in (which is good, as your own voice is important), but each of your characters will have different personalities and see the world in different ways. Just like you use the right verb and the right noun to craft a well-written sentence, use the right words and phrasing to craft a well-developed character voice.

You've been working on people and plots for a while now, so let's shift gears and focus on the descriptive nature of your novel.

Workshop Five: Description Work

The Goal of This Workshop: To strengthen your description and stage direction, find told prose, and eliminate unnecessary descriptive details.

What We'll Discuss in This Workshop: How to analyze your description and identify weak or overwritten areas. You'll also look at the best ways to tighten and streamline heavy description, revise told prose, spot and eliminate infodumps, determine the right details to add, use tone and mood, and enhance the emotions in the manuscript.

Welcome to Workshop Five: Description Work

Writers tend to focus on characters and plot first, but the real workhorse of a novel is description. It's the unsung hero, existing in every word, but never getting the respect it deserves. When you think about it, *everything* in a novel is description—you use it to tell the entire story, from descriptions of action, to dialogue, to how a character thinks.

All too often, writers treat description like we're taking notes. Here's what something looks like, here's the general lay of the land, here's what's going on. Not only does it do a disservice to the description (I'm guilty of this myself), it does a disservice to the novel.

Luckily, description doesn't *want* to be the hero; it wants to be the sidekick. It's happiest when it's blending into the background and making everything and everyone around it look good. And what's good for description is also good for you.

This workshop focuses on general descriptions. Character descriptions are covered in Workshop Two: Character Work, and setting and world-building-specific details are covered next in Workshop Six: Setting and World-Building Work.

Analyze the Descriptions

Description problems tend to fall into one of three categories: too much, not enough, or too vague. Too much description results in bogged-down scenes and infodumps that slow pacing. Too little description creates white rooms and talking heads, and can lead to reader confusion. Too-vague descriptions are confusing, forgettable, or just plain boring.

In this session, the goal is to examine your descriptions and identify weak, overdone, or missing sections; find told areas, unnecessary info-dumps, and awkward stage direction; and evaluate the emotional layers of the story.

A note about description: Different genres will have different expectations for how much needs describing. Action-focused genres might do very little, while literary novels tend to paint larger word pictures. Take your novel's genre or market into account when deciding what the "right amount of description" is.

Determine if the Descriptions Are Working

If your descriptions are working as intended, readers will flow through the story without realizing how much information they're absorbing. They'll visualize the action, see the characters striving for their goals, and feel as if they're along for the ride.

Step One: Examine the General Descriptions

Refer to any notes made during your manuscript analysis, or skim through each scene. Look for heavy blocks of text or multiple short lines in a row. These could indicate areas that need less (heavy blocks) or more (short lines) description.

▶ **Is there too much description?** Not every item in a scene needs to be described, only what's important to understand the scene, the setting, the characters, or the problem, or to set the mood. If you're unsure, try highlighting or changing the color of all the descriptive text in a scene to quickly spot heavy areas that might need trimming.

▶ **Is there too little description?** Look for blank "rooms" where there's little to no description at all. Passages with a lot of short lines or white space on the page are often places that could be heavy on dialogue, light on description.

▶ **Are the descriptions vague?** When you use vague words to show what something looks like, you're missing an opportunity to bring that something to life for your readers. Also look for generic words, such as tree, room, smiled. In most cases, a more specific word paints a stronger picture.

▶ **Do the descriptive details tell readers anything they didn't already know?** Soft, fluffy, and white all describe a cloud. That's like saying, "He dived into the wet water." If the words don't provide additional information than what the detail itself conveys, consider revising.

▶ **Do the descriptive details show judgment on the point-of-view character's part?** This is a good test to see if you're the one telling readers what something looks like or if the point-of-view character is describing it in her own words. How often do you walk outside and think, "Gee, look at those soft, fluffy, white clouds drifting gently across the sky." You'd more likely think, "Pretty day" or something that fits your personality and the situation.

▶ **Could you describe something better through action?** Since description is often adjective heavy, and adjectives describe other words, a precise noun or verb that suggests action might work better. "A hard rain fell against the windows" could turn into "Rain pounded the windows."

▶ **How do the descriptive details affect the rhythm of the prose?** Several descriptive words in a row can feel list-like if you don't vary them. For example, "She was a tall, thin woman with flowing, curly blond hair and wide-set ice-blue eyes. Her long dress swirled around her, a dark royal blue, with small, round, gold buttons along a narrow waistline."

However, putting the right word in the right spot adds an extra beat that can make a line sing. Such as: "He was tall and dark, with eyes of sin and moonlight." The double beats at the end balance the beginning in an ear-pleasing way. It wouldn't sound the same as: "He was tall, with eyes of sin and moonlight." All the music is gone.

▶ **Is the point-of-view character describing details the same way no matter what she's feeling or doing, or is she seeing it based on how she feels at that point in time?** Point of view is your best tool for figuring out how to revise description. Think about the point-of-view character in the scene and what her emotional state, personality, and goals are. Someone waxing philosophical after a profound experience will probably see the garden courtyard a lot differently than someone running through it with zombies on their tail. One would notice the beauty, the poetry, the fragility, while the other would notice the potential weapons, exits, and ambush spots.

▶ **Is the point-of-view character noticing the same types of details all the time, or does she see what she feels is important in that scene?** What gets noticed tells as much about the person noticing as what she sees. This can be tough if you need to slip in a clue and it's something your point-of-view character would never pick up on, but you can have her notice something that fits within her personality. It's also an opportunity for characters to misunderstand something important.

▶ **Does the point-of-view character have a reason to look around, or is she doing it so you can tell readers what she sees?** People don't usually notice everything about what's around them. The details that stand out catch their eye for a reason. Many times they're looking for something specific, which gives you opportunities to describe as they search.

Overall, is there a good sense of what objects and people look like? Gut feeling—are your instincts telling you an area needs work? Trust those instincts.

REVISION RED FLAG: Be wary of taking the easy way out and letting the characters describe *everything* in a room or scene. If they're looking for a hidden trap, or a burglar, or a secret door, they'd check different spots than someone looking for a place to put a painting, or someone looking to buy their first home.

Problems Found?

If you find any description issues, spend some time doing the exercises in If You Want to Strengthen the Descriptions on page 227.

Step Two: Check for Told Prose

"Show, don't tell," has annoyed many a writer, and it's a common comment in critiques. It's easier to fix than you'd think, as long as you know what to look (and listen) for.

▶ **Are there any detached or distant-feeling scenes?** Look for scenes that read (and feel) as though you're watching them from a distance.

▶ **Is there an abundance of common telling red flag words?** Look for words such as: when, as, to (verb), which, because, to be verbs. These are often found in told prose.

▶ **Are there any scenes with a lot of explanations?** Watch for places where you stop the story to explain some aspect of it—how something works, why a character is acting, reasons for events to unfold as they do are common areas for telling.

🚩 **REVISION RED FLAG:** Your narrative distance and point-of-view style will determine what feels told and what feels natural, so take that into consideration when examining your scenes.

Problems Found?

If you find any telling issues, spend some time doing the exercises in If You Want to Show, Not Tell on page 232.

Step Three: Check for Unnecessary Infodumps

A quick test for infodumps is to look at the information and ask, "Is it for the character's benefit or the reader's benefit?" If it's to inform the reader, it's dumping.

▶ **Are there passages of information that seem more like notes than story?** Infodumps often seem like the author inserting information readers "need to know."

▶ **Are characters telling each other information they already know?** Infodumps through dialogue can turn characters into walking encyclopedias.

▶ **Is there a history lesson any time the protagonist enters a room or meets another person?** Infodumps often appear when something new is introduced, be that a character, a place, or a situation.

Problems Found?

If you find any infodump issues, spend some time doing the exercises in If You Want to Eliminate Unnecessary Infodumps on page 237.

Step Four: Check for Awkward Stage Directions

It's not necessary to describe *every* step a character takes to get from one place to another, or to compete a task. Too much focus on the individual steps can seem clunky and bog down a scene.

▶ **Are there extra action tags in the dialogue?** Clunky stage direction is most often found in dialogue, as characters speak-move-act-speak-move again.

▶ **Are there a lot of common stage direction red flag words?** Look for words such as, while, when, and as. These often connect multiple actions in one long (and confusing) chain.

▶ **Are any characters trying to do too much?** Look for places where the characters perform multiple actions at the same time.

▶ **Are characters "trying" a lot?** Try is a red flag word, since characters often "try" to do what they actually accomplish. It could indicate unneeded steps in the action, or vagueness about what occurs. "She tried to stand, swaying heavily as she grabbed the chair." Did she stand or didn't she?

Problems Found?

If you find any stage direction issues, spend some time doing the exercises in If You Want to Streamline the Stage Directions on page 240.

Step Five: Check for Weak or Missing Emotional Clarity

A scene meant to be scary and foreboding with a point-of-view character who isn't a bit scared or worried will likely result in an emotional disconnect for readers. Take a look at your scenes and make sure the characters are feeling (and conveying) the right emotions for that scene.

▶ **Is it clear how each character feels at the start of the scene?** Make sure you know how the point-of-view character or protagonist is feeling, especially if there's a change in emotion in the scene.

▶ **Do emotions change in the scene?** While not every scene will have a shift in emotion, too many scenes in a row with the same emotion could indicate a lack of stakes, or a problem with the plot.

▶ **Do you know what you want your readers to feel in the scene?** Think about the emotions you want to evoke in your readers. Readers who care are more invested in the story.

▶ **Is it clear why the character is having any emotional reactions?** Readers should be able to determine why a character is feeling the way she does by what's in the scene (or what has led up to that scene). Sudden or out-of-the-blue emotional reactions or changes can indicate a problem with the character arc or motivations.

REVISION TIP: *Don't forget to check the emotions for all the characters in the scene. Each one will react differently based on their moods and personalities.*

Problems Found?

If you find any emotion issues, spend some time doing the exercises in If You Want to Deepen the Emotions on page 242.

Step Six: Check for Clarity of Tone

Tone is like a soundtrack playing in the novel's background. It tweaks the emotions at the right moment and nudges readers toward what you want them to feel. Not every scene has to have the same tone, but if you're writing a light, fun romance, a lot of heavy, dark scenes can make the book feel out of whack.

▶ **Does the opening scene convey the tone of the novel?** A cozy mystery probably shouldn't start off with a room full of people being slaughtered. It sends all the wrong signals for what the novel is about.

▶ **Does the tone of each scene match its emotional core?** Tone can help underscore the emotional layer of the scene, so be wary if the tone conflicts with the scene's emotional core (unless the point is to show a stark contrast).

▶ **Do the imagery and word choice of the descriptions reflect this tone?** A scene aiming for dark and foreboding probably isn't going have a lot of descriptions of bright flowers and sunny skies. Let the details you use support the tone you're aiming for.

▶ **Does the tone enhance individual scenes to bring about the desired emotional impact on the reader?** Tone can rise and fall, same as tension, manipulating your readers' emotions for the greatest impact. The right tone at the right moment can put readers in the right mindset for a key emotional scene.

▶ **Does the tone change over the course of the novel?** Should it? Some variance in tone is expected, but be wary if the tone is inconsistent or conflicting. That could indicate uncertainty over what you want the novel to be.

Problems Found?

If you find any tone issues, spend some time doing the exercises in If You Want to Strengthen the Tone and Mood on page 249.

Step Seven: Check for Clarity of Mood

If tone is the novel's soundtrack, mood is its lighting. A scene's mood creates the right emotional reactions in readers and characters. Mood and tone play off each other to heighten emotions and raise tension. For example, a foreboding tone paired with nervous characters will put readers on edge, waiting for something to happen.

▶ **What mood do you want the characters to convey?** The emotional state of the characters usually determines what mood they're in when they start a scene. It's also a clue for how readers ought to feel.

▶ **What mood do you want the scene itself to convey?** The scene's mood can lay the emotional groundwork for what's about to happen.

▶ **Would conflicting tone and mood enhance the scene?** Contrast can work well to heighten tension, such as characters in a dire situation joking around to keep from being scared (make sure it's clear they *are* scared to maintain the right tone and emotional state).

▶ **Does the mood of the scene change?** If the emotions don't shift, the mood might, as characters see hope for their goals, or realize help isn't coming.

▶ **What do you want readers to feel in this scene?** Does the mood reflect that? Manipulating reader emotion is what tone and mood do best.

Problems Found?

If you find any tone issues, spend some time doing the exercises in If You Want to Strengthen the Tone and Mood on page 249.

If You Want to Strengthen the Description

Descriptions are a common weak spot for many first drafts, because you're focused on getting information down as it pours out of your head. *How* it flows isn't as important in these early stages, and you end up with a lot of details and generalizations that need some fine tuning.

In this session, the goal is to examine your descriptions and ensure they're painting the right picture for your story.

Step One: Flesh Out Blank Scenes

First-draft scenes often put the focus on the action or character, not the description, and can feel like events are happening in a blank room. Look for ways to fill in the details and bring that scene to life.

Add details that someone in this situation would notice: Take the protagonist's emotional state and goals into account. If you were in her shoes in that situation, what would you pay attention to?

Add items the character might use to complete the scene's goal: This might be the perfect scene to add a critical element you'll need later, or show a skill or possession that has relevance in a future scene.

Take advantage of opportunities to describe something important to the story: This could be a chance to show the world in action, hint at backstory, or show an aspect of the world's inherent conflict.

Add details that might hinder the character's goal, add conflict, or raise the stakes: Don't just toss in whatever details come to mind; look for objects that can help or hinder the protagonist, or cause trouble.

Cut details that reveal more by *not* describing them: Look for foreshadowing opportunities or ways to add subtext. For example, an orphanage mysteriously devoid of children could hint that something sinister is afoot.

As you add or tweak your descriptions, think about what they can do besides show what something looks like. For example, if you want to describe a street, think about what types of elements exist on that particular street. Could certain details show more about the world? Could they give the protagonist a reason to react in a way that shows her character?

Step Two: Add More Sensory Details

While you certainly don't want to approach description like a fill-in-the-blanks template, if you know this is a weak area for you, it's not a bad idea to look through each scene for details that involve all the senses. Not every detail needs to affect every sense, but aim for at least one detail for each sense in each scene (unless of course, it reads awkwardly or is inappropriate for the scene).

Describe what the characters see: Typically, this is the primary sense for the description, so unless the scene is sparse on description in general, you won't need to add much here.

Add the sense of touch: Let the protagonist touch items in the scene and experience tactile sensations of various surfaces. Don't forget to let objects touch the protagonist as well, such as wind or rain or even people.

Add the sense of smell: Odors are strongly connected to memory, so associating smells with backstory or world-building details allow you to do more with fewer words.

Add the sense of sound: Noise is all around us, so don't forget about the background sounds of a scene. Sounds help set tone or create a mood.

Add the sense of taste: If the protagonist isn't eating, taste is a tougher sense to include, but plenty of situations can "leave a taste" in the protagonist's mouth to suggest flavors.

REVISION TIP: *Take each sense, close your eyes and imagine the scene with that sense in mind. List all the details you come up with and pick the best ones to add to the scene. Don't go for the obvious ones—dig a little deeper for the details unique to your world, story, or characters.*

Step Three: Enhance the Descriptions

If the description just sits there and tells readers what details look like, odds are it's not helping your story. Use your descriptions to layer in additional information.

Add details that suggest something about the world: Instead of details that could apply to any place anywhere, use something specific to your world or locale.

Add details that foreshadow an event: Find objects that will have greater meaning later, or work thematically to suggest something brewing in the story.

Add details that could be clues to a plot twist or plot point: A detail readers see, but ignore, early on could be the perfect trigger for characters to remember later to move an important element of the plot.

Add details that help create tension or suspense: Slip in details associated with foreboding concepts, or details that foreshadow or mirror a problem yet to come.

Add details that trigger an emotional response: This is handy when you need to send a character into a different emotional state.

Add details that evoke a memory: If a character needs to remember something, use a detail that would naturally trigger that memory.

Revision Option: Personalize the Descriptions

This is where all that point-of-view work you did in Workshop Four will pay off. If a point-of-view character notices something, there's a reason behind it, which can make the world feel that much more personal and inviting to your readers.

As you go through your scenes, consider:

Why does the character notice *that* detail? You chose that detail for a reason—was it something the character would pick up on, or did you as the author want it noticed?

What is the character most likely *to* notice? What's notable to a character will change based on personality and emotional state. Someone worried about being spotted will notice potential witnesses, or someone having an emotional meltdown might not notice much of anything at all.

How does a particular detail make the character feel? Details with different levels of importance or meaning will have different impacts on a character. Something that reminds her of the worst day of her life might dredge up those feelings, while something colorful that catches her eye just distracts her.

Revision Option: A Closer Look at Problem Scenes

If a scene has the right level of detail, but you still think something is off (or your beta readers have told you something is off), it could be that you're using the wrong details, or the details aren't clear enough yet. Context might be lacking and what's in your head isn't making it onto the page.

Which details might mean more to you than to readers? It's possible you're bringing more context to what's on the page. Look for important details and determine if someone who knew less about the book would get the same impression.

Which details need a little more explanation? If there are foreign terms or made-up words in the description, readers might not understand what they mean or their significance in the story.

Which details could be giving readers the wrong impression or setting up the wrong expectation? Some details come with a set of preconceived ideas, such as the default "medieval village" setting for fantasy. Check that you're not inadvertently making readers picture or assume something different from what you intended.

Which details aren't specific enough? If you wrote "tree" but picture a cactus, what's in your head isn't making it to the page. Look for any too-general details that don't paint a solid enough picture.

Optional Exercise: Brainstorm Your Description

If you're looking for a fun way to develop more interesting descriptions, try this:

1. Pick a sense. Or for fun, use a random number generator and pick one the five: (1) Sight. (2) Smell. (3) Hearing. (4) Touch. (5) Taste. If you use dice, try adding a "sixth" sense for intuition.

2. Pick a scene in your novel. What's the dominant emotion in that scene? Use that as the base for your description.

3. Brainstorm details for the chosen sense, based on the dominant emotion.

For example, if you picked smell, and the dominant scene emotion is joy, then think about all the smells the protagonist associates with joy. Look at the scene and ask (adjust sense and emotion to fit your details):

- What in the scene smells joyful (sense + emotion)?
- What smells (sense) would make the protagonist feel happy or think about something joyous (emotion)?
- What smells (sense) would the protagonist notice only because she is happy?
- What unpleasant smells (sense) would be judged favorably because of the emotion? Such as, a normally icky smell makes the protagonist happy instead.
- Why would smell (sense) be the thing the protagonist notices most in this scene? (Could speak to something in the character's backstory)

- What joyous smells (emotion + sense) might affect the protagonist in a *negative* way, such as the joy of others makes her unhappy or angry?

Looking at a scene with a particular sense + emotion combo in mind encourages you to think more creatively about what you describe. It's not
the same basic "what's there" details, but unique elements that enhance
the scene in a memorable way. It also helps you layer the senses, since
most of the time sight is the number-one sense used for description.

Ways to Mix it Up

Choose the least obvious or least likely sense to work in that scene:
For example, if the scene takes place outside at night, sight would probably be the hardest sense to work with.

Choose the opposite emotion: For example, if the dominant emotion
for the scene is joy, what if the protagonist saw the scene from a sad or
miserable standpoint? Obviously this will only work on scenes where
the contradiction fits.

Pick two emotions and/or senses: If the scene is emotionally charged,
try doubling up on the senses. For an extra challenge, pick contradic-
tory emotions or senses and play off the contrasts.

Go wild with your descriptions. Not only will it be more fun for you to
revise, but you might add a unique and compelling aspect to a scene.

 REVISION RED FLAG: Be wary of going overboard with descriptions and accidentally shifting into purple prose.

Now that your descriptions are dazzling your readers, let's make sure
you haven't slipped into telling anywhere.

If You Want to Show, Not Tell

Showing is dramatizing a scene to make readers feel in the moment
with the protagonist as the story unfolds. Telling is hearing about it all
secondhand. It's describing the situation, not the story. It's like reading
a review of *The Lion King* vs. going to see *The Lion King*.

In this session, the goal is to find told prose and revise it to show.

You'll be using the search function of your writing program heavily this session, looking for common red flag words often associated with told prose.

But remember, just because you find one of these words doesn't mean you have to eliminate or rewrite it. If the word is doing its job and the sentence says what you want it to say, in the way you want to say it, leave it. Searching for these red flag words is just the easiest way to find told prose in a manuscript without reading the entire thing one more time.

If you're unsure if something is told or shown, imagine yourself acting out what the characters are doing. If you can do what they do, you're probably showing. If not, you're likely telling.

Step One: Determine Your Narrative Distance

Telling is a sliding scale. A close narrative distance (where the reader feels deep inside the point-of-view character's head) is less forgiving on telling slip-ups, while a distant, omniscient narrative distance feels more told, because someone other than the point-of-view character is telling the story. The deeper the point of view and closer the narrative distance, the more you need to show.

Determine where your narrator is, and you'll be able to judge where that novel's show, don't tell line is.

Step Two: Revise Motivational Tells

Motivational tells explain motive, frequently before the character has even exhibited the action. For example, "To stop the mugger, John threw a rock at the guy's head." This tells readers why John threw the rock before he throws it, explaining the action instead of showing it.

Look for ways to rewrite any motivational tells in a way that readers can guess the motivation by the way the character acts, thinks, or speaks, such as, "John threw the rock at the mugger's head. The man yelped and crashed to the sidewalk." We can guess he threw the rock to stop him.

Common red flag words: to (action), when, as, while, causing, making, because.

Step Three: Revise Emotional Tells

Emotional tells explain feelings or state the character is feeling an emotion, but readers never *see* that emotion exhibited by the character. If you've gotten feedback such as, "I'm just not feeling it, even though the character says she's upset," this could be the reason why. For example, "She screamed in anger and flung a rock at his head." In anger tells the emotion the scream and rock flinging clearly show.

Look for ways to convey the told emotion by using details that evoke that emotion, such as, "Gritting her teeth, she screamed and flung a rock at his head."

Common red flag words: In (emotion), and with (feeling).

Step Four: Revise Descriptive Tells

Descriptive tells explain actions. These are trickier because they often sound fine until you notice you're telling readers what they should be able to determine from the character's actions or how the scene is described. For example, "She sneaked across the room, trying not to be seen" or, "The sound of a gun echoed across the stadium."

Show the action and let readers decide what's going on by what they see. "She sneaked across the room, scurrying from chair to chair in the shadows," or, "A gunshot echoed across the stadium."

Common red flag words and phrases: Realize, could see, the sound of, the feel of, the smell of, tried to, trying, in order to, to make.

Step Five: Revise Placeholder Adverbs

When you see an adverb, there's a good chance you can improve the sentence by using details that show what that adverb means. How would someone who did something "adverb-ly" look and sound? For example, "She said angrily," and, "He walked nervously," are stronger as, "She yelled," and "He scurried."

Examine each adverb and decide if the sentence would be stronger without it.

Step Six: Revise Passive Tells

Passive tells are found in passive writing using to be verbs—such as, was (verb) and is being (verb)—where the subject of the sentence gets all the action instead of the subject *doing* the acting. For example, "Bob was bitten by a zombie," vs., "The zombie bit Bob."

Common red flag words: To be verbs—is, am, are, was, were, be, have, had, has, do, does, did, has been, have been, had been, will be, will have been, being.

While using a to be verb isn't passive on its own, these verbs *are* frequently found within writing using the passive voice, especially when paired with a past participle, such as: "Bob was greeted by the nurse," vs., "The nurse greeted Bob." By is another red flag word often seen mixed in with passive voice.

Do a search for these words and look at how they're used in each sentence. Determine if the subject is acting or being acted upon, and rewrite any passive sentences that don't need to be passive. Sometimes, the passive voice is exactly the right thing for the sentence, so you don't need to change every instance of it.

Step Seven: Revise Mental Tells

Some words fall into a telling gray area—they can feel told depending on their usage, but sometimes they read fine. They're good words to examine if you're getting "show more" feedback and you've eliminated all the other common tell words.

Common red flag words: realized, thought, wondered, hoped, considered, prayed, etc.

Realized: Unless the point-of-view character is referring to something she'd realized in the past, this word will likely feel told. Realized isn't a word you use when you "realize" something. You just do it.

Thought: If it's used as a tag, there's a good chance it can go. After all, everything your point-of-view character thinks are her thoughts, so saying "she thought" is redundant.

Wondered and hoped: These words are often fine because you *do* think, "I wonder what's for dinner," and, "I hope it's something I like." But they can feel told, especially if they're tucked in with a lot of other told-ish or distant prose.

Considered: Considered is like thought. When used as a verb it reads fine, but as a dialogue tag or descriptive summary it often feels told.

Prayed: Stopping the story to show the prayer would most likely bog it down, so this is a good example of a word that works better when told. Readers don't need to see the prayer to get what's going on.

If the mental tell word is used conversationally, as in, "I thought I'd run out to the store," or, "She'd hoped they'd make it back okay," then odds are it's working and showing. It's part of either the internalization or dialogue.

If it's used as a dialogue tag or description of the action (and action can mean thinking and realizing here: whatever "act" your character is taking), there's a good chance it's telling.

Revision Option: Dramatizing Summarized Scenes

There's nothing wrong with a summary or an explanation scene if that's what the story calls for, but sometimes the wrong scene is being shown and there's something mentioned in that summary that has more inherent conflict and is far more compelling. It's as if you wanted to tell readers something significant happened that affected the protagonist, but you didn't do a full-blown scene about it.

Take a peek at your draft, especially those "something's not right and I'm not sure why" sections. Ask:

Are you summarizing something that would make a compelling scene if you dramatized it? Look for places where decisions were made off screen. If the protagonist was faced with a choice, readers will want to see it.

Are other characters relaying information to the protagonist that would be more interesting if the protagonist had been the one to discover it? If the summary is a few lines, chances are it's fine to keep as a summary. But if it takes a few paragraphs—or worse, *pages*—to explain the situation, consider showing that scene unfold somehow.

Do you have a lot of scenes where the protagonist is learning plot-driving information by talking to people she knows who do the work, (such as, she has other characters uncovering plot details and she's only hearing reports)? If the plot is moving forward based mostly on other characters acting, that could indicate you have a reactive protagonist who's not driving the plot. Note: This applies less to mysteries, since investigating is the point of the book.

Are you glossing over something that has a strong influence on the protagonist's decisions in another scene? Choices made are typically important moments in the plot, and readers want to understand what motivated those decisions. If the reason seems more like an afterthought, or you think you had to explain why the character suddenly changed her mind, that could indicate a problem with the overall motivations or even the character arc.

Not every summary or exchange of information needs to be dramatized, but sometimes, you find the perfect scene is one you already told yourself about.

Red flag words will catch most telling issues, but some larger explanations might get missed. Let's look at telling's big brother—infodumps—next.

If You Want to Eliminate Unnecessary Infodumps

Building a story world takes a lot of effort, and usually a lot of research. After doing all that work, it's understandable that you'd want to share all the intriguing tidbits you'd uncovered or created for your novel. Unfortunately, you can get a little *too* excited and dump all that information into the story and bog down the novel.

In this session, the goal is to identify any infodumps and trim back what you don't need.

Step One: Identify and Eliminate Unnecessary Infodumps in Description

There's a fine line between conveying information and dumping information. If it's information readers need to know to understand what's going on at *that* moment, in *that* scene, it can usually stay (even if it needs a little trimming here and there). If it's there to explain an aspect of the story, world, or characters, but that information isn't relevant to the current scene or state of mind of the character, it can usually go. Be ruthless. Infodumps slow down the pacing and can make a novel drag.

Here are some common places infodumps like to hang out:

Introduction of characters: Cut out any information that diverges into histories or behaviors that aren't relevant to the scene or state of mind of the character.

Beginnings of scenes: Cut out any information that explains what readers are about to read. Summing up what happened between this scene and the previous one is also a common infodump. Unless what happened off screen is critical to know, or is a quick transition paragraph, skip it.

Walking into a new place: Setting the scene in a new location is useful, but cut it back if it starts to go into detail about elements the protagonist doesn't care about or know, and would certainly never think about at that moment in time.

History lessons: This is probably the most common infodump—be it a history about a person, a place, or an item in the novel. The story stops to tell readers all about it, why it's important, and how it works.

Insights into characters: Characters reflect, and sometimes that's good, but when they start musing philosophically about the past, the future, or what some detail means in the grander sense, it might be time to hit the delete key.

 REVISION RED FLAG: To spot potential infodumps, look for words such as: because, knew, since, and realized.

Step Two: Identify and Eliminate Unnecessary Infodumps Through Dialogue

Not all infodumps lurk in the text, so check your conversations for information stowaways.

Common dialogue infodumps include:

"As you know, Bob" conversations: Infodump-as-dialogue's biggest offender is one character explaining in detail what both characters already know. Get rid of anything that starts with "As you know..." and watch out for characters who tell another "how everything works around here."

Explaining everyday objects: This is found more in genre novels or novels that aren't set in the familiar world of the reader. Characters explain how some piece of technology or item works so readers know what they're talking about. If the characters take it for granted, they're not going to explain it. Would you explain how a phone works?

Catch-up dialogue: Characters catching each other up on what happened can't always be avoided, but cut it where possible. A good example of necessary catch-up dialogue is when the other characters will need to know that information later, but having them "know it" without showing how would seem like a mistake.

Revision Option: Ways to Fix Infodumps

The easiest way to fix an infodump is to cut it, but that's not always feasible. It's a good first step, so try cutting it and reading the page or scene. If it reads fine without the infodump, leave it out. If cutting the infodump makes what's happening unclear, then look for the critical details that have to be there and add them back in. Rewrite if necessary.

Infodumps should flow naturally with the rest of the scene. Try to:

Keep them in the point-of-view character's voice: Character opinions sound natural to the scene, and not like the author stopping to explain a detail.

Naturally trigger them by what's going on in that scene: If you need to stop the story and explain something, make sure there's a reason for it to happen. Look for places in the scene where something can make the character pause to reflect on that information.

Keep them short so readers aren't overwhelmed with information: A sentence or two here and there usually glides seamlessly by and doesn't jump out at readers. It's also easier for them to absorb that information, which is probably vital if you're stopping the story to explain it right then and there (if it's not vital, cut it).

Let them do more than dump information: If the information matters to the scene, it'll affect something in that scene. If it's a bit of history, have that knowledge affect how the character behaves. If it's backstory, let that history influence a character's choice or action.

Once the infodumps are under control, take a look at how your characters are moving through the world and how you're handling the stage direction in your scenes.

If You Want to Streamline the Stage Direction

Stage directions help get characters from place to place, whether it's across the room or across the galaxy. They're necessary to keep the story moving, but also common places to find awkward prose—we've all written a sentence where the character is essentially doing four things at once and needs three hands. It's also common to try to explain too many steps when one basic phrase would get the point across just fine.

In this session, the goal is to identify cumbersome stage direction and revise to smoothly describe your characters' actions.

Step One: Identify Awkward Stage Direction

Awkward stage direction usually slips in when your characters do too many things at once. Characters speaking, "while doing this, and moving toward that, while being this" is where you'll find most of the confusing or awkward stage direction.

Look for:

Common stage direction red flag words: Clunky stage direction is frequently connected by the words, as, while, or when. If your scenes read awkwardly, try searching for these words first.

Characters who try: Characters "try" to do a lot in stories. They try to get up, they try to hide, they try to hold back tears. Sometimes the act of trying is valid, but a lot of times, what you mean is that they *do* something, not *try* to do something. For example, "She tried to stand, dragging herself up by the curtains." At the end of this, is she standing or not? If so, then she "dragged herself up by the curtains" and there was no trying involved. She did it.

Do a search for "try" and make sure it's saying what you mean and not creating awkward or ambiguous directions. Ask:

- Is the person doing what she's trying to do? If so, rewrite to eliminate the try.

- Are you intending to show the struggle or failure of that action? If so, trying is probably the right word.

- Does the use of try show an action or explain a motivation? If it's explaining motivation, you might be telling and this is a good spot to rework.

Revision Option: Ways to Fix Awkward Stage Direction

The easiest fix is to break the (usually too long) sentence into multiple sentences. For stage directions with way too many steps, trim them down to the steps that matter.

Let readers fill in the blanks: Think about the stage direction as a dotted line. Give enough details to show the line and where it's going, but let readers fill in the logical missing pieces.

Skip the obvious steps: If readers will know the various steps to do something, such as starting a car or getting dressed, there's no need to describe them.

Flesh out what's *not* obvious: If readers won't be able to discern a character's actions or movements, then focus a little more on what she's physically doing. For example, disarming a bomb or moving through an unusual setting.

After your characters are moving around smoothly on the outside, take a look at how they're working on the inside. Let's develop the emotions of the scene next.

If You Want to Deepen the Emotions

When revising the emotions of a scene, take your character into consideration. People react differently to objects and situations, and you can use that to maintain variety in your descriptions. Maybe someone is quite physical and notices how their body reacts, while another is more cerebral and thinks through their emotions. Someone might hide what they feel while another announces it. Use the emotions to reflect the personalities of your characters.

When one person reacts in a certain way, the other has a chance to *also* react, so emotions can build off one another—for good or for bad.

In this session, the goal is to identify weak or unclear emotional responses and areas in your scenes that could benefit from emotional development.

Step One: Clarify the Emotions in the Scene

When a character is emotionally in the moment, that moment becomes real to readers. The stronger the connection, the more they'll like the book. Make sure what the characters are feeling is clear—even if they're all mixed up emotionally.

Look for emotional reaction words: Search your story for emotional reaction words, especially if you've gotten feedback with questions about why a character felt or did something. Look for those two-word sentences: I smiled, he groaned, she frowned, I bristled, she chilled, he shivered, I jumped, he twitched, she gasped, etc. Now ask yourself:

- Would a little internalization (or dialogue) help clarify what the protagonist is feeling?
- Is the emotion clear if you took *out* that I-verb phrase?

Often, such placeholder words can go once you've fleshed out the emotion. Of course, sometimes the I-verb phrase is exactly right for the paragraph, and adding more would only bog down the scene and might even add some redundancy.

Each character will react differently to the same emotion, so understanding who that character is can guide you on how to describe how she feels.

Step Two: Ensure Characters Are Emotionally There

As the writer, you know if a problem is a minor blip or major deal, and it's not uncommon to write the characters' emotions with that knowledge—so the emotions don't ring true to the situation from the character's point of view. Make sure your characters react realistically to what happens to them in every scene.

Show how the character feels right then and there: What's her gut reaction, or that instantaneous response she can't help but feel, even if it's the totally wrong response to the situation? For example, insane jealousy for a good friend who received good news, or joy to hear something nasty happened to someone a character can't stand. What is the raw, unfiltered emotion?

This can help pinpoint the emotional center of the scene.

Show the emotion the character is struggling with: Sometimes we know when we're feeling something we shouldn't and it bothers us that we felt it at all. Or we know an emotion isn't going to help us and we try to block it out to get whatever we have to do, done. We might even have conflicting emotions that affect our judgment or ability to handle the situation.

This can help determine the inner conflict of a scene, or add some conflict to a scene that needs it.

Show what gets pushed completely out of the character's head: A character caught up in an emotional moment (whether good or bad) might forget critical details, not be somewhere they should, or misread a situation.

This is useful if a character needs to miss something important for the plot or story.

Show what the character does that she wouldn't have done otherwise: Good judgment is often the first thing to go when someone is emotional. They make decisions based on the heat of the moment that they might not have made if they were thinking clearly or rationally.

This is useful if a character needs to make a bad decision.

Show how this moment affects behavior after it's over: Strong emotions linger, and they affect us even after the crisis (or celebration) has passed. A big scare is likely to make someone skittish or overprotective, happiness might make them more agreeable or more forgiving, or anger could cause them a short period of selfishness and cruelty.

This is useful to cause a character to act *out* of character and still be believable.

Show the character looking for clues in the people or items around her: Someone on the run might notice dangers or ways to escape. Someone who thinks she's about to be proposed to might be looking for signs that her guy is about to pop the question. A guy who isn't sure if he's on a date or out with a friend might be looking for clues to help him decide which it is.

This can help determine which details to include and which you can skip.

🚩 **REVISION RED FLAG:** Be wary of being *too* in the moment—avoid the old "time slowed down so now I can describe everything in minute detail" cliché. What gets attention are the details related to the moment itself.

Revision Option: Ways to Freshen Up Tired Emotional Descriptions

It's not uncommon to use the same words to describe basic emotions, such as smiling, frowning, trembling, etc. These keep your momentum going in a first draft, but once you've identified what emotion you want, it's good to swap those tired, old words for something more original and unique to your story.

Look through your common emotional words. Can you:

Express the emotion with a synonym? Swap smiled for grinned, or trembled for shuddered.

Express the emotion through internalization? A quick *What a jerk* might convey the same idea as a frown.

Express the emotion through dialogue? "You're hysterical!" can replace a smile or laugh.

Express the emotion through movement? "Her lip twitched and her eyes sparkled" might work better than a smile.

Express the emotion through bodily functions? "Tears slid down her cheeks" could work instead of, "She cried."

Express the emotion through involuntary reactions? "She jerked away, eyes shut tight" might show more than, "She cringed."

Express the emotion through senses other than what's expected? Fear is often shown by how the stomach or throat reacts, but what about sounds or smells? Ears might ring, or sounds might be distant and muffled. Scents might trigger memories that evoke the emotion you want to show.

Express the emotion through subtext? Sometimes what we *don't* say is more telling. "Why of course you can stay," she said, ripping her napkin into small pieces.

Revision Option: Ways to Enhance the Emotional Responses

Describing outward emotions can often sound forced because people in the moment feeling those emotions aren't usually thinking, "I want to stare deeply into his eyes." It's the *effect* of that deep gazing that's on their minds, not the gazing part.

To deepen the emotional response of a character, think about what that person would feel.

What physical symptoms would she experience? Emotions trigger physical reactions. Racing heart, shaking, numb fingers, sweaty palms. Some reactions are involuntary like clenching a jaw or blushing.

What thoughts would she think? Emotions also trigger a mental response, which can convey both real and conflicting emotions. Maybe the character would silently urge the other person to act, or they'd have a moment of self-reflection.

What response does she want the other person to see? What a character feels can be different from what she wants others to *know* she feels. Holding back tears, biting a lip, swallowing a reprimand. Or she may want to open up and let the feelings flow by gazing longingly, punching, or hugging.

What response does she want herself to feel? Sometimes we lie to ourselves. We try to convince ourselves we're not feeling what we are, or that it means something different from what it does. Thoughts paired with conflicting reactions are quite possible, and can get across a complex emotional state.

What external sensations would she notice? Heightened emotions can also heighten the senses, so perceptions might be stronger. Fear can induce a hyper-awareness; love can increase sensuality. Details that enhance a mood are noticed first.

Revision Option: Add Emotional Layers

Nobody feels one way all the time, or even one emotion at a time. A myriad of emotions float around in our heads at any given moment. We might be happy for a friend who received a promotion, but also jealous because we were passed over for one. Or thrilled for a sister marrying the man of her dreams, but worried because he's been married four times already. Layers add complexity and realism to a scene. Consider:

What's the protagonist's primary emotion for this scene? There's often one feeling or mood that takes precedence—the emotion that's driving the protagonist to act in that scene. This will typically determine the kind of scene it is. Fear = a suspenseful scene, lust = a love scene, sadness = a reflective scene (but not limited to these of course).

Conflict layer: To add more conflict or tension to the scene, look for ways to make the protagonist feel the opposite emotion of the primary mood.

Stakes layer: To raise the stakes of the scene, look for ways to add fear, worry, or apprehension about something in the scene.

Character layer: To flesh out the character, look for ways to add inappropriate emotions that show another side of the character.

What are the protagonist's secondary emotions? No matter what major emotion is driving the character, there's usually more going on under the surface.

Conflict layer: How might this secondary emotion cause a problem with the goal or the scene?

Stakes layer: How might this secondary emotion cause the protagonist to make a mistake?

Character layer: How might this secondary emotion reveal an aspect of the character?

What are the protagonist's conflicting emotions? Stories are about conflict, so there's a good chance your characters are feeling conflicted over something in any given scene. Where are their feelings ambivalent? Where do they emotionally disagree with other characters in the scene? What *shouldn't* they be feeling, but they feel anyway?

Conflict layer: How might this emotion deepen the protagonist's internal conflict?

Stakes layer: How might this emotion cause the protagonist to fail?

Character layer: How might this emotional conflict cause the protagonist to make the *wrong* choice?

What are the protagonist's hidden emotions? People feel emotions they'd rather not feel. Sometimes we don't even know we're doing it. Are your characters hiding anything? Is there anything they're trying *not* to feel? This is a good spot for those unconscious goals or feelings to leak in.

Conflict layer: How might the hidden emotions foreshadow later events or problems?

Stakes layer: How might the hidden emotions cause the protagonist to react in a way that adversely affects her?

Character layer: How might the hidden emotions hint at or show what the protagonist's character arc or emotional journey will be?

What are the *other* characters in the scene feeling? Your protagonist isn't the only one who gets to show a little emotion. If other people are in the scene, what do they feel? What are they hiding or pretending to feel? This is one way to drop subtle hints or add tension to a scene if there's clearly an issue no one is talking about.

Conflict layer: What clues might the protagonist pick up on (or not) that show another character doesn't agree with her—and that this might be a problem?

Stakes layer: Where might an emotional non-protagonist character cause a problem or make a problem worse?

Character layer: Where might added emotions show a deeper side to a secondary character?

Are there any forced emotions? Sometimes a character is trying hard to pretend to feel a certain way, even when she feels nothing. It might be out of compassion (little white lies to spare someone's feelings) or life-saving (pretending to still be the friend of the person you discovered betrayed you). Is this a scene where your characters are faking it?

Conflict layer: How might this faked emotion spark the opposite effect from what's expected?

Stakes layer: How might this faked emotion make the situation more personal for the protagonist?

Character layer: How might this faked emotion become real, either in this scene or later in the story (create bonus conflict if this causes unforeseen troubles)?

Emotional layers are also a useful way to weave in subplots or character arcs. Even if the plot portion of the scene isn't related to a subplot, the emotional layer can connect the plot to that scene and give the scene multiple layers of complexity. A character who's struggling with a blackmailer might act suspicious or distracted during a critical meeting at work and lose an important client (and maybe the job). Happiness or love might make someone oblivious to dangers they'd normally spot right away.

REVISION TIP: *If you have a scene that's not working, try changing the emotional state of your protagonist. How might she approach this situation if she was in a totally different mood? Try it with the other characters in the scene as well.*

It's not always about how something looks, or what someone does. More often it's what they feel or think that conveys the most emotion. Reinforce (or contradict) those feelings with what the character does, and you can craft emotional responses as rich as the emotions themselves.

Now that your characters are feeling all emotional, let's add a little mood lighting.

If You Want to Strengthen the Tone and Mood

Crafting the right mood and setting the right tone can go a long way to drawing readers into your story and keeping their attention. Choose words that create the mood or tone you want them to feel, and show them emotions they haven't seen a hundred times before. Don't go for the easy or familiar. Unfamiliarity creates uncertainty, and uncertainty leads to anticipation. Once you have that, you have the reader wondering what will happen next.

In this session, the goal is to set the right tone for your story, and ensure the mood of every scene supports the emotions you're trying to evoke.

Step One: Examine the Tone and Mood of the Scenes

The mood of a scene is like the scary music in horror movies. With the sound on, the scene makes us nervous—we jump at the slightest provocation—and it adds to the overall mood. Turn the sound off and the scene isn't scary anymore. It's just events happening in front of us.

What mood do you want for the scene? The emotional center of the scene determines the mood it's trying to evoke.

What details conjure that mood? Brainstorm a moment and free-associate words and images that fit the scene's mood. Are you using any of them in the scene? Should you be?

What tone do you want to set? You'll likely have a general tone for the entire novel, but some scenes might diverge for emotional impact. If the scene is too far off the novel's tone, that might indicate a problem with its emotional center.

Can you increase the tension by using details that reflect your protagonist's mood? Mood can help a scene that's weak on tension or feels emotionally disconnected.

Are you lessening the tension with the wrong descriptions? A conflicting tone or mood can create the opposite emotion in readers.

Step Two: Enhance the Tone and Mood of the Scenes

For every scene that feels emotionally empty, add a little mood to the descriptions.

Use imagery that conveys the scene's mood: Certain images convey certain emotions, and you can use those to your advantage. If you want to evoke sadness, look for images that tend to make people sad—injured animals, crying, rain, friends dying, etc.

Replace generic words with specific ones: Look for words associated with the tone and mood you want to evoke. Someone "skipping" down the street is different from someone "creeping" down it, though they're both "walking."

Use the sentence rhythm to reflect the mood: Snappy banter is fast-paced, with short sentences and little or no exposition or dialogue tags. It's light, funny, and playful, and it reads that way. Anger is often portrayed with choppy sentences, and sudden starts and stops as people yell, then pause to think and yell again. Sadness is often shown through longer, slower sentences and lots of internalization.

Put the characters in the right mood: How the characters feel can underscore the tone and set the right mood. No matter how serious a situation is, if the point-of-view character is flippant and blows it off (and that's not the point of this scene), it won't seem serious. Same as how a character being overly dramatic in a situation that clearly doesn't call for it can feel melodramatic. If the character feels one way, and the rest of the scene backs that up, then you'll create that same feeling in your readers.

At this stage, your descriptions should be solid and rich, with deep emotional layers and the right tone for your story. Next, let's focus a little more closely on the setting and world building and make sure they're just as well developed.

Workshop Six: Setting and World-Building Work

The Goal of This Workshop: To strengthen your setting and story world and eliminate unnecessary descriptive details.

What We'll Discuss in This Workshop: How to analyze your setting and world. You'll also look at the best ways to describe your setting and ground readers in that world.

Welcome to Workshop Six: Setting and World-Building Work

Setting and world building are often used interchangeably, but I've found it helpful to treat them as two separate aspects, especially during revisions, because they focus on different elements.

Setting is the location the *scene* is set in. It should contain all the information and details needed to understand and picture that scene. It might be a kitchen, or space station, or even a plane of existence.

World building is where the *story* is set. It should contain all the information and details needed to understand and picture how the world works, and why this is where the story had to happen. It might be a town, a world, or even a single room.

Separating them mentally is useful because you want to use details that matter to the scene, character, or world. A particular descriptive detail might not be relevant to the scene goal, but it is relevant to the world and establishes *why* the protagonist would be after that goal in the first place.

"Life in the big city" conjures different images and societal rules than "life in the country," but both can have a scene set at a restaurant in those respective worlds. What details you choose to show for that restaurant will vary based on which world it inhabits.

It can be extremely helpful to keep these subtle, yet important differences in mind as you revise your settings and story worlds.

Analyze the Setting

Without a clear picture of where a scene takes place, readers can feel as if they're listening to characters talking in a blank room. A sense of place grounds your readers and helps them imagine the scene and lose themselves in your story.

In this session, the goal is to make sure every scene establishes the location and provides enough details to ground readers in that scene.

In the next session, you'll delve more into world building.

A note about setting: Just like with description, different genres will have different needs for how much setting is required. Created-world genres like fantasy or historical fiction typically need more detail to place readers in those worlds, while novels set in the real world need less. Take your story into account when deciding what the "right amount of setting" is.

Determine if the Setting is Working

The majority of setting details are usually found when the character first enters that location, or at the beginning of the scene set in that location. Look at your scene and ask:

▶ **Are details introduced right away to ground readers in the scene?** Even a few words can be enough to establish where and when the characters are.

▶ **Is it clear who's in the scene?** Characters appearing out of the blue halfway through a scene can jar readers right out of the story and make them think they missed something.

▶ **Have the characters changed location since the last scene?** New locations will need grounding, but it's not a bad idea to add a word or two to remind readers where they are in a new scene or chapter even if it didn't change locations. Scene and chapter breaks are common places to stop reading.

▶ **Have the characters changed times?** If time has passed, let readers know, otherwise they'll assume the next scene happens immediately after.

▶ **Does the point-of-view character spend more time talking about what the location looks like than doing anything in it?** People exist and move through the world; they don't stop and evaluate it without good reason.

▶ **Are there a lot of sweeping word paintings that focus on the landscape or weather?** While poetic descriptions of the landscape can add to a story, they *are* red flags for setting description overload. If the character isn't in the mood to muse about the weather, it might be too much.

▶ **Do interior scenes read like articles from an interior design magazine?** Too much attention on the details of furnishings is another red flag that the focus is on details that aren't serving the story and might need to go.

Problems Found?

If you find any setting issues, spend some time doing the exercises in If You Want to Clarify the Setting on page 257.

Analyze the World Building

How unique your world is will likely have determined how much world building was done prior to writing the novel. A fantasy world probably has pages and pages of information, while a novel set in the real world might not have much beyond a list of specifics. However, if the real-world story centers around a topic readers aren't familiar with (such as a spy novel, police procedurals, or anything involving highly specialized skills), it could have just as much world-building information as a world created from scratch. To your readers, it *is* a unique and unfamiliar world.

In this session, the goal is to examine your story world and determine if you have the right balance to understand that world without overwhelming readers.

Determine if the World Building is Working

World building permeates a novel, from the sweeping vistas of the geography to the smallest glance from its people. How characters exist in your world and what they do are shaped by what that world is like and the rules of living there.

As you review your world, think about how these questions pertain to your story and how your world serves that story.

▶ **Are there enough specific details to show the special rules of this world?** The more unusual your world is, the harder it is for readers to picture it correctly or understand the rules around it. For example, if everyone flies, show someone flying right away to establish that.

▶ **Are people interacting with the world or is it just a backdrop?** If the world-building details and passages could be cut and not affect anything in the scene, that could indicate a world that lacks relevance to the story.

▶ **Does the point-of-view character share her thoughts and views on the world around her?** People have opinions about the world they live in, and those opinions cause the characters to act, and affect their decisions when they do act.

▶ **Does the world offer inherent conflicts that make the protagonist's goals harder?** The whole point of a world is to provide an environment for a story and a place for the characters to evolve. If the world doesn't create or add to the conflict, why is the novel set there?

▶ **Does the world allow you to make a point you couldn't otherwise make?** Worlds that work on a thematic level add depth and meaning to the actions that take place within those worlds.

▶ **Does the world provide challenges you couldn't otherwise have for the characters?** Living in this world should affect how the plot unfolds and how the characters experience events.

▶ **Does the world pull its own weight as far as the story is concerned, or does it just sit there looking pretty?** Be wary of details that do nothing but look or sound "cool." These are often the first to go if you need to trim world description.

▶ **Does the world building continue to the end of the novel, or does it fade out after it's established?** It's not uncommon for much of the world-building setup to occur early on in the novel, so it's easy to forget about it and thus, the level of description fades away as the novel unfolds.

▶ **Are there areas that read more like a textbook than a story?** If the world feels more explained than lived in, that could indicate a lot of infodumping or telling.

▶ **Do the details help readers understand the conflicts or problems in this world?** If the details don't directly serve the plot, they'll likely show why the plot matters or why the actions of the characters are necessary.

▶ **Are the rules of this world clear?** If readers don't understand how a world works, odd are they'll get lost or confused in that world.

▶ **Do the rules make sense in the context of the story?** Make sure the world works in a way that helps the plot unfold and allows the characters to grow as they need to.

▶ **Are there contradictions in the world?** No world makes perfect, logical sense. Contradictions, weirdness, and bizarre elements help make a world feel real, but be wary of contradictions that defy credibility.

▶ **Is the world complicated and layered?** People have different beliefs, and varied ways of approaching or solving issues. Let your world reflect the complexities of life.

▶ **Does the world feel like it exists when the main characters aren't there?** If everything in the world exists for the characters alone, it can feel two-dimensional and stagnant.

▶ **Does this world have a history that logically influences the story events?** The world developed to the point of the story and created whatever situation requires fixing by the protagonist. This might be a vast political system spanning galaxies, or it might be the office rules that cause everyone in accounting to revolt.

▶ **Is the infrastructure sound?** Make sure the world mechanics and rules hold up to questions. If you can't answer why something is the way it is (beyond, "because the plot needs it that way") then the world probably isn't developed enough. Also be wary if the aspects of the world don't depend on each other to function.

▶ **Are the people varied?** No group is all any one thing, be that race, gender, faith, or opinion. Aim for differences that lead to conflicts and a variety of beliefs on whatever the story is about.

🚩 **REVISION RED FLAG:** If you find the focus of your world building is more on the past and not the present, that could indicate too much backstory and not enough relevance to the plot. If the opposite is true, that could indicate the world is too tailored to the plot and isn't a fully realized world on its own.

Problems Found?

If you find any world-building issues, spend some time doing the exercises in If You Want to Balance the World Building on page 260.

If You Want to Clarify the Setting

Setting is the stage dressing, providing the environment in which characters act in your story. The best settings offer more than a place to "do stuff," and can underscore a theme, create a mood, provide conflict, or even show a character's personality.

In this session, the goal is to make sure each scene has enough setting to ground readers so they understand where and when they are in the story.

Step One: Clarify Your Setting

A common problem in early drafts is a setting filled with generic details. It's a house, a store, an evil empire, but there's nothing that sets the story in a *particular* house, or store, or evil empire.

Describe what's unique to the place or situation: Everyone knows what a town looks like, or a spaceship, or a medieval village, but what makes *your* town, spaceship, or village different? Try adding three or four key and unique elements that readers need to know when they enter this setting.

Describe what will be assumed incorrectly: If your setting is a forest and you say "forest," readers will likely imagine tall, green trees, birds singing, and sunlight filtering in between the leaves of the canopy. But if your forest is comprised of white, crystalline trees that resonate with musical chimes when the wind blows, that's an entirely different forest than the default "forest" setting. Rework default setting images that give the wrong impression (this is especially true in fantasy settings).

Describe what's relevant to the scene: If your protagonist is trying to escape a madman by running into a maze of crumbling buildings, it's not a good time to describe the overlay of the entire city. Revise to focus on elements important to the setting at that moment.

Describe what's relevant to the character: If the protagonist doesn't know the difference between a palm tree and a maple tree, she won't be describing the local landscape in meticulous detail. But if she's an architecture fanatic, she might describe the buildings in more detail (if this is an important thing for readers to know, of course). This will also help you show instead of tell, as you'll see the world through your point-of-view character's eyes.

Describe by showing it in action versus explaining it: Setting details work best when they're in the background of the scene and flow seamlessly with the rest of the text. If it's raining in a city, show people stepping over puddles on the sidewalk, pulling on raincoats as they leave cafes, the squeak-thunk of windshield wipers. Pick details that make it clear it's raining without saying, "It was raining."

Optional Step: Setting Exercise

If you think your setting still isn't as rich as you'd like, try this exercise:

Grab a blank sheet of paper (or a new file) and take a look at your own setting.

1. Write down the setting. (short answer: a street in New York, Geveg, 1672 Mexico, high school)

2. Add the first details that come to mind when you think about this setting.

3. Picture this setting and think about why you chose it for your novel. Look past the basics and think about this place.

4. Now add the details you found after looking more closely.

5. Picture your point-of-view character. Put *her* in the scene and look out through *her* eyes.

6. Add the details *she* sees.

Odds are you'll come up with more interesting details that carry not only setting information, but character and theme information as well. Details in the setting will now be noticed because they mean something to the point-of-view character.

The first details that pop into your head will likely be the same details most of your readers imagine. Because of that, the scene can feel flat, typical, or just plain boring. Readers have seen it before and it offers them nothing new.

Pull out unusual details and you'll surprise them. A typical setting becomes fresh, perspectives are interesting, and readers pay more attention. The right setting details can put readers in the right mindset for the scene, and provide a richness that makes that location seem real.

After you get your settings into shape, take a look at the larger world and how it can support these locations.

If You Want to Balance the World Building

It's not unusual to have an imbalance in your world building in a first draft. Either you do too much and your worlds are packed full of unnecessary details, or you do too little and those worlds fail to come alive. But once you see how the story turns out, you can judge the right amount of detail to include that will show your world without turning it into an encyclopedia.

In this session, the goal is to ensure your world feels real and immersive, but isn't distracting from the story.

One caveat here: This advice is aimed at finished worlds, not suggestions on creating a world from scratch. It assumes you've done your research, created the rules of your world, and have already developed it to fit your plot and story. It might need some tweaking, but the world itself is sound.

Step One: Check if You're Maintaining the World

Discovering new aspects of your world helps hook readers and draw them into the story. If you set up your world and then forget about it, you risk making the back half of the novel feel flat or empty. Take a minute to ensure you're showing aspects of your world (and revealing new aspects) all the way to the end of your novel.

What details have changed since the novel opened? The characters will probably have had some kind of an effect on the world as they acted to resolve the plot. Or they might have learned enough to see that world differently.

What details have been uncovered? Secrets often exist in the story world, and are revealed at various points throughout the novel.

Are there any recurring details that connect to a theme or symbol? Details might show how a thematic element has changed, or provide visual proof that the world is indeed changing (for good or ill).

Are there reasons why the point-of-view character might notice new details? A change in attitude or beliefs could affect how a character sees the world or understands it.

Are you showing the same details, or building off of what you've already done? Let readers delve deeper into the world and experience all its complexities as they move through the story. Details that might have bogged the story down in the early chapters often resonate well after readers get to know the world.

Revision Option: If You Have Too Much World Building

Too much world building is most often found in the description, with heavy infodumps and large passages of what objects look like and why they work they way they do.

If you're unsure what to keep and what to cut:

Use objects the characters interact with: Two paragraphs on what the blacksmith's shop looks like doesn't matter if the characters never interact with him, and being a blacksmith has zero effect on the story. If characters *only* look at something as they go by so you can describe it, you probably don't need that detail or need only a brief mention.

Keep multi-leveled details: If a detail creates mood, shows an aspect of the culture, gives a reason for the protagonist to feel a certain way, *and* paints a picture of what the town looks like, it's a *good* detail. But if it does nothing more than show what something looks like, go ahead and cut it (or develop it so it does more, and get rid of other details that don't).

Show important details about the world through character experience: This is the essence of "Show, don't tell." If the detail is important enough to tell readers about it, show that detail in action and have a character experience it, such as the protagonist being hassled by police in a story about a corrupt police force. This puts the world (and those interesting tidbits) in context.

Show details that have inherent conflict—especially if it affects the plot or character arc: The world is filled with examples of the problems the protagonist faces, and reasons why her life is as bad as it is in the story.

Show details unique to your world: If the details of your world are common to pretty much every book in that genre, you can skip lengthy descriptions of it. Readers don't need to know in great detail what the horses and their tack look like, but they *do* need to know if the horses have six legs or are controlled by cybernetic implants.

Keep details that show something new and interesting to readers: Revelations of new information and secrets keep readers hooked, and secrets about the world can work as plot revelations—if they're interesting. Focus on the interesting details that give the world its character. Keep the bizarre, the unusual, and the weird contradictions that make it seem human.

Overall, cut all details that don't serve the story: No matter how cool an aspect of your world might be, if it does nothing to help advance the plot, deepen the story, enhance a character, explore the theme, or otherwise shed light on the tale, it can usually go.

Revision Option: If You Have Too Little World Building

Fleshing out a world after the story is done is sometimes easier because you know exactly what details will affect the plot and change the characters. You can pick and choose the best details from your research that illustrate your multi-faceted world.

Look for places where the characters physically interact with the world: Put the details in the action and let them affect the outcome of those actions.

Look for moments where the protagonist judges or conveys an opinion about something in the world: These are moments where the theme and conflicts often come into play. They show not only how the world works, but the type of person the protagonist is by how she feels about that aspect.

Look for places where readers need to know more about the world to understand a plot point: Magic or unusual social norms typically need more attention because readers aren't familiar with them going into the story.

Look for moments when the protagonist is figuring out something about the world: These are useful moments to explain why something matters without resorting to infodumps.

Once you've found the best places to do a little world building, add details that:

Show the rules of the world or society: Readers want to know how the world works, especially if the rules are interesting and will affect the protagonist during the plot.

Enhance the tone or mood of the scene: If your world is dark and dreary, find the best dark and dreary examples you can. Put them where you want readers feeling apprehensive.

Help foreshadow a later scene or event: In most cases, you want details that affect and serve the scene those details are in, but sometimes a little foreshadowing is required, especially if the scene is a precursor to a later event.

Help clarify a character's motives: We're shaped by the world we live in, and characters should be affected the same way. Living in your story world should have left its mark on your characters, and influence how they act and feel about their lives and the world they live in.

Revision Option: If You Need to Shore Up Your World's Foundation

A first draft often focuses on the world-building details that affect the plot, so by the time the novel is done, the world seems a little thin. If you think your world could use more attention, start with the foundation and add elements as they pertain to your story.

Use climate details to give a sense of place: People living in the cold lead different lives from those who live in the tropics—and it's not just what they wear, but their morals can also be affected. If a culture is always covered up, there could be a taboo against bare skin, or it might be considered risqué. Rain, or snow, or a particular season may play a role in the plot.

Use agriculture and food to add visual flavor: Food might be a way to designate social classes, with hard-to-get items illustrating wealth or indulgence. Food can also say a lot about a character. Are they a risk taker trying exotic meals, or do they always stick to meat and potatoes?

Certain places have unique cuisine that reflects the culture, and you can add local flavor with unusual dishes.

Use plants and animals: People use what's available to them, so you could pull some interesting details using plants and animals common to a particular region. Animals can also add a fun layer to settings as well. Imagine finding an alligator under the car for Florida settings, or dealing with migrating crabs. Animals and weird animal behavior could provide just the right touch to spice up a plot and provide something unusual to set the story apart.

Offer glimpses of how people in that world make a living: Jobs vary by area. If the protagonist lives in a small town, everyone might work at the same plant or factory, or an area might all be heavily employed by a certain industry, like steel in Pennsylvania or cars in Michigan. A big city could have jobs unique to that area, such as music in Nashville or movies in Hollywood. A more fantastical world might have complex (and fascinating) social and economic structures, or it could reflect these aspects of our world.

Show the entertainment and recreational options: What's considered fun is often tied in to the morality and ethics of a culture, and you can show right and wrong behaviors by what the characters do in the off hours. Different cities can also have different activities. Local festivals or events can add as much color as food or a job. Instead of sending the protagonist on a date of dinner and a movie, maybe she goes to the annual wine tasting or strawberry festival. Or maybe the entertainment can show the values of that city, such as strip clubs that cause a stir in the community, or one that's a normal and accepted part of the town.

Suggest education levels: Education might be used to separate classes or genders, or show roles and attitudes about gender or class. Different areas have different expectations about education, so how far along your protagonist might be scholastically may depend on where she's from. This might cause conflict or embarrassment for her if she's from a vastly different background than her friends, co-workers, or love interests.

Use religion to show various views and beliefs: Remember that no culture has a population that believes exactly the same thing, so there will be ranges of belief and even some radical thinkers. You may not mention religion at all, but your protagonist might wear a cross or a Star of David, given to her by a favorite grandmother. Religion is all around, so it could provide an answer to a plot problem, or it could be used to show the ethics or morality of a character, especially if she's facing an ethical dilemma.

Use art and architecture to show culture and aesthetics: Music, dance, painting, sculpture, bead work—art evolves from where people live, what they believe, and what materials they have available. Art is even seen in how those cities are built—skyscrapers vs. stucco, or glass vs. adobe brick. Different regions have their own looks that can provide the right style for the story. Specific or unique details also add realism to the setting to make readers feel like they're there.

As you finish your story world, take a moment to congratulate yourself. You've completed all the harder, developmental aspects of your revision (characters, plot, description, setting). There's still more work to do, but the tough part is over.

Let's dive into dialogue and voice work and make your novel sound as good as it now looks.

Workshop Seven: Dialogue and Voice Work

The Goal of This Workshop: To examine the manuscript's dialogue and character voices, and craft believable conversations and unique voices.

What We'll Discuss in This Workshop: Common dialogue pitfalls and ways to correct them, and ways to develop strong voices for your characters.

Welcome to Workshop Seven: Dialogue and Voice Work

Dialogue is connected to nearly every aspect of a novel—from how characters convey information, to how they interact, to how they move the plot from scene to scene. When it works, you have real people guiding your readers through the story. When it doesn't, you have bad actors on a cheap stage.

How a character sounds helps readers identify who that character is—in a literal and philosophical sense. Characters who sound the same are hard to tell apart, and can leave readers confused about who is saying what. Bland characters can also rob the story of its uniqueness, offering nothing but cookie cutter people who do nothing to affect the world they live in. They're there to spout their lines, though it doesn't matter which one says what, since they all sound exactly alike and say whatever is required to check off elements on a plot list.

Strong, well-developed characters deserve strong, well-developed voices. Take advantage of all the work you put into them and make sure they sound as real as they feel.

Analyze the Dialogue

Stilted dialogue can stop a story cold or make it sound melodramatic and cheesy. Good dialogue captures the essence of real-life conversations without the awkward pauses and interruptions that actually happen.

In this session, the goal is to examine your dialogue and identify weak spots.

You'll look at the external dialogue, as well as character voices.

Determine if the Dialogue is Working

Dialogue walks a fine line between sounding realistic and conveying necessary information. It's easy to slip over that line into infodumping and character lectures, or have characters who sound like they're reading from a script.

Look over the dialogue in each scene and ask:

▶ **Do the characters sound like real people?** Real people speak from their own world experience and personal views; they don't read lines on a page. Look for dialogue that sounds forced, overly formal, or stilted. A lack of contractions often indicates too-formal dialogue, as does always speaking in grammatically perfect sentences.

▶ **Is the dialogue an *actual* conversation or two people stating information at one another for the reader's benefit?** Conversations have give and take, with one character speaking and another responding to what was said. Look for stretches of one long speech followed by another long speech in reply. Characters should be talking, not spouting information.

▶ **Are characters telling each other what they already know?** Look for any infodumps through dialogue and "as you know, Bob" conversations, and either cut or rework so it sounds natural.

▶ **Are there empty dialogue phrases?** Look for pointless small talk, unnecessary greetings and farewells, and awkward prompts to speak. Trim out the dialogue that does nothing to serve the story.

▶ **Is the dialogue advancing the plot or story?** A conversation might be interesting, but if it isn't serving the story, it's bogging the pacing down. Make sure your characters' conversations have a point to them.

▶ **Are the dialogue tags clear?** Look for spots where the speaker is ambiguous or it's hard to know who's speaking.

▶ **Are there too many dialogue tags?** Only tag where necessary. Also look for places where characters repeatedly use names. If it's clear who's speaking without the tag, cut it.

▶ **Are there any over-written or impossible dialogue tags?** Tags should be simple and words you can physically "say." For example, yelled is a manner of speech, sigh is not. You can't sigh a line of dialogue, but you can yell it. Look for any places where you're trying too hard not to use some form of "she said."

▶ **Are characters giving away too much information for no reason?** Be wary of characters who answer questions with as much information as they can. Not only is it unrealistic, but it could also indicate infodumps through dialogue or places where the goal is achieved too easily.

▶ **Are you summarizing any conversations instead of dramatizing them?** Watch out for conversations explained instead of dramatized. Dialogue is active and keeps the story moving. Summarizing when the characters are standing right there seems told and static.

▶ **Is there subtext? Is it clear what's *not* being said?** Good dialogue is more than what's said, it's also what's not said. Look for places where too much is revealed and nothing is being held back.

▶ **Is the language appropriate for the intended market?** A middle grade novel with a lot of swearing and sexual innuendo is going to have problems with its intended audience. Make sure the language fits who'll be reading it.

Problems Found?

If you find any dialogue issues, spend some time doing the exercises in If You Want to Strengthen the Dialogue on page 271.

Analyze the Voice

Voice is important in a novel, but there's more than your author's voice. Characters have voices too, and making those voices distinct helps readers keep track of who's who. It's also a good way to help you develop your characters into solid personalities. Knowing what they sound like can help determine who they are (and vice versa).

In this session, the goal is to identify weak or too-similar voices in your manuscript.

Determine if the Characters' Voices Are Working

A character's personality is at the core of his or her voice, so keep in mind who a character is as you develop your voices. Look at your characters and ask:

▶ **Does each point-of-view character have his or her own voice and style of speaking?** Be wary of characters who all sound the same, especially in multiple point-of-view novels. Look for ways to vary how characters speak and interact with other characters.

▶ **Can you tell who's speaking even without identifying the character by name?** The goal is for readers to know who a character is, even without a name. It's the individual speaking style, verbal ticks, the tangible elements that make one person sound different from another.

▶ **Can you get a sense of who the character is by the voice?** Personality shines through in how we speak, even if we use the same exact words. Make sure the characters sound like the type of person they are (or are trying to be).

▶ **Does the point-of-view character's outer voice sound like her internal one?** Unless the character is trying to appear as a different person, the internal and external voices will be similar. Variations due to social situations and direct attempts to hide a true personality are acceptable, but watch out for interior voices that sound nothing at all like the way a character speaks.

▶ **Do characters use language suitable to their status, age, or cultural situation?** Characters should speak in ways appropriate to their life experiences and place in the world. For example, five-year-old children don't typically sound like college professors unless there's a reason.

▶ **Does the voice change depending on the situation?** A teen sounds different when talking with peers versus talking to parents or authority figures. Are there situations where a character's voice will change? Are there rules for that in your story or world?

▶ **Do the non-point-of-view characters all sound the same?** If you can change the speaker and it doesn't change how the dialogue is spoken, the character voices probably aren't varied enough. While some lines might be interchangeable, most shouldn't be. Aim for every character expressing themselves in a distinctive way.

▶ **Are any of the character voices annoying?** Be wary of whiney, mean, overly sarcastic, or otherwise attitude-laden characters. A little goes a long way, and it's easy to push a strong personality into an irritating character (young adult and women's fiction authors be especially wary of this).

▶ **Are any of the character voices stereotyped or clichéd?** Does the jock sound like a bully? The cop tough and hardnosed? The librarian meek and mousy? People speak in ways that show who they are (or who they want people to think they are). Avoid the voices we've all seen before.

▶ **Is there an overabundance of dialect?** Dialect is hard to read and often unnecessary. A word here and there to establish an accent can work, but if readers need a translator to understand the character, it's gone too far.

▶ **Does every character use the same vocabulary or is it varied?** Different cultures and educational backgrounds will influence what words a person uses. Your poor farmer from the lowlands shouldn't use the same words and phrases as the royal princess with the private tutor.

▶ **Does every character speak with the same rhythm or pattern?** Someone born and raised in Manhattan sounds different from someone raised in Mississippi. Does a character use clipped sentences or does she ramble? Is she curt? Eloquent?

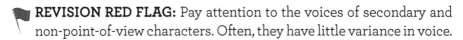 **REVISION RED FLAG:** Pay attention to the voices of secondary and non-point-of-view characters. Often, they have little variance in voice.

Problems Found?

If you find any voice issues, spend some time doing the exercises in If You Want to Vary the Voices on page 277.

If You Want to Strengthen the Dialogue

Dialogue makes up a sizable chunk of a novel, but it's also a common area to find weak prose. In first drafts, it's not unusual to let your characters ramble on, give them unrealistic dialogue, and even steal their unique voices from them.

In this session, the goal is to clean up and strengthen your dialogue.

Step One: Eliminate Empty Dialogue

In real life conversations, people use small talk and break up what they say into bites. For example:

"Hi."

"Hey, John."

"Did you see that new movie?"

"The one with the robot?"

"Yeah."

"Not yet, you?"

In a novel, this will slow the pace down and make readers impatient to get back to the story (and use a lot of unnecessary words). Realistic dialogue is condensed to keep the pace moving:

"Hey, John. Did you see the new movie with the robot?"

"Not yet, you?"

This takes a lot fewer words to get to the same place, and nothing in the story is lost.

Look through your dialogue for any lines that can be condensed, combined, or cut. The beginning of a conversation is a common place to find empty dialogue, as characters get up to speed to have the real talk. Also check the ends of conversations as they wrap it up and say goodbye.

If you're unsure if the dialogue is needed or not, ask:

If you took it out, would the meaning of the conversation change? Empty dialogue is empty because it adds nothing to what's being said.

Could you combine several lines into one, tighter line that accomplishes the same task? If four lines basically say, "Hello, how are you, long time no see," or the like, then one line is probably all you need. Skip the delays and get to the meat of the conversation.

Are you *trying* to delay the scene? Sometimes you add empty dialogue because you want the scene to convey someone dragging her feet. Instead of throwing in words that mean nothing, look for ways to deepen the scene or add additional information *while* giving the impression of time passing awkwardly.

One benefit to empty dialogue is that it's easy to get rid of since it's not necessary. If you're trying to trim down your word count, this is a good thing to add to your words-to-cut list.

Step Two: Revise Stilted or Too-Formal Dialogue

Overly formal dialogue often appears when you're trying to sound "writerly" and forget that characters should sound like real people.

Go through any dialogue that doesn't sound like real people talking and rework to sound natural. Use contractions and sentence fragments, let characters interrupt each other, and make sure the conversations sound like conversations.

Step Three: Revise "Share Everything" Conversations

Not every character should be forthcoming about every bit of information she knows. Real people lie, they fudge, they withhold information, they steer conversations back to what *they're* interested in (usually themselves), and they don't offer information that will make them look bad.

Review character conversations and revise anything that's a little too helpful or forthcoming. Consider what a character might be hiding or trying to achieve in the scene or conversation. Not only will you make the conversations more interesting, but you'll likely raise the tension and conflict as well.

Things to consider:

What's more interesting if it's left unsaid? Look for opportunities to add in subtext that deepens the scene.

How does the body language underscore or contradict what's being said? Our bodies can give us away when we're lying, or support us when we're telling the truth. Someone who sounds cheerful and agreeable while clenching her jaw and hands is sending mixed signals.

Where might characters lie or hide information? Even if they're not trying to hurt the protagonist, characters can cause trouble by wanting to keep secrets.

What are characters afraid to say? Dancing around an issue can heighten tension and create conflict in a scene. It also helps develop character.

Step Four: Revise Awkward Summarized Dialogue

Dialogue is about the spoken word, but once in a while you might gloss over it and summarize a conversation when you don't need to. It's another form of telling, and often readers want to see these conversations unfold in real time in the novel. For example, I walked into the kitchen and asked Mom about the gun I'd found in her suitcase. She dodged the question and asked me what I wanted on my eggs instead.

This is a missed opportunity to create tension and probably a compelling moment in the novel. What would Mom say? How would she dodge the question? What was her body language like?

Look for any summarized dialogue and dramatize sections that would be stronger if seen.

Step Five: Eliminate Infodumps as Dialogue

If you revised your dialogue infodumps in Workshop Five: Description Work, you can skip this step.

Infodumping doesn't just happen to prose. Look for characters talking about subjects they'd never talk about. A good rule of thumb: If the information is for the *reader's* benefit, chances are you're dumping. If the information is for the character's benefit (or detriment), chances are it's fine. For example:

Reader's benefit: "I'll rig up a small explosive device to blow open the door. That's the way we did it when I was deployed in Afghanistan as a Navy SEAL."

Character's benefit: "Um, Kevin, where'd you learn to make bombs?"

"The Navy."

One advantage to *not* explaining everything to readers is that they won't know exactly what's going on or what's going to happen. If they don't know, then they'll read in anticipation of what will happen next. Don't explain the magic trick before you perform it.

Common places to find infodumps in dialogue:

"As you know, Bob" conversations: Look for characters explaining in detail what both characters already know. Find ways to convey the information naturally, while at the same time, giving readers the important details.

Catch-up dialogue: One character finds out critical information the other characters need to know, but *not* having them tell the others would seem odd, and readers might wonder how the other person learned about it. Try adding more information or giving the reader something new so it isn't so repetitive. Or use slightly different language so you're not repeating what you just showed in another scene.

If you have to dump information into your dialogue, keep it in the character's voice.

Step Six: Revise Awkward or Confusing Dialogue Tags

Dialogue tags are part of any novel, keeping them from sounding repetitive can be a challenge. Said gets old fast. Nodded, shrugged, frowned, and smiled can only be used so often. Having a character push back her hair or clench his hands clogs up the narrative after a bit and can even seem melodramatic. Too much stage direction feels clunky, but not enough makes a scene unclear.

Dialogue tags work best when they're invisible—either by not drawing attention to themselves or by blending in and doing more than identifying the speaker. The harder *they* work, the less work *you* have to do to craft the scene.

Bad dialogue tags can range from cumbersome to ridiculous, creating missed opportunities to flesh out a scene.

Common areas to check for trouble:

He said adverbidly: In most cases, an adverb in a dialogue tag is a missed opportunity to show, not tell. Check your tags and make sure you have good reasons for any adverbs used, and there isn't a better way to dramatize the adverb instead.

Non-said tags: Said is a perfectly good word. It's invisible to readers, so they gloss right over it. Avoiding it, or using solely action dialogue tags, can give the prose a clunky, list-like feel since it's technically one short sentence after another.

Internalization overload: Internalization tags dialogue without using said or stage direction, but be wary of large chunks of internal thought that create awkwardly long pauses between bits of dialogue. If there are nine lines of thought between "Did you go?" and "Yes, I did," readers might forget what the character was asking about.

Characters as mind readers: Sometimes a character will think something, but the other characters in the scene react as if the words were spoken. Make sure characters act based on dialogue they heard.

Awkward dialogue tag placement: Tagging every line of dialogue at the end feels repetitious and list-like. Listen to how the words flow and look for the right spot to add a pause, since a tag often works like a comma to slow the dialogue down. Ask yourself if you can you get more dramatic punch if the tag is in a different place. This is especially true for zingers or those "dum-dum-DUM!" moments.

The goal with dialogue and tags is to find a balance between them. Use enough exposition to set the scene and make it clear who's talking, but not so much that it detracts from what's being said. Let the stage direction add to the suspense of the scene and provide details that flesh out the setting instead of just sitting there.

A general rule of thumb (and this can vary by genre and story): Anything more than six exchanges of dialogue in a row without a break risks losing readers. The longer the conversation, the faster it will likely overwhelm them. Be particularly wary of long passages with characters speaking *at* each other instead of having a conversation (as in dumping information or backstory via dialogue).

Step Seven: Flesh Out Talking Head Conversations

Sometimes a conversation reads like two heads talking with no sense of place. Look for passages with a lot of dialogue but no description or additional information. Add enough dialogue tags, description, and stage direction to ground readers in the scene. If you find a lot of these scenes, consider returning to the exercises in Workshop Six: Setting and World-Building Work on page 252.

Step Eight: Prune Unnecessary Dialogue

Dialogue is a critical part of a story, so it's rare to have too much. What's more likely is either dialogue that isn't helping convey the story, or there's too *little* of something else—too little internalization, description, stage direction, or action. If you think there's too much dialogue, check to see what might have gotten left out.

Also check for "too much dialogue" sections filled with empty dialogue. You'll often find a lot of small talk that can easily be trimmed out.

REVISION TIP: *Zoom out on your page and see if you have a lot of short lines or a nice mix of lines and gray areas (where a text paragraph looks like a gray box). A dialogue-heavy/narrative-sparse page will have a lot of white space and look more like a list than a page from a novel.*

Many dialogue issues can be found by reading the scene out loud. Awkward phrases tangle our tongues, alliteration hits our ears funny, and telling speakers apart becomes much harder. Also, if you get a little winded or forget who's speaking, that's a red flag that there isn't enough text to support all that dialogue.

Once your dialogue is looking and sounding good, move on to your character voices.

If You Want to Vary the Voices

Fantastic character voices can overcome minor flaws in a novel, because readers will forgive the sins of a story for characters they love to hang out with. That doesn't mean you can slack off on writing a strong book, but it does take some of the pressure off getting it perfect.

In this session, the goal is to develop strong voices for all the characters who need them.

Step One: Vary Too-Similar Character Voices

Ideally, characters should sound as different as they look, but it's not uncommon to have secondary characters with basically the same voice. You could change who says a line of dialogue and not have to change the dialogue itself. For example, "Maybe this is a bad idea," Bland Character said.

If you had to describe the way a character spoke, how would you do it?
Describe the type of character and what he or she sounds like. Your gut reaction can guide you in determining the right voice for each character.

Revision Option: Ways to Develop Character Voices

Character voices bring our character to life, so it's important that they sound like the unique people they are.

Start with the character's general personality: The voice will reflect that personality and color every line of dialogue and internal thought. Even better, it'll help you develop richer characters because they won't be two-dimensional people spouting lines on a page. Those lines will come from someplace real, because you'll know why those characters speak like they do.

Consider how the character greets people: People say hello differently. Sometimes it's a regional or cultural tradition, or even a personal style. Is your character a "Yo what's up?" kind of gal, or a, "So good to see you," type? How she greets someone suggests where she grew up, where she lives now, and how open she is toward others.

If she's a boisterous greeter, she's boisterous in other ways as well. Or maybe she likes to draw attention to herself, so she's the one who interrupts or always has something to add to a conversation. If she gives a weak, "Hi," then she might be the quiet one who rarely gives more than a one- or two-word answer.

Consider how the character answers questions: Does she give one-word answers or way-too-much information? Does she get right to the point or is there a story attached to it? Someone who's reluctant to answer might also be a gal who doesn't like to talk a lot or reveal too much about herself. A gal who says *too* much might be a talker in all aspects of her life and have a hard time getting to a point. The reluctant gal might be a "Hey" kind of greeter, while the Chatty Cathy probably never *just* says hello.

Consider how the character reacts to situations: Someone who faces a situation and immediately decides what to do is a different personality type from someone who questions it before making a decision. The jump-to-it gal always "knows" what to do (even when she's wrong) and might sound bossy or confident. The thoughtful gal might appear hesitant or meek (even when she's not) or might seem wise because she always asks the right questions.

Consider the character's education level: Education plays a role in how people communicate. Is this a gal with a large vocabulary who likes to use it, or someone with a limited vocabulary who uses a lot of slang or clichés? Take it a step further and think about why she speaks as she does. Maybe she's self-conscious about her Ph.D. and purposefully tries to sound dumber to fit in. Or she might be a smart gal who never graduated high school who tries hard to sound more educated.

Maybe that boisterous greeter who makes statements instead of asking questions is insecure about her lack of education, and overcompensates by always acting like she knows what to do or what's going on. Or the meek greeter asks questions because she's not sure she understands what's happening and doesn't want to appear dumb. The friendly greeter might ask a lot of questions to determine the best course of action, because she truly wants to help and has the smarts to offer good advice. (See how these all build upon each other?)

Consider where the character grew up: Where a character grew up will leave traces on her speech. If her hometown has a distinct accent or speaking pattern, it makes it even easier to determine how someone from there would speak. Saying pop versus soda, crayfish versus crawdad, everyone versus y'all.

Consider how the character organizes thoughts and words: A thoughtful thinker might be precise in how she speaks, while a free spirit might ramble or use vague, poetic terms. Careless personalities probably speak without thinking, while control freaks want to make sure everyone understands exactly what they're saying.

Consider the character's favorite sayings or quips: People use different expressions and react in different ways. Maybe one character swears, and another is genteel. One might relate every situation to stories her grandmother once told, or pepper her speech with another language. Look for common expressions and revise so each character has a unique way of expressing themselves (within reason, of course. Some expressions are universal).

Step Two: Develop the Voices of Non-Point-of-View Characters

Voice is a bit harder for non-point-of-view characters because internalization is a large part of character voice, and without that, you have to rely on the dialogue and how your point-of-view character sees and hears that character. But there *are* ways to help differentiate your characters and know what dialogue and traits go with what person.

Revision Option: Ways to Develop Voices in Non-Point-of-View Characters

You'll see voice exhibited through dialogue and body language in non-point-of-view characters. Look for ways to:

Reflect the type of information the character typically conveys: If she often has the answers to technical questions, her voice is going to reflect those technical skills. If she's more the trust-your-emotions kind of confidant, her voice will reflect that trust-your-gut attitude.

Support the character's role in the story: A character's role and relationship to the protagonist influences the voice. The best friend will interact with the protagonist differently than the antagonist or the love interest would. A comic relief character will be funny, while a cautionary tale mirror character might echo the darker traits of the protagonist.

Limit (or increase) how much you want that character to stand out: Strong voices draw attention, so be wary if a small, walk-on character is more memorable than a major character. The most important characters should have the strongest and clearest voices. Make sure you have the right balance of attention.

Character personality shines through no matter what that character is doing or saying, so take advantage of all the opportunities you have to show who your characters are.

You've been focusing on creating rich worlds, strong stories, and compelling characters, and now it's time to make sure all the information is unfolding at the right pace.

Workshop Eight: Pacing Work

The Goal of This Workshop: To examine your manuscript's pacing and adjust as needed to create a well-paced novel.

What We'll Discuss in This Workshop: Determining the right pacing for your novel, smoothing transition between scenes and chapters, developing strong hook lines and foreshadowing, and tightening the narrative focus.

Welcome to Workshop Eight: Pacing Work

A well-paced novel means something different to everyone, and much of it depends on the genre and type of story. Readers expect thrillers to be fast paced, literary novels to have a slower pace, and everything in between to be paced fast enough to keep the story moving and slow enough for them to absorb that story.

In general, pacing works like an ever-growing wave. It rises, then slacks off, then rises again, but it rarely drops as low as the previous wave (similar to stakes). The pacing increases as it nears the end of the story, with the climax being the most fast-paced section of the novel. The speed of that pacing is relevant to the novel, so a high-octane thriller will have a different definition of fast for the climax than a bittersweet character journey of self-discovery.

Pacing is the speed at which information is conveyed to readers to achieve the best impact. There's no one ideal pacing—it varies by novel and genre—and using typically fast-paced techniques (like short sentences and lots of dialogue) can bore readers if what's going on in those sentences doesn't make them want to read on, while slow-paced techniques (description and exposition) can be riveting if readers are dying to know what happens in those scenes.

Chapter length is also a factor. One novel might use long chapters with multiple scene breaks to pull readers through the story, while another novel might use short chapters that flow together seamlessly to achieve the same goal. If the pace works, don't feel the need to comply with arbitrary structures. Keep the reader turning the pages, however it works for you.

Analyze the Pacing

If the pacing of your novel is off, it can derail the entire story. A slow start never draws readers in; a too-fast ending rushes past the payoff and leaves readers feeling unsatisfied. No matter what speed you aim for, you want that steady wave that gets faster and faster as you near the end.

In this session, the goal is to examine your pacing to ensure it's moving at the right speed for your novel.

Missing or weak hook lines, a lack of foreshadowing, too much telegraphing, or a loose narrative focus can also affect the pacing, and you'll look at those in more detail next.

Determine if the Pace is Working

Grab your editorial map and look at the pacing as a whole:

▶ **What's the common pace for your genre?** Is your pace consistent with that genre? For example, a slow-paced thriller could indicate a problem (or suggest it's more of a suspense novel).

▶ **Is it well paced overall?** Slow or fast, a well-paced novel keeps the story moving from start to finish. Look for a good rise and fall in the pacing to pull readers through the novel.

▶ **Does it grab you, does it hold your attention, do you want to read on?** Look for any slow spots or scenes that are weak but you aren't sure why.

▶ **Does something change in every scene?** If nothing changes in the scene, odds are there's nothing new being revealed to keep the story and plot moving forward. Look for what's different about the characters or situation at the end of a scene compared to the beginning.

▶ **Does the pace speed up during major plot moments?** Aim for a rush and urge to read faster as you close in on the critical plot moments of the novel.

▶ **Are there waves of fast and slow pacing throughout the novel?** Tense plot moments will typically be faster paced, while emotional or reflective moments tend to slow down. Aim for a mix of both.

▶ **Are there any spots that read too fast and readers might have trouble absorbing the information?** Check the big action moments or reveals. In the excitement to write these scenes, it's not uncommon to rush through them.

▶ **Are there any slow spots that might lose readers?** Check the transitions or reflective scenes, as these are common slow-down areas. Also look at scenes where characters catch each other up on information.

▶ **Are there any spots that encourage readers to skim?** Check any scenes that introduce details, such as a setting, a new character, or a world-building detail. When the description starts to get heavy, it often bogs down the pace.

▶ **Does every scene have an emotional hook?** Check for an emotional reason why readers want to know what happens in that scene. What will evoke an emotion in them?

▶ **Does every scene have a mental hook?** Check for a plot or informational reason readers will want to keep reading. What puzzle or mystery is being offered?

🚩 **REVISION RED FLAG:** If the pace doesn't vary much and maintains a predictable and even march forward, that could indicate not enough high (or low) points in the story.

Problems Found?

If you find any pacing issues, spend some time doing the exercises in If You Want to Adjust the Pacing on page 292.

Analyze the Transitions

How you move from scene to scene and chapter to chapter leads readers though your novel. The smoother those transitions are, the easier it is to draw readers in, while jarring jumps, awkward shifts, and missing information can all knock a reader right out of the story.

In this session, the goal is to examine your transitions and how your plot moves from scene to scene.

In the next sessions, you'll look more closely at your hook lines, examine the foreshadowing, and check on the narrative focus.

Determine if the Scene and Chapter Transitions Are Working

Any time you break a scene, you give readers an opportunity to set the novel down, since scene breaks are natural stopping points. You might even want to *create* good stopping points, such as having a character go to bed or set off on a trip, something that tells readers, "Yeah, we'll pick it up here tomorrow, 'kay?" But without something to entice readers to read on, why *would* they come back tomorrow?

Scene breaks are typically softer than chapter breaks, relying on the building sense of doom to carry readers forward. A decision has been made, the stakes have been stated, and now it's time to see how it works out. Chances are, you've have nice tension building, so start out the next scene in a way that builds on that tension and keeps it going.

Look at the final few paragraphs of every scene (and the first few of the next scene) and ask:

▶ **Does every chapter end with something that compels readers to turn the page?** It might be a cliffhanger, a secret revealed, the revelation that there *is* a secret, a foreboding piece of dialogue or image, a major decision, etc.

▶ **Is there a sense of anticipation about what will happen next?** Both the characters and the readers should feel that something is brewing, and they must keep going forward.

▶ **Is there a sense of where the plot or story is going?** Check that the plot and story move forward, and there's a sense of progression to keep readers intrigued.

▶ **Does the *next* chapter's opening scene satisfy reader curiosity, or does it jump ahead in time or location and flash back to deal with the previous chapter's end?** The opening of the *next* chapter is as important as a chapter's ending—probably more so since this is where you can lose readers if you don't make them happy. Check that chapter openings fulfill the promise of the chapter endings and isn't a trick to fool or mislead readers. For example, be wary of a chapter that ends with someone creeping up the stairs toward the protagonist, and the next chapter opens with the "danger" being the protagonist's husband coming home early. The tease that something bad was going to happen isn't real, so readers can feel manipulated.

▶ **In multiple points-of-view novels, did the next point-of-view character's scene start off with something equally interesting or did the pacing drop and the tension start over?** It's not uncommon in multiple point-of-view novels to break points of view and basically start over with a new character and rebuild the tension. Drop it too low, however, and by the time readers come back to the exciting chapter, you've lost all the tension you created.

▶ **Does the scene end with something to draw readers forward, or does it let the protagonist sleep, travel, or do something else that drops the tension and pacing?** Check that every scene ends with or gives a reason to turn the page.

▶ **Does the next scene start with the plot in motion or does it set up the scene to come?** Keep an eye out for any scenes that end with a character winding down, and the next scene starts with the character winding back up again. For example, a character going to sleep, followed by that same character waking up and getting dressed. These are inherently low-tension, low-interest activities.

▶ **REVISION RED FLAG:** Checking the transitions is a good way to spot (and fix) a problem when something isn't working but you're not sure why. If it seems like all the right pieces are there (and they often are), but the scene drags, feels clunky, or isn't grabbing the attention it should, try adjusting how you transition from scene to scene. Maybe you're not giving readers a strong enough reason to stay with the story.

Problems Found?

If you find any transition issues, spend some time doing the exercises in If You Want to Smooth the Transitions on page 298.

Analyze the Hook Lines

Hook lines evoke an emotion in readers. They cause a chuckle, tug at heartstrings, instill dread, or pique curiosity. They're the reward for reading, and often the lines fans quote or cite as their favorites.

In this session, the goal is to ensure you have strong hook lines pulling readers through the story.

In the next sessions, you'll look at the foreshadowing, and check on the narrative focus.

If you found any pacing issues during your analysis, a lack of hook lines could be a reason. Look at the problem scenes first and determine if there are indeed hook lines that need strengthening, or if they're missing.

Determine if the Hook Lines Are Working

Scanning your entire manuscript for hook lines is time consuming, but hook lines are often found alone in their own paragraph for emphasis, or as the last line in a paragraph. Try looking for single lines first in a scene or chapter. If you don't find any, that could indicate a lack of hook lines, or that your hook lines are lost in the text itself. Look through your scenes and ask:

▶ **Does every page have an emotional hook line?** If you go more than a page or two without some emotional tug, that could indicate the scene won't connect with readers.

▶ **Does every page have a mental hook line?** If you go more than a page or two without something to pique curiosity, that could indicate there's not enough conflict or action.

▶ **Are there funny or poignant one-liners scattered throughout every scene?** If no personal lines evoke some kind of response from readers, that could indicate too much description or backstory.

▶ **Are there lines that make you smile as a writer on every page?** Strong hook lines often make us feel like "writers," and they're typically our favorite lines in the book. If you have no favorite lines on a page, that could indicate a weak scene that lacks reasons for readers to care what happens in it.

Aim for a balance of hook lines overall, between emotional, mental, funny, and poignant. The more layers you hit, the more likely you'll keep readers invested in the story.

🚩 **REVISION RED FLAG:** If you find a lot of hook lines in the middle of a paragraph, that could indicate the best lines are getting lost in the text. Move them to either their own line, or to the beginning or ending of a paragraph.

Problems Found?

If you find any hook line issues, spend some time doing the exercises in If You Want to Strengthen the Hook Lines on page 300.

Analyze the Foreshadowing

Foreshadowing is a powerful technique, but one that requires a deft hand to use well. There's a fine line between hints to enhance the mood and mystery of the story, and giving it all away.

In this session, the goal is to ensure your foreshadowing works, and you aren't telegraphing the reveals of your novel.

In the next session, you'll check on the narrative focus.

Determine if the Foreshadowing is Working

A lack of foreshadowing could slow the pacing, because there are no hints or clues to indicate something is amiss, and no subconscious clues simmering in a reader's mind. Clues dropped too hard might give away the details you're trying to keep a mystery until the big reveal.

Step One: Examine the Foreshadowing Details

The right foreshadowing details can raise tensions and make future surprises seem inevitable. A lack of foreshadowing can make those same surprises seem out of the blue and even a little contrived. Make sure you're foreshadowing the right events and laying the groundwork for those plot twists and turns. Ask yourself:

▶ **Are you foreshadowing the major events or reveals in the story?** A lack of foreshadowing can indicate that events happen without build up and with little impact, as there was never a chance to worry about them. If you drop a few hints first, then readers can anticipate what's coming—even if they don't know what that is.

▶ **Are there any slow or weak scenes that could benefit from adding some foreshadowing?** An event or clue with greater meaning could fix a problem scene by layering in more complexity.

▶ **What emotional scenes might benefit from a little foreshadowing a few scenes earlier?** If a character has a major breakdown or dark moment, get readers to start worrying about it earlier—even if they don't know what's wrong, they'll have an unsettling sense that *something* is coming. You can put them in the right headspace for a scene to have maximum emotional impact.

▶ **What "out of the blue shocker information" would seem inevitable with a little foreshadowing to lay the groundwork?** Major surprises can sometimes seem like they come from nowhere if there's not a single clue that it could have happened. Sometimes you want that shock, but these surprises are often more believable if subtle clues were there all along.

▶ **Are there any setup scenes that could do double duty as foreshadowing scenes?** Sometime you need to have certain events happen for later plot events to work. These scenes can be opportunities to add deeper meaning or foreshadow the future.

Problems Found?

If you find any foreshadowing issues, spend some time doing the exercises in If You Want to Strengthen the Foreshadowing and Reveals on page 302.

Step Two: Check for Any Telegraphing

While foreshadowing is good and can heighten tension and make the reader eager to know what will happen, telegraphing steals all the tension and takes the mystery out of those hints. It shines a light on the elements you're trying to be subtle about, which can kill the pacing since it all seems predictable.

Telegraphed clues often seem stuck in, because they aren't a natural part of the events or thoughts the protagonist is currently experiencing.

▶ **If you had no idea what a clue meant, would it still fit the scene?** Be wary of clues or details that only make sense after readers know the truth. The goal is to have a clue that means *more* after the truth is revealed, but still makes sense in the scene it's in.

▶ **Is the clue there *specifically* to be noticed by readers?** Be wary of details that have no reason for the protagonist to look/think/say/notice, aside from hinting that whatever she's seeing/thinking/saying/noticing means something.

▶ **If the reader picked up on this clue and figured it out right then, would it ruin the suspense?** Readers are smart. If knowing what that clue means will kill the story, don't make it so obvious. If you have any "hopefully they won't figure this out this until later" feelings, you might consider cutting that clue.

🚩 **REVISION RED FLAG:** If you're drawing attention to a detail because you want readers to remember it for later, there's a good chance you're telegraphing. Drop hints; don't point out the clues.

Problems Found?

If you find any telegraphing issues, spend some time doing the exercises in If You Want to Strengthen the Foreshadowing and Reveals on page 302.

Analyze the Narrative Focus

A strong narrative focus keeps the text flowing smoothly from one idea to the next, and prevents the story from wandering off and making readers wonder what the point is. Losing your narrative focus is a sure way to knock the pacing out of whack.

In this session, the goal is to tighten the narrative focus and ensure that the story is leading readers exactly where you want them to go.

Determine if the Narrative Focus is Working

Confusion often results from a lack of narrative focus, pulling readers in different directions so it's never clear what the point of a scene is.

Step One: Examine the Narrative Focus

The larger, macro focus issues should have been taken care of in Workshop Three: Plot and Structure Work as you made sure your plot was advancing well and in a logical fashion (if not, or if yours still needs work, you can continue to work on that here). Those larger steps will guide you through these smaller, scene-by-scene steps.

Although there are two checks here (scenes and paragraphs), it's fine to check them both in one pass. In most cases, there's no need to edit the scene twice unless it's severely unfocused and needs the extra attention. Most scenes will need only a quick scan to ensure nothing was shoved off focus.

If you did a fairly detailed editorial map, you might be able to check the scene-level focus there instead of in the text.

Step Two: Examine the Scenes

Make sure each scene has a point and the text is supporting that point, as well as advancing the ideas behind that point. Start with the goal for the scene and ask:

- ▶ **Is the goal clear?** A lack of a clear goal could indicate the scene isn't unfolding toward a specific resolution, but wandering aimlessly.
- ▶ **Does the goal move the scene forward?** If the protagonist isn't taking steps to achieve the scene goal, then the scene will read as if it's not going anywhere and the story will drag.
- ▶ **Is the bulk of the scene's information supporting this goal?** Not every scene needs to be 100 percent on topic, but if you notice multiple ideas or goals all pulling the protagonist in different directions (and

not in a good, conflict-inducing way), that could indicate the scene is unfocused and trying to do too much.

▶ **Does the goal lead to the next scene?** The scene should lead the pro-tagonist (and the plot) forward. If not, that could indicate the scene is simply dumping information, and isn't working to advance the story.

You can have multiple goals in a scene; ensure that what the scene is trying to accomplish is moving in the same direction. If subplots inter-twine or overlap with the main plot, aim for clear paths that show where each plot thread is headed and how they interact.

🚩 **REVISION RED FLAG:** If you can't identify the point of the scene and why it's there, the narrative is either out of focus, or there's no goal. The scene is likely providing information that serves no point at that moment.

Step Three: Examine the Paragraphs

Since this check can require reading the entire manuscript again, focus on any scenes you flagged with pacing problems or clarity issues (as a lack of focus can also affect the description).

Skim through the individual paragraphs to make sure they're not a col-lection of disconnected details. During the drafting stage, it's common to throw in details as they come to you without considering how they fit in the existing paragraph. When this happens, the story flow looks more like a spray and you end up with a scattered sense of what's going on.

For example, a paragraph might open with the character looking at the room in search of a clue, then shift to talking about a world-building detail, then end with a statement about how she's feeling. Readers will likely be confused about what that paragraph was trying to say.

🚩 **REVISION RED FLAG:** Consider doing a paragraph-level check of the narrative focus if you've received feedback with a high percent-age of comments that question what's going on in the scene, show con-fusion over character actions, or say that the pacing was too slow.

Problems Found?

If you find any narrative focus issues, spend some time doing the exer-cises in If You Want to Tighten the Narrative Focus on page 306.

If You Want to Adjust the Pacing

Pacing problems generally come in three flavors: too slow, too fast, and inconsistent. If you think your pacing isn't keeping readers hooked, try looking at ways to adjust how your novel unfolds.

In this session, the goal is to adjust the pacing so it pulls readers through the story at the pace you want.

Step One: Fix a Pace That's Too Slow

A slow pace typically results from not enough new and interesting information being conveyed to your readers. There are no surprises or reveals, and the story drags or becomes predictable.

Here are some options for fixing a too-slow pace:

If There Are Too Many Words

While any number of issues can contribute to a slow pace, too much of "something" is frequently the culprit—long sentences, heavy exposition, speeches—any information readers have to slog through to get to the story. The more unnecessary words you add, the slower the pace will be.

Trim out heavy or repetitive description: Look for long descriptive passages, especially if the scene is supposed to be fast-paced or has a lot of action. Trim it back or spread it out to help pick up the pace.

Cut empty dialogue: Look for dialogue that adds nothing to the story, such as greetings and good-byes, and single questions used solely to keep someone talking. For example:

"You won't believe what Bob said."

"What? Tell me!"

"He said..."

In this case, "What? Tell me!" can easily go.

Cut extended internalization: Look for spots where there's so much internalization that you forget what the last line of dialogue was or what the next speaker is responding to. If the dialogue and responses are supposed to sound snappy and come right after each other, don't put a lot of internalization (or anything else) between them.

Smooth clunky or overdone stage direction: Skip the obvious details that don't add value to the scene. Be especially wary of places where a character speaks, moves, speaks, moves, speaks, all in the same paragraph.

Have something change: At the core, pacing is based on revealing information to readers. If nothing changes there's nothing new, and the pace drags. Make sure something changes in every scene and readers learn new information as a result.

If Important Information is Left Out

Missing key scene-driving elements can result in a pace that drags, because there's nothing pushing the story forward.

If nothing seems too wordy, look for:

Unclear or weak goals: Most times, if a well-written scene drags there's a goal issue. The protagonist isn't proactive, she doesn't want anything, and readers watch her go about her day in some fashion. Try adding or strengthening (or stating) the goal to drive the scene and make the protagonist actively work to accomplish something.

A lack of stakes: The next biggest offender here is a lack of stakes. The protagonist *is* acting, she *has* a goal, but readers don't care if she achieves it or not. Try making the consequences of the goal matter more on a personal level. Give readers something to worry about as the scene unfolds.

A lack of conflict: If there's nothing standing in the way of the protagonist's goal, there's no mystery whether or not the protagonist will succeed. No struggle = boring, and that slows everything down to a crawl. Find ways to add or strengthen the conflict so the outcome is uncertain.

Weak character development: Sometimes the protagonist isn't "in" the scene even when she is. Readers feel detached, as if they're watching from a distance rather than experiencing the story with the character. This usually happens when there's little internalization or personal input from the protagonist or point-of-view character. She acts, but readers don't know why or why it matters so they can't connect to her and thus don't care.

If the Structure is Out of Whack

Sometimes structure is the issue, and how you break up the novel affects how it reads. The scenes themselves might work okay, but they're not unfolding in the best sequence for the strongest impact.

The problem might be with:

Bad chapter or scene endings: Chapters and scenes typically end with something unresolved or left hanging. If the chapter just stops with nothing to entice readers to read on, the novel doesn't feel like it's going anywhere. Try breaking slow scenes where something is left unresolved, or places where readers will want to know what happens next. Or add a reason for readers to continue with the story in the existing ending.

Not enough scene breaks: A lack of scene breaks can indicate a lot of unnecessary transition description bogging the story down (traveling to get somewhere, filler between scenes that change location). Look for transition summaries between events. Chances are you can cut those and break the scene.

🚩 **REVISION RED FLAG:** If the scenes work at a text level, but the pacing is still slow, or you're getting feedback that the story isn't holding your reader's attention, that could indicate a larger macro problem with the stakes, conflict, or general premise. You might need to go back and examine the core conflict and main goal of the novel. If there's an inherent flaw in the core story, that will affect how the novel reads.

Step Two: Fix a Pace That's Too Fast

Dialogue is fast-paced, as is action, but if you focus too much on those, you'll end up with a breathless ride that goes by too quickly for readers to enjoy.

If There's Too Much Information at Once

A too-fast pace often comes with a lot of action thrown in at the same time, so too much is going on to absorb it all as it goes by. Nothing sticks and readers get confused and stop trying to keep track of it.

To make it manageable, try:

Detangling complicated complications: Having plans go wrong is good, but if every little thing that *can* go wrong *does* go wrong, they all start merging together. Do you need all those problems? Can any be combined or eliminated? Try breaking down the steps of your scenes and see how many tasks the protagonist has to do (and overcome) to reach the end. If the number looks high, or the obstacles are delaying tactics with no consequence (or the same consequence as the other steps), trim a few out.

Adding breathers between action scenes: If the protagonist never gets a chance to catch her breath, readers won't either. Look for places where you can let the protagonist pause and reflect on what's happened to her. These include: right after a problem is discovered, when one is resolved, when she learns something new, when she's stuck and unsure what to do next, etc. Reflection gives you a chance to remind readers why all this matters.

Pruning scenes containing large crowds: A sudden influx of characters (and the names that come with them) can trigger "you can skim over this part" to readers. It's clear they're not supposed to remember all these people, so the scene takes on less importance and flies by. Try naming only those who need to be remembered and limiting the number of people in the scene.

If There's Too Much Action

An all-action plot might be missing the emotional depth that brings its characters to life and fleshes out the world they live in.

Be wary if you see a lot of:

Flat characters: You know those action movies where you can't remember the hero's name? Skimping on characterization is the book equivalent. Give readers time to get to know the characters and care about what happens to them. Offer glimpses into their personalities to slow the pace down when the story is going full tilt for too long.

Blank rooms with no settings: Are you describing the setting enough? Are there enough details for readers to put everything in context? Setting can also be used to raise tension and heighten conflict, and a little goes a long way to slowing a too-fast pace.

Weak motivations: Is the protagonist going through the motions and acting out plot for the sake of plot? If she's just a body "things happen to," the action has no point and becomes background noise. Try showing why you chose this protagonist to handle these problems. Let readers get to know her so they understand *why* she's going through all this trouble. Adding moments of internalization or discussion helps transition scene to scene at a more manageable pace.

If the Text is Too Short and Choppy

Short sentences, short chapters, short scenes. They all pick up the pace, but when used too much, it can be overwhelming.

If everything else seems right, try to:

Smooth choppy sentences: Short sentences are fast. We read them quickly, and the staccato nature adds to the tension of the scene, but there comes a point when it reads like a strobe light, showing freeze-frame images in a row, not a story unfolding. Try mixing it up, using long sentences *and* short quick ones. Use the length of the sentences to adjust the pacing where you need it.

Combine super-short chapters: There is no average size for a chapter, but too many short ones in a row can start to feel disjointed. It's the nature of chapters, since they usually end on that, "Oh no!" moment, but a cliffhanger every few pages never allows for the tension to build. Look at where combining small chapters into one larger chapter would provide a better (and slower) narrative flow. Perhaps turn the small chapters into individual scenes and ease up a little on the dramatic endings for a slower transition.

Add description to talking heads: Dialogue is also fast-paced, but a lot of it without any exposition or stage direction makes it hard for readers to keep up. Check for large sections of dialogue and make sure you have some narrative breaks in there to remind readers who's speaking and provide context for what's happening.

🚩 **REVISION RED FLAG:** If everything is rushing by too fast, that could indicate a weak character arc. The plot side of the novel is working, but there's no character side to provide internal conflict and character growth. Look at how the character arc unfolds and where those more reflective scenes can slow down the story where you need it.

Step Three: Fix a Pace That's Inconsistent

Though more uncommon, sometimes the narrative style contradicts the pace intended, such as having a lot of short sentences and dialogue in a scene you want to unfold slowly.

If the pace doesn't seem right, you might need to:

Map out the pace per scene: Go through the scenes and list the speed of the pacing. If the pace changes in that scene, show that, such as fast > slow (fast, then goes slow). Are there long stretches of one speed? Quick jumps between speeds?

Check the pace against your turning point map: If you have slow-paced scenes during traditionally fast-paced moments (such as key turning points in the plot), try shifting the scenes or changing the pace of those scenes.

Check the sentence and paragraph length vs. the pace desired: Slow-paced scenes typically have longer sentences and more information to absorb. They're also often the more emotional scenes in the novel. Fast-paced scenes use shorter sentences and paragraphs, and contain more action-focused language. If your fast-paced scene has a lot of long and complex sentences, that could be the problem.

🚩 **REVISION RED FLAG:** Sometimes an inconsistent pace results when the novel isn't sure what it wants to be. Check to make sure you're not trying to pace your novel to fit a different type of story or genre from what you wanted to write. For example, if you want a fast-paced thriller, but the novel is paced more like a romantic suspense, you'll want to revise to pick up the pace.

If the general pacing is working, let's take a closer look at how you transition from scene to scene.

If You Want to Smooth the Transitions

Awkward transitions can cause pacing issues, even when your scenes are working well to hold readers in the story. Once readers get into the chapters the text smooths out, but it's a rocky start every time. This can make it tough for readers to start that next chapter, knowing the story is going to drag again before it gets better.

In this session, the goal is to smooth any rough transitions and eliminate jarring areas between scenes and ideas.

Step One: Smooth or Fix Transition Issues

If the pacing is choppy due to rough transitions, identify and revise so the scenes move smoothly from one to the other.

Look for:

Awkward time or location changes: Readers can stumble if the location or time changes without clues to alert them that they've moved. This can also be confusing if the story jumps ahead in time, but it isn't clear how *much* time has passed. Inform readers about a shift, either at the end of one scene or the beginning of another.

Confusing shifts in topics: A shift in ideas that comes out of the blue can also leave readers struggling to catch up. This often happens when the character needs to realize or remember something for plot reasons, but there's nothing in the text to trigger that realization. Try adding that trigger and showing what makes the character suddenly change topics.

Unnecessary travel: Too much time spent showing the transition will cause the pace to drag. Travel is a common problem area for this type, with the character moving from one place to another, often describing everything she sees along the way. In fact, this is sometimes the only reason *for* the travel—an excuse to describe the setting. Break the scene and jump to when the next interesting thing happens.

Scenes that just stop: Be wary of scenes that end with the character going to sleep or stopping, with no sense of something left hanging or where the story might go next. Perhaps end the scene before the action is over, or add a suggestion about what comes next to hand off to the next scene.

Scenes where no decisions are offered: Scenes often end with a character making a decision or choice. No choices means there's nothing to move the scene forward. Try adding a choice or options so the protagonist has several ways to advance the plot.

REVISION RED FLAG: If you have a lot of transition issues, this could indicate a stagnant plot or lack of goals. The scenes focus on individual events, not on a protagonist working to achieve a goal, so the story is a series of, "...and then this happened, then that happened, then this happened."

Step Two: Eliminate Too-Similar Transitions

Since scene beginnings and endings often have similar phrasing, it's not unusual to encounter the same general line repeated throughout the first draft. This can lead to a story that seems predictable and repetitive, even when the scenes *are* different.

For example, be wary if a large percentage of your scenes start with:

- "As I walked into..." and then it describes the room.
- "I stood with..." and then it lists who is in the scene.
- "They waited while..." and then it sets up what's about to happen.

The same opening every time makes readers think they've read the chapter already. The same thing applies to the way you end your scenes and chapters. Look for:

- Characters who go to sleep.
- Declarative "doom and gloom" sentences: "If he didn't find it fast, he was dead."
- Questions about what might come next: "Could they make it to the park in time?"

The same ending can sap the tension from a scene because readers have already seen how that basic ending has turned out. Even if the resolution *is* different, readers might assume they know the answer and thus not wonder or worry about it.

Write down the first and last lines (or paragraphs) of every scene and look for similarities. If you have multiple scenes that start and end in the same way, rewrite to vary. Also, look for repetitive time frames, such as, every time the protagonist has to wait, it's always ten minutes.

Aim for a good mix of transition types, and if possible, try to create a sense of rising tension toward the climax with *only* your opening and ending lines.

REVISION RED FLAG: If most of the scene endings are the same type, that could indicate the scenes themselves are all similar and there's not enough unpredictability in what happens. Make sure every scene has a different fundamental goal, conflict, and stakes so it's not the same scene over and over with different details.

If moving from scene to scene is working well, let's look at how you keep readers turning the individual pages.

If You Want to Strengthen the Hook Lines

Hook lines continuously re-engage your readers and keep your story questions alive. They remind readers what's important, why they like the characters, and what's at stake, so they have reasons to turn every single page of your novel.

In this session, the goal is to strengthen your hook lines to maintain a solid pace for your novel.

There's no set formula for how many hook lines you want per page, so trust your instincts to find the right balance. Put in too many and the manuscript will start to seem like a slew of one-liners. Too few, and there won't be enough to draw readers through the story.

A general rule of thumb: Aim for one to three hook lines on most pages, unless it's an action scene where the high stakes themselves do the hooking. If you don't have at least one hook line per page, that could be a red flag that something is off. You might have too much description or backstory, or your protagonist wasn't driving the scene.

Revision Option: Ways to Develop Hook Lines

Hook lines work well when they're playing on an emotion—joy, sadness, hope, fear, regret, even sarcasm, as that's often covering for strong or repressed feelings. There's a hint of something happening in a good hook line, either a goal stated outright, or a subtle sense of danger or failure.

Develop hook lines in:

Places where you want to emphasize something: A strong hook line can underscore a point for greater impact.

Places you want readers to remember: Good hook lines stand out, so readers tend to remember them.

Places you want to resonate with the theme: Hook lines can summarize and encapsulate an idea or theme that sheds greater meaning on the entire scene—or even the entire story.

Places where you want to create a mood or set a tone: Hook lines can nudge emotions where you want them to go, and help you create the right tone or mood for the situation.

If you're unsure how to craft or develop your hook lines, try to:

Use humor: Make readers laugh and they'll stay with you. Look for places where your protagonist can think or say something funny.

Use emotion: An emotional connection gets readers invested in the story, so bring out points of strong emotion.

Suggest there's more: A hook line combined with a story question is a powerful draw for readers. Can you hint that there's more going on than is being revealed?

Add danger: Hook lines can foreshadow trouble on the way. Can you remind readers of the stakes in a subtle (or not-so-subtle) way?

Get personal: Hook lines usually aren't descriptions. A beautifully written line *can* make readers pause, but it typically will be static, whereas hook lines are active. Personal connections make hook lines *about* something, which draw readers in and pushes them on.

Put them at the ends of the text: Hooks tend to be the last thing readers read, either at the end of a paragraph or all alone on a line. It's the punch right before a pause, so it stands out even more.

⚑ **REVISION RED FLAG:** Don't add a hook line because there's not one on that page. Hook lines work because they fit the scene and highlight some aspect of it that rekindles a reader's interest in the story. A joke for the sake of a joke probably won't work. A joke that fits the scene and says something deeper about it will. Don't force the hooks, *bring out* the hooks.

Hook lines aren't the only way to keep readers on the page though. Sometimes, you need to tease them a little with promises of things to come.

If You Want to Strengthen the Foreshadowing and Reveals

Well-crafted foreshadowing puts readers in the right mindset long before they reach a scene, and makes them anticipate that scene. Secrets unfold in surprising, yet inevitable ways, and readers feel as though the clues were there all along if only they'd seen them—because they *were*.

In this session, the goal is to strengthen your foreshadowing and eliminate any telegraphing that gives the story away.

Step One: Create a Mystery Arc

Do a quick mystery arc to see where critical secrets are revealed, clarify who knows what when, and to determine where the clues are found or hidden in plain sight—you might sneak in a clue but not draw attention to it, knowing it will become relevant later. This will help ensure the protagonist isn't acting on information not yet learned, and allow you to see how your mystery arc unfolds with the rest of the plot.

Look at how the mystery side of your plot unfolds and where readers encounter clues and reveals.

If you're unsure how these elements should unfold, consider:

When and where you want readers to start suspecting the truth: Establishing patterns is a useful foreshadowing technique. Tension builds when readers are expecting something and waiting eagerly for it to happen.

Don't forget the value of the Rule of Three here:

- The first time someone sees something, they merely see it.
- The second time, they notice it, because it stands out now.
- The third time, they're *looking* for it because you've established a pattern to anticipate.

For example, if you want to foreshadow a misunderstanding that has dire consequences, you might have the protagonist misunderstand something minor in the first few chapters. Later on, she might get something else wrong due to distraction. Now you've established a pattern that the protagonist doesn't always listen and misunderstands what she hears. Readers will be looking closely at all her assumptions from then on to see if she's missing something important. When the big moment occurs, tensions will be higher because readers won't know if she's right this time, or if she's missed something yet again.

Or you might drop hints about an item to be used later. When the protagonist arrives at a quaint bed and breakfast for a yoga retreat, she is surprised to see a shotgun hanging above the fireplace and makes a comment. The next guest to arrive notices the gun and makes a joke about it. When the third guest arrives, readers expect the gun will come up again. And that will make them wonder when, where, and how that gun will be used in the story.

Or, you can be more subtle about it and tap into a reader's subconscious. Say you want to foreshadow that blue means bad. You might have the protagonist get into an accident with a blue car early on. Then she has a run in with an office rival who knocks blue ink all over her. You might toss in her snagging her new blue skirt and tearing it right before she goes into an important meeting. After that three-step setup, readers will be *looking* for blue things and anticipating the problems they might cause.

These types of hints can happen over the course of one scene or the whole novel. It's the creak in the night, followed by the thump, followed by the guy in the ski mask jumping out at you.

When and where you want the protagonist to start figuring it out: Readers often spot details long before characters do, but if the clues are *too* obvious, then the characters look dumb if *they* haven't figured them out as well. Check to make sure you have a good balance between reader hints and character hints. If your protagonist needs to know something by page 45, make sure you've left enough clues so the realization feels plausible.

FORESHADOW TIP: *One mystery-writer's trick is to hide important clues in the middle of the paragraph. Readers don't pay as much attention to what's in the middle of a paragraph, but they do focus on the beginning and end of that same paragraph. So they see it, but it often doesn't jump out at them.*

Step Two: Break Any Patterns That Are Too Predictable

Patterns that don't go where we expect them to surprise us. This is the way jokes work: They set up a pattern, then throw in something unexpected as the third item and shock us.

> How do you get to my place? Go down to the corner, turn left, and get lost.

To keep the story unpredictable, lead readers in one direction, then break the established pattern with humor, drama, or even pathos. It works with scenes or a single line. Two scenes set up the pattern, then the third starts off to satisfy that pattern, then—wham!—it changes direction and offers a surprise.

REVISION RED FLAG: Beware of foreshadowing too much. If you're dropping clues every chapter, readers will figure out the secret long before they get to the reveal.

Step Three: Eliminate Telegraphed Details

Telegraphed details can show up anywhere, but here are some common areas to find them:

The deny-it-early conversation: Early in the story, the characters discuss and deny whatever it is that ends up happening later on. It draws attention to the detail you don't want readers to consider, and of course, now that you've mentioned it, they do.

The not-so-random stranger: Someone walks into a scene and gets noticed (often described with more detail than the scene warrants), but is then ignored. At a key moment later in the story, the protagonist remembers this person and it's exactly what's needed to save the day. Or worse—that stranger appears out of the blue when needed.

The obvious pointed-out item: The badge left on the desk, the burning candle, the drip—an item that carries significance is focused on and the protagonist pays a little *too* much attention to it while acting like she's *not* paying attention to it. Readers know this item is going to be important later. In movies and TV shows, this is a slow close up while dramatic music plays.

The overheard news: This *can* be done to great effect, but it can also be a neon sign that something is going to happen. The TV is on as a character walks into the room and the newscaster is talking about something the protagonist will need later. Or the protagonist is out somewhere and encounters two locals arguing about a myth or local legend that will be encountered in a few chapters. The detail *seems* like it's slipped in naturally (it's just background noise after all) but it's obvious instead of seamless because it stands out.

The "little did they know" cliché: Be wary of any phrase that shifts out of the point-of-view character to let readers know something bad is going to happen. For example, "She had no idea what was really in store for her."

Step Four: Add Suggestive and Evocative Details

There have been a slew of movies, TV shows, and Vegas acts that have the protagonist—usually some type of con man—setting up a mark (the victim) to think or respond a certain way. They use subliminal clues to suggest what they want the mark to think or say. Drop enough clues with the numbers three and six in front of someone, then ask them to pick a number between ten and forty, and you'll get a lot of thirty-sixes.

To put ideas in readers' heads, plant a few suggestive clues. Don't explain or draw attention to any of them, but if you want readers to think "blue means bad," then put in something blue whenever something bad happens. Associate blue with bad in their minds, so by the time your protagonist reaches why blue is bad, readers will already feel apprehensive.

Foreshadowing is a handy way to raise tensions, and a well-planned story puzzle leaves lots of clues that readers can look back on and see that the answers were there the whole time.

The final pacing session focuses on your narrative focus, making sure all the work you've done is channeling the story exactly where you want it to go.

If You Want to Tighten the Narrative Focus

Tightening the narrative focus is a time-consuming process that requires going through the entire manuscript and reworking it at the prose level. Not every manuscript will need it, but if all other pacing options haven't cleared up the issues and the manuscript still seems off, it's worth doing.

In this session, the goal is to refocus your narrative to tighten the novel.

To maintain your own focus, try revising one scene or chapter at a time, taking a break between revision sessions. The more focused you are, the easier it will be to focus your narrative.

Step One: Go Scene by Scene and Eliminate Extraneous Details

Look for any off-topic ideas or goals in the text and either cut or revise the text to bring it back on topic. In some cases, you might be able to move the extraneous text to a better scene where it is on topic.

Step Two: Go Paragraph by Paragraph and Refocus the Details

Break up any unfocused paragraphs and regroup them by idea, then add transition sentences to lead readers where you want them to go story-wise. Show what's important and take readers to the next important detail. If you find summarized ideas that feel sluggish or tell-y, you might try dramatizing them instead.

Step Three: Go Sentence by Sentence and Clarify What's Going On

Look for complex sentences where multiple actions are happening at once. "As" is a red flag word here, for example:

> She shed her raincoat as she walked through the door and into the kitchen, dropping her purse on the table as she picked up the note left by her husband.

So much is going on it's hard to tell what the point of the sentence is. Break convoluted sentences apart so each idea is clear and easy to follow, and relates to the paragraph and scene.

Overall, if a detail bogs down the text or goes off on a tangent, consider getting rid of it, or moving it somewhere else where it flows naturally. Beware of irrelevant details that draw focus away from what's important and cause readers to miss the critical information (unless of course, the point is to hide a clue).

You should now have a solid draft (or close to it) that mirrors the vision you had in your head when you came up with the novel's idea. Some manuscripts will be ready for the final look, and if so, skip ahead to Workshop Ten: A Final Look on page 317. Others might have a solid story, but either be too long or too short for the target market or audience. If you need to adjust your word count, continue on with Workshop Nine: Word Count Work.

Workshop Nine: Word Count Work

The Goal of This Workshop: To determine if you need to adjust the word count of your manuscript.

What We'll Discuss in This Workshop: How to cut words from a too-long manuscript, and how to add words and flesh out a too-short manuscript.

Welcome to Workshop Nine: Word Count Work

Word counts provide a framework for your novel and a guide to your chosen genre, but the goal is to tell your story to the best of your ability, however many words that is. If a word isn't pulling its weight, cut it. If it's a star performer, let it shine.

Your novel should grab readers from the start, offer them a story they can't put down, and hold that attention until the end. The trick is to make sure every word you use does exactly that. If you have 75,000 words that don't grab a reader, the book will fail, but if you have 140,000 words that grab a reader and don't let go, the book will succeed. It's the story that matters. A great book is a great book.

That said, a published novel *is* a product, and as a product, certain rules apply. These rules exist, for example, to cover the cost of making the book versus what it can sell for, and a book that will cost twice as much due to size isn't economical to sell. Readers won't pay thirty dollars for a 2,500-page paperback (never mind how they'd even *hold* the thing). With e-books and e-book-only publishers, word counts are changing, but the guidelines still do exist, and if you plan to pursue a traditional publishing path, you do need to consider all facets of that.

No matter which path you take, ultimately, it's not how many words you have, but what those words do, that counts.

Analyze the Size of the Novel

When determining the right size for a novel, consider the general ranges of your chosen genre. They will guide you to what readers—and publishers—expect. You want every word used to help the story. It's not about reaching a certain limit, it's about writing the best story you can.

In this session, the goal is to see if your word count is within your target market range and personal goal, and adjust if need be.

A word about word counts: Some writers will be revising a novel with a particular genre, market, or publishing path in mind and need to be within a certain range to sell or publish it. For example, category romances have specific rules that must be adhered to for a particular imprint. If you're not one of those writers, you're not as constrained by word count.

Determine if Your Word Count is Working

Word counts for a typical novel run between 80,000 and 100,000 words. If your novel falls in that range, chances are you're fine for most adult fiction genres and markets. Children's fiction runs 30,000 to 50,000 for middle grade, and 50,000 to 80,000 for young adult. Chapter books run 5,000 to 25,000 words. Picture books come in at under 500. Mysteries often go as low as 60,000 and historical fiction and epic fantasy rise as high as 140,000.

These are *very* general ranges, but if the average size of the genre and market you're aiming for is 60,000 words, your 120,000-word novel is too long. That's like trying to pitch a movie for a 60-second commercial slot.

Be wary of the word-count trap. For every person who says, "You'll never get published with a 145,000-word novel," another will say, "But Best-sellerBob's book was 145,000 words." It does happen, but it's important to remember that those novels succeeded *in spite of the word count,* not because of it. You stand a much better chance at success if you fall with-in the norms, but if the novel absolutely without a doubt must be that size, then, let it be that size. Just understand that it could be an issue down the road if you plan to publish.

Your chosen publishing path—traditional or self—also affects what's an acceptable word count for your novel. For example, if your goal is a traditional publisher, staying within the standard ranges gives you the best chance at selling your novel. If you plan to submit to an e-book-only publisher or self-publish, word counts can fall outside the norm. No paper means no printing costs and no bulky books, so additional pages aren't as problematic.

Problems Found?

If you find you want to cut back on your word count, spend some time doing the exercises in If You Want to Cut Words From the Manuscript on page 310. If you find you want to increase your word count, spend some time doing the exercises in If You Want to Add Words to the Man-uscript on page 314.

If You Want to Cut Words From the Manuscript

Cutting words from your manuscript doesn't have to be a huge hack and slash deal. You don't have to rip your baby to shreds. In fact, hack-ing away whole scenes often hurts more than helps, because you're kill-ing the story, not the extra words. You want to get rid of the words that *aren't* helping the story.

In this session, the goal is to trim down your manuscript to your target word count range without losing any of your story.

Cutting Words Isn't so Hard. No, Really.

Cutting thousands of words from your manuscript seems daunting, and cutting *tens of thousands* of words can make you want to curl up in a ball and cry, but it's much easier than you think.

Let's look at what "cutting words" really means:

A common "too-long" manuscript is 120,000-words, roughly 480 pages (based on the traditional 250 words-per-page format). You can cut 4,800 words if you delete ten words per page. Ten words is nothing—it's one sentence in most cases, and even in polished and published novels you can still find one sentence per page that can go and not lose any important information. Cut twenty words per page and that's almost 10,000 words gone with little effort. A 150,000-word novel? 600 pages, and 6,000 or 12,000 words gone. Cut thirty words—18,000 words down.

Approaching your edit on a words-per-page basis is much more manageable and allows you to trim consistently across the entire novel, not just certain sections of it.

Step One: Decide How Much You Want to Cut

You might have a fixed number in mind, such as 90,000 words, or a range, such as 80,000-90,000 words. You might also decide to cut in stages, taking out half of the target and then seeing how the manuscript flows before doing anything else.

Step Two: Decide Where it Needs Cutting

Most manuscripts can be trimmed overall, but some will be heavy in one area and need specific trimming. Looking at the novel's structure is an easy way to determine where the extra words are coming from.

Using the basic Three-Act Structure, list the word count of each act (or use whatever structure you prefer and adjust your percentages to fit your structure). Act One is the first 25 percent of the manuscript. The second 25 percent fills the ramp up in act two to the midpoint. The third 25 percent is the ramp down in Act Two from the midpoint. The final 25 percent is in Act Three. So, if your manuscript is 100,000 words, you'd have four chunks of 25,000 words each. At the end of each act, you'd have a major plot turning point.

Remember—these guidelines aren't exact, but if (using the above example) you discover the first act is 35,000 words, but the rest fits the target size for your novel, there's a good chance the beginning is too long and your extra words should be cut from there.

A 10 percent variance in size is fairly normal, but anything beyond that bears a closer look. If you decide an act is working even though it's longer, that's okay. The goal is to use structure to diagnose and identify potential trouble areas, not force your manuscript to fit a particular template.

Step Three: Cut Down the Manuscript

Now comes the tough part, but you can do it. Take it step by step, page by page, and be ruthless. If your instincts tell you what needs to go first, trust them.

Common Areas for Extra Words

Extra words can be found anywhere, but there are a few places where writers tend to babble. Check these areas first when trimming words.

Stage direction in dialogue tags: If the speaker is clear, getting rid of the "she said" tag can help eliminate hundreds of words.

Repeated ideas or thoughts: It's not uncommon to say the same thing in different ways in a scene. Look for multiple details in descriptions, emotional internalizations, and introductions of pretty much anything—these are frequently areas to pile on extra information.

Unnecessary or redundant words: For example, is someone sitting down on the floor? If so, down can go—unless something weird is going on with gravity, sitting on the floor *always* means down. Check your prepositions as well, as most of those can go.

Extra description: A few implied words are often enough to give readers the idea of what something looks like. Let them fill in the blanks so you can save the words.

Characters questioning themselves: Often narrators and protagonists will ask what they should do or wonder about something. It usually reads a lot like them talking to themselves. More times than not, you can trim out these phrases or combine them so they use fewer words.

Overwriting: Look for places where one word can replace several, such as "we went around back to the rear of the store" vs. "We went behind the store."

Tightening the overall writing eliminates the extra words without changing anything.

Revision Option: Tricks to Make Cutting Words Easier

If your words-to-cut number is daunting, it might help to trick your brain into thinking it's not as bad as it looks.

Do the easy cuts first: Empty words, empty dialogue, unnecessary tags—cut all the words that commonly bloat a novel first. You might be surprised at how many "only" "just" and "of the" a novel has.

Cut back to front: If you're cutting words-per-page, start on the last page and work your way toward the beginning. Not only will this keep you from getting caught up in the story, it also won't adjust the page and cause you to cut more words from the front than the back as the novel tightens and becomes shorter.

Cut one chapter at a time in a new file: Copy the chapter into a new file before you trim. It's a lot easier to hit that goal when you can see those words dripping off. And a bonus: By isolating the chapter, you can look at it more objectively and judge the pacing and flow.

Cut one act at a time in a new file: Same principle, with more pages. This can help ensure the cuts are applied evenly throughout the novel.

Set time limits on your cutting sessions: The longer you edit, the more likely it is you'll let something slide because you're tired and want to move on to the next part. Take a break between editing sessions and avoid this temptation.

It's not unusual to need several editing passes to cut down a manuscript. The easiest words tend to go first. Then, if you still need to trim, you have to make harder and harder decisions.

If you need to add words, move on to the next session.

If You Want to Add Words to the Manuscript

We spend a lot of time talking about what to cut from our manuscripts, but there are times when we do need to add words. Maybe you have a novella you want to make larger, or a NaNo (National Novel Writing Month) novel that needs fleshing out, or you fell short of your genre's target range. Even if a novel is the right size for the intended market and genre, you might think the story needs deepening to make it stronger.

In this session, the goal is to find the best way to add words to your manuscript without hurting the story or bloating the narrative.

Step One: Diagnose What's Missing

Before you add anything, determine if you have a sparse manuscript that needs some fleshing out, or a novel that's short on plot. A sparse novel may not need any macro work, while a short-on-plot novel will need some larger additions. Your editorial map will help here, as will your draft analysis from Workshop One.

Plot Check: Look at your plot. Is it too easy to go from inciting event to resolution? Did you skip any steps? If you haven't, do any events need a step or two more to accomplish?

Look for places where if the protagonist didn't win, or outcomes didn't go in her favor, you could tack on a scene or two and add more conflict. Be cautious here though, because you don't want scenes that *take* longer, there needs to be real conflict.

Also look for places where the stakes will go up if the protagonist fails instead of succeeds. Or places where you can raise the stakes if she fails. You want to maintain that sense of problems getting worse and worse or you'll end up with a lot of empty "stuff" happening that doesn't move the story forward.

Subplot Check: Take a peek at your subplots. Are there any points on your main plot line that can be complicated or hindered by braiding in an existing subplot? Can you deepen any of them to give something else in the novel greater meaning? Can they affect the stakes? Do you *have* any subplots? The amount of subplots varies by genre and book, but on average, you usually see one or two subplots in a novel.

Tangent Check: Were there any scenes with goals or ideas you started to explore but decided against it? Those might be subplot ideas your subconscious thought would be fun to develop but didn't, which could be exactly the subplot you need.

Conflict Check: Look for spots where decisions are made. Are the choices too easy? How can you make them harder? And not just physically harder, but emotionally tougher as well.

Clarity Check: Is everything clear? Is the stage direction solid and can readers follow what's happening in every scene? Are the dialogue tags clear so there's no confusion over who's speaking? Is there enough backstory to inform readers about the significance of events? Often these elements get left out because you're terrified of having too much.

World Building Check: This is true for real worlds as well as crafted worlds. Have you done enough with your setting so the world feels real? Real-world writers—have you used enough specific details to make your setting come alive? It's easy to say "New York" and let readers fill in the blanks, but you could end up with flat and lifeless worlds that way. And if your world is created, then you might find some confused readers who feel ungrounded, especially if you used a lot of made-up words.

Internalization Check: Are you in your point-of-view character's head enough? You know why your characters act as they do, but are you getting that all on the page? Pretend you know nothing about them or their history. Are the details readers need to know clear? Short novels often have lots of action, but the emotional aspect is missing—and vice versa.

Action Check: Are you in your point-of-view character's head *too* much? Are you telling or summarizing what's happening and not letting it unfold? Strange as it sounds, action scenes can be boring to write, so it's easy to scrimp on them to get to the more interesting emotional scenes. But it's the balance between head and heart that make the story work.

Backstory Check: Is there an element of the backstory that might be dramatized or illustrated to shed new or better light on something already in the novel? You don't need to add a flashback (unless you do), but a memory of something might cause a different action or response somewhere and take the story to a new place, or even offer a new obstacle to overcome.

Step Two: Flesh Out Where Needed

Once you've identified what's missing, return to the specific workshops and redo the exercises until your manuscript is the right size for the story you want to tell.

The key thing to remember when you're bulking up a novel is to be true to the story. Look for ways to tell that story, deepen those characters, and keep readers guessing what will happen next.

All that's left now is to take one, final look at your manuscript.

Workshop Ten: A Final Look

The Goal of This Workshop: To do a final review to catch any issues not previously caught and fixed.

What We'll Discuss in This Workshop: How to know if you're done revising, and how to review your manuscript like a reader.

Welcome to Workshop Ten: A Final Look

By the time you get to the final look, you probably want it over. You're sick of the novel, you're tired, and you want to move on to the next step (this is normal, so don't worry). It's a dangerous time, because the urge to send the manuscript out—either to agents, editors, or publishing it ourselves—is high.

Resist the urge.

This is when those "I can't believe I didn't catch that" mistakes happen. You stop seeing what's on the page and see what you want or expect to see. You ignore any nagging thoughts that you *should* fix that subplot, or third chapter ending, or too-similar names, and tell yourself no one will notice.

And someone always does.

Take a break from revising if you need to (a good idea, as it lets you forget what you wanted to do and see what's there), then come back and look at that finished draft and decide if it truly is finished.

Are the Revisions Done?

How do you *know* when a novel is done? When *do* you stop revising? Ultimately that's up to the writer, but you usually have a sense of when you're making novel-changing edits and when you're delaying the inevitable. Declaring a novel "finished" carries a lot of weight and even expectations, so it can be as scary as it is exhilarating. Sometimes, you'd rather keep fiddling with it than send it out.

In this session, the goal is to determine if you are indeed finished with your revision. If you know you're done, skip this session and move onto the final read through.

The easiest way to tell if you're done is to look at the type of changes you're still making.

If You're Making Minor Changes

If all you're doing is tweaking a word here and a comma there—style changes not substance—you're probably done. However, one or two tweaks per page suggests one last proof-reading pass will benefit you. One or two tweaks per chapter suggests it's probably good to go. One caveat here: If the tweaks are errors, keep proofing until you get them all.

If You're Making Story Changes

If you're still tweaking the story, the revisions are not done. In fact, if the story is changing significantly at this stage, that's a red flag that the novel itself isn't finished. You might need to nail down the story and fix it before you can return to the revision.

If You're Making Text Changes

If you're still getting the text right, revising sentences, or moving text around, the revisions *could* be done. If the tweaking isn't changing the story or scenes any, you can skip ahead and polish the text—approach it as a proofreader or copy editor. If the tweaks change the meaning of the sentences and scenes, then you're still revising.

If You're Making Word Count Changes

If you still need to adjust the word count (up or down), the revisions are not done.

If You're Making "Scared it's Not Good Enough" Changes

If you're tweaking out of fear, you're probably done revising. This is a normal fear, and self-doubt about a new project happens to pretty much everyone.

If You're Making "It's Not Quite Right" Changes

If everything *feels* like it's done, but there's something that still bugs you, it could go either way.

On one hand, being tired of the manuscript can easily make you think that it's done when it isn't.

On the other, a finished manuscript you've read dozens of times can seem boring because you've read it so many times.

If the *story* is boring you, that could indicate the story is, well, *boring*. Be objective and determine if this feeling is due to those countless re-reads, or if that scene has always felt blah. Be especially wary of scenes you tended to skip over during revisions because you felt they were "good enough" and didn't want to deal with them anymore. If you were skimming to get through it, you might want to reconsider that scene. Ask yourself:

What about the work feels wrong? If you can pinpoint specific problems, then you're not finished, even if the text is polished to perfection. The issue is likely a macro problem that has nothing to do with the quality of the prose, but a structural or story issue, such as, the pacing is slow in chapter nine, or the goal isn't clear in chapter six, maybe the front half is too long or the stakes are too low overall.

Has that scene or aspect ever bothered you before? Some scenes you know aren't right, but you ignore the warning signs. Often it's because you like the scene and want to keep it, even though you know deep down it should go. Listen to those nagging suspicions that you "ought to do something." Ignore that whisper that says, "No one will notice," or, "I can get away with it." That's a red flag you should fix it.

Uncertainty about a manuscript's readiness is normal, so don't fret if you have doubts. But also know you *can* cross the line between improving your manuscript and editing the life out of it. Stop before you change the text or story *just* so it sounds new.

Review it Like a Reader

Before you declare the novel finished, it's wise to let it sit for a few weeks and then read it straight through, same as if you'd bought it off the shelf. You're not a writer during this read; you're a reader, dying to find your next favorite author and a book you can't stop talking about.

In this session, the goal is to treat your novel the same as the toughest critics you'll ever have—your readers.

Go to wherever you most enjoy reading, using whatever device you prefer—hard copy or e-reader. Review your manuscript as if you were a reader who paid full hardcover price for this book (which means be tough—you deserve a great book for your money!).

When through, answer these questions as honestly as possible:

- ▶ Did the first line intrigue me?
- ▶ Did the first paragraph hook me?
- ▶ Did the first page make me want to read more?
- ▶ Did the first scene grab me?
- ▶ Was there a mystery or story question I wanted to see answered?
- ▶ Was there a suggestion or anticipation that something was about to go wrong?
- ▶ Did every scene make me want to read the next scene?
- ▶ Was there a reason to keep reading on every page?
- ▶ Did the chapters feel like they were going somewhere?
- ▶ Did the middle connect the opening goal and/or the core conflict goal?

- ▶ Did the stakes keep escalating and drawing me through the story?
- ▶ Were the mysteries and story questions interesting?
- ▶ Was I consistently learning new details about the story, world, plot, or characters?
- ▶ Was the voice consistent and enjoyable throughout?
- ▶ Were the characters consistent throughout?
- ▶ Was the final battle worth waiting for?
- ▶ Was the resolution satisfying?
- ▶ Would I tell my friends about this book (be honest)?

If you answered no to any of these, that's a red flag you still need a little more work in that particular area. Return to that session and re-do those exercises.

To check the general pacing and flow of the novel, answer the following questions:

- ▶ Did my mind ever start to wander?
- ▶ Did I notice any unnecessary scenes?
- ▶ Did I skim any scenes?
- ▶ Was I in a hurry to get through any scenes?
- ▶ Did I stumble over any of the text?

If you answered yes to any of these, that's a red flag the manuscript could still use some trimming or editing. Re-examine those scenes and determine what needs fixing.

If you *really* want to dig in for a final analysis, look objectively at the individual story pieces more than the novel as a whole (some of these questions are similar to your analysis from Workshop One).

Look at the Characters:

- ▶ Did I like the point-of-view character(s) and find them interesting and/or compelling?
- ▶ Did the characters and their actions seem real?

- ▶ Did the characters feel balanced in their views, attitudes, and opinions (or were they mouthpieces or yes men for the protagonist)?
- ▶ Did the characters behave in a credible fashion?

Look at the Plot:

- ▶ Did the plot make sense?
- ▶ Were the characters' goals clear?
- ▶ Did those goals advance the story?
- ▶ Were the goals believable?
- ▶ Were the stakes high or compelling enough to keep me interested and worried?
- ▶ Did the stakes seem genuine (not manufactured for the sake of drama)?
- ▶ Did the overall structure hold together?
- ▶ Was the plot predictable or did it surprise me (did it read as a fresh story or the same as other novels in its genre)?

Look at the Point of View:

- ▶ Did the narrative style fit the genre and book style?
- ▶ Did I feel connected to the point-of-view character(s)?
- ▶ Were there any points of view that felt unnecessary?

Look at the Description and Setting:

- ▶ Was I ever bored by too much backstory, exposition, or description?
- ▶ Did the world feel real and fleshed out?
- ▶ Was I ever uncertain about what something looked like?

Look at the Dialogue:

- ▶ Were the dialogue tags clear?
- ▶ Were the character voices different?
- ▶ Were there any talking heads in white rooms?

Look at the Pacing:

- ▶ Was the pacing good?
- ▶ Was I engaged in the story?
- ▶ Did I need a break at any time in the story?

If you find anything you'd like to tweak or fix, make those changes now. If everything checks out, declare your revision done!

Bonus Workshop: Salvaging Half-Finished Manuscripts

The Goal of This Workshop: To find ways to fix and finish a manuscript you've been unable to finish.

What We'll Discuss in This Workshop: How to identify the fatal flaws of a half-finished manuscript and how to fix them.

Welcome to the Bonus Workshop: Salvaging Half-Finished Manuscripts

Although it happens to us all (even the pros), it's not uncommon for an early novel to wind up as a half-finished manuscript (HFM). You're still learning and figuring the whole writing thing out, and you don't always have the necessary skills yet to fix whatever is wrong. It's not even unusual for seasoned writers to lose steam halfway through, because you don't know where a story will take you and it takes you someplace *meh*.

These manuscripts can be terribly frustrating, because you usually love the story and want to make it work (which is why you keep going back to it). It can even make you doubt your writing ability.

Don't let a HFM undermine your confidence or sap your creativity. Some ideas take more effort and time to make them work. Sometimes, an idea hits you before you're ready to write it, and you'll find if you let it sit while you figure it out, or first learn the needed skills to write it, when you go back it starts flowing again.

If you're facing a half-finished manuscript, take a deep breath, roll up your sleeves, and let's get to work fixing whatever is holding it back.

Salvaging Half-Finished Manuscripts

Fixing a half-finished manuscript is often more frustrating than a regular revision, so prepare yourself for a lot of hair pulling and self-doubt (this is totally normal and happens to almost everyone). Keep reminding yourself that it's not you, it's the tricky *idea* that's causing the problems. It's a giant puzzle you just need to find the edge pieces for, and then the rest of it will fall into place.

When you get stuck, keep asking yourself: What does my protagonist want? Why does she want it? What's in her way of getting her goal? These three questions will get you around almost every wall you hit and allow you to keep moving forward.

In this session, the goal is to provide additional guidance in revising half-finished manuscripts.

Step One: Re-Read the HFM

It's probably been a while since you last worked on it, and it's important to re-familiarize yourself with the manuscript. It might even surprise you and not be as bad or as hopeless as you remember. You'll probably want to tweak as you read, but don't start editing just yet. You'll want to gain some perspective before you dive back in. Otherwise, you risk running into the same issues that made you stop writing in the first place. Make notes on elements you like and dislike. This read through is about getting your bearings. It's not a bad idea to create your editorial map at this time.

Step Two: Find the Sticking Point

Determine why you stopped working on it. Was it a story flaw? A lack of conflict or real stakes? Maybe you didn't know what to do next, or the love was gone and it no longer interested you. Each issue will require a different plan of attack to fix and get that manuscript back on track.

Step Three: Fix the Fatal Flaw

Some stories are inherently flawed and nothing you do will save them until you fix those flaws. If you received feedback on the work, the critique should have clues to help you pinpoint the problems. If you haven't shown the manuscript to anyone yet, your instincts are probably poking at you with similar thoughts. You did set it aside for a reason, remember? What is that reason? Be honest here.

The most common reasons for a stalled manuscript include:

Problems with the premise: The flaw is part of the original idea, and that's spilling over into the entire novel. Something about the premise isn't working, and needs to be revamped or reworked.

The wrong protagonist: You thought the hero was the main character, but it turns out she has no stake in the plot. If she walked away, nothing in the story would change.

The wrong story: You started out wanting to tell one tale, and somehow everything veered off track and the story shifted to a subplot or new idea and abandoned the core conflict.

The wrong point of view: This might be character related, or style related. Maybe the epic tale is too big for a single, first-person point of view, or you need more points of view to fully show the core story.

A lack of conflict: You know what the protagonist has to do, but there's nothing trying to stop her.

A lack of stakes: Nothing about the protagonist or the problem makes readers care if the problem is solved or not. It's hard to keep working on a story if even *you* don't care how it turns out.

No one likes the protagonist: Unlikable protagonists are hard to root for, especially when you know deep down your hero is a jerk.

The characters aren't credible: You have to believe your characters would do XYZ to make the plot happen, and when you don't, the story falls apart and seems contrived.

A lack of narrative drive: If you're not sure where the story is going or how it ends, the plot can ramble aimlessly and seem like the novel isn't going anywhere.

If any of these sound like your novel's fatal flaw, do the exercises that apply in Revision Options: Fixing Common Fatal Flaws.

Step Four: Move Forward

Once you've identified your HFM's problems, fix them and finish the manuscript.

The biggest obstacle to a HFM is figuring out why you stopped in the first place. Solve that problem (or problems) and the ideas will start flowing again—even if the best idea is to retire that manuscript and work on something new.

Revision Options: Fixing Common Fatal Flaws

Fatal flaws can sink a story, but don't lose hope if you find one in your manuscript. They require a bit of work to fix, but they usually *are* fixable. Review your manuscript objectively, pinpoint where the problem lies, and then take steps to repair the flaw and get the story back on track so you can finish the novel.

Fixing a Faulty Premise

Sadly, some ideas just don't work, or readers just don't get them. This is one of the harder flaws to fix, but understanding what's turning off your readers can help.

Common feedback symptoms include: "I can't believe the protagonist would do this." "I'm having a hard time accepting the story would unfold like this." "No way, I'm not buying this." "Are readers going to believe this?"

Look at where the critiquers have doubts (or where you feel that nagging suspicion) and ask:

Is it a motivation issue? Do you see a lot of "Why are they doing this?" Then it's likely character based and working on your characters' motivations might solve your problem. Frequently, it's the motivation that causes credibility issues, because there's no good reason for the character to be doing what's needed for the book to work.

Is it a situation issue? Do you see a lot of "This would never happen"? Then it's likely breaking rules your readers can't suspend disbelief to accept. Odds are they've told you what that rule is, so either find a solid way to explain breaking that rule, adjust what you have so it follows the rules and still works for plot, or toss the idea aside and think up something else.

A premise problem can be daunting, but sometimes, you just need to write a chunk of it before you can fix it.

Fixing the Wrong Protagonist

Sometimes you pick the wrong protagonist. You have an idea in your head and think the story is going to be about one person, but as it unfolds, another is clearly the one driving the story.

Common feedback symptoms include: "I want to know more about X." "X is way more interesting than Y." "X seems to be the one doing everything, and Y just goes along for the ride."

Look at your protagonist and story and ask:

Is **the protagonist wrong?** If so, change who the protagonist of the story is. Consider doing the exercises in Workshop Two: Character Work: If You Think You Have the Wrong Protagonist on page 62 at this time.

Is the protagonist not enough? It's possible the story needs more than one main character to drive it, and the protagonist is only doing half the necessary work. Take a look at the character critiquers ask about. Could that person become a major character and do more in the story? If yes, do it.

Does the protagonist need reworking? Maybe you have the right character, but she needs a total makeover so her personality or situation better serves the story. Take a fresh look at her, and decide what kind of person she needs to be to resolve all the issues your critiquers had trouble with.

Often, changing the protagonist doesn't require as much rewriting as you fear. The scenes are right, but the character navigating them is wrong.

Fixing the Wrong Story

Sometimes, you write an idea and as it plays out, you lose interest in it. Or you discover that what you thought you were writing isn't at all what's on the page. Somewhere you became lost in the weeds and have been writing in different directions looking for a way out.

Common feedback symptoms include: "What about the X plot? Are we ever going to find out how that worked out?" "What happened to So-and-so?" "This subplot is much more interesting than the main plot." "I skimmed through here, but it really took off here." "Why are they doing this when that is way cooler?"

If you think you're writing the wrong story, ask:

What story do you *want* to tell? It's possible you lost sight of what your goal was, so take a moment and remember what drew you to this idea in the first place. But it's also possible that once you delved deeper into the story, it wasn't as interesting as you first thought. There's no shame in setting aside an idea that didn't pan out.

Is a subplot more interesting to you? Maybe a subplot has taken over and is far more interesting than the main plot. Brainstorm to see if that subplot *can* carry the entire novel. Don't be afraid to hack off a main plot that has died on the vine, even if that means re-plotting the entire novel with this new (and better) direction.

Are your beta readers more interested in a subplot than the main plot? Maybe your readers are ignoring the core conflict, but are dying to know more about a throwaway subplot you tossed in there on a whim. It's possible you stumbled into a better story without realizing it. Consider what the novel would look like if you cut the core conflict and promoted this other idea instead.

Sometimes the only way to salvage a HFM is to start over with the right idea. It's disheartening to throw away all that work, but look at it as writing that needed to be done to find the true story in your idea.

Fixing the Wrong Point of View

Shifting perspectives can change the entire feel of a novel, turning what was once distant and told into close and personal.

Common feedback symptoms include: "This would be better in first/third." "If you did first/third you'd be able to explore X better." "Have you thought about doing this in first/third?" "Why are we seeing this character's perspective?"

Look at your point-of-view style and ask:

Is the scale off? An epic tale that spans continents may be too large to be told by a first person point of view without access to the larger elements of the story, same as a third person point of view might feel too detached for a personal journey. Look at your novel's scope to see if the point of view matches the scale. It could be the narrative distance is too close, or too far away. It's also possible that the novel works in that point of view, but you don't like how it reads in that style and it's keeping you from writing.

Are there too many point-of-view characters? Even when you have the right point-of-view style, if too many characters are involved, the story can feel clunky and hard to follow. Look through the points of view and decide if you *really* need to see the story unfold from that character's perspective.

A point of view problem is one of the easier flaws to fix, since you can write a new chapter or two in a different point-of-view style and compare. If you like what you see, the rest of the novel should go smoothly. If you're still unhappy, you can try another style, or reexamine the flaw—maybe point of view isn't the real issue and it's a character or protagonist flaw.

Fixing a Lack of Conflict

Conflict drives a novel, and without it, the story can seem like it's not going anywhere or nothing is going on. A lack of conflict can take many forms, but most often it's because A) there's no goal so there's nothing to conflict with, B) there's nothing preventing the protagonist from acting, or C) every obstacle is easily overcome.

Common feedback symptoms include: "Everything's too easy for the protagonist." "There's nothing in the protagonist's way." "Stuff just falls in her lap." "There's nothing going on." "What's this about?"

Look at your novel and ask:

Is it a goal issue? The fault might be with the core conflict itself. What is your protagonist trying to do? The goal should be external and something the protagonist can physically do. Internal goals are vital for character arcs, but they don't help drive a plot. If your protagonist is trying to do something ambiguous, such as "overcome her grief," that's probably the problem. The external actions she *does* take to overcome that grief is where the goal will lie.

Is it an antagonist issue? A protagonist (and a conflict) is only as strong as the antagonist. Who or what is preventing the protagonist from acting? If no one is actively trying to keep your protagonist from her goal, this could be the problem.

Is it an easy-obstacle issue? How hard is it for your protagonist to solve her problems? If every problem encountered is solved with no effort or skill, then there's nothing in the way even though it may look like it. Conflict = struggle + hard choices.

Is it a character arc issue? The lack of available hard choices could be because there's no character arc to create the inner conflict needed to create the tough choices in the first place. Try adding a stronger character arc, or doing the exercises in Workshop Two: Character Work on page 51.

Often, the conflict is weak because the actions are for plot reasons only, not because the characters want to do what they're doing. Nobody's trying to stop anyone because nobody cares—it's a play, not their life.

Fixing a "Why Should I Care?" Lack of Stakes

Not caring is almost always a personal stakes issue. If there's no risk for the protagonist, why should readers care about her problem? The fun is in the fear that doom is just around the corner, and terrible consequences will befall those who fail.

Common feedback symptoms include: "Does it matter if she does this?" "What will go wrong if she fails here?" "Why is she going through all this? Can't she just leave?"

Look at your major turning points and ask:

Are there personal and life-changing consequences for failure? What happens if your protagonist fails? If she won't lose something that matters a lot to her, why put herself at risk? How might you make it personal? How will it change her life forever? If the protagonist can walk away and nothing bad happens to her, that's the problem.

Is the only thing at stake "the protagonist dies" or "the world ends?" Huge stakes *seem* big, but we all know the hero rarely dies and the world doesn't end, so readers don't worry. If death or bodily harm is the *only* reason and the *only* consequence, find or create a few more reasons to make failing personal and compelling.

Finding the right stakes can be tricky, because it's not always easy to answer the classic, "Why should I care?" question. A consequence can feel enormous, but readers still don't care, while a small little risk can yank at their heartstrings. Typically, the more personal they are, the higher the stakes feel.

Fixing an Unlikable Protagonist

If readers don't like the protagonist or aren't intrigued by her, they won't read about her. There should be something about the protagonist that makes readers curious to know more about her. For example, Dexter is a serial killer, but you like him anyway because he's compelling to watch.

Common feedback symptoms include: "I'm losing sympathy for the protagonist." "I don't like the protagonist much." "The protagonist seems mean here." "I've lost all respect for the protagonist." "Watching the protagonist do X makes me uncomfortable."

Look at your protagonist and ask:

Is it an understanding issue? You might have reasons for your protagonist to do what she's doing, but something isn't coming through on the page. Look at the motivations and internalization. There's a good chance that readers don't understand the protagonist's actions because the motivation behind the action is unclear. Also check the backstory. You might need to adjust the past to make the character more sympathetic.

Are the problems inherent to the character's actions or personality? The smallest thing can turn readers off and color everything that character does in ways you never expected. Look at where your comments come from. Do readers not like what the character is doing or who she is? The behaviors will highlight which aspects of your protagonist aren't coming across well.

Is the protagonist likable or compelling? Just because you love your creations doesn't mean everyone else will. Be honest. Is the reason you like the character due to knowing where she ends up or what she goes through in the story? Don't judge her based on end-book information, but on how she appears in the first few pages.

Is the protagonist mean to a beloved character? No matter how nice a gal is in every other way, you see her kick a puppy, you don't like her. Is your character mean to someone in the story readers love? Maybe it's time to adjust a few behavioral quirks.

Is the protagonist whiny? Nobody likes a whiner. If the protagonist is annoying—even if she has good reasons for whining or complaining—it could irritate readers. Consider cutting back on the "woe is me" and giving the protagonist a little backbone.

Since you're so close to your protagonist, you might need to seek outside help to pinpoint exactly what's wrong here. However, be wary if the obnoxious aspects are *why* you love the character. That's a red flag you might enjoy the character for what she does, not for who she is.

Fixing a Lack of Credibility

Sometimes characters act in ways that make no sense. Everyone knows the killer is waiting in the dark, but the character goes into the basement to check the weird noise anyway. Or a character has a skill set that stretches credibility, or breaks a law of physics with no explanation. Whatever goes wrong, readers say, "Nope, not buying it."

Common feedback symptoms include: "Why would they do this?" "Why didn't they do X instead?" "This seems like a lot of work when they could have done X." "Doesn't this go against what they said before?"

Look at where your characters might be stretching credibility and ask:

Is it a motivation issue? Characters need solid reasons to act, and when they act against their own best interests, readers cry foul. Look at what your characters do and why they do it. Is it plausible? Would they do the opposite if this was real life? Give characters solid and believable reasons to act as they do.

Is it a realism issue? The suspension of disbelief is vital to fiction, but there's a fine line between a little reality finagling and outright impossibility. Check any rules you might be breaking—both in your own story world and in the real world. Fix it so it adheres to those rules (or gives a darn good reason why not), even if it messes up the plot.

Is it an over-thinking issue? People usually try the option of least resistance first. If a simple action can solve the problem, they won't come up with a huge elaborate plan. If every problem requires a Rube Goldbergesque plan to resolve it when a simple act will fix it, there's a good chance the plot is getting convoluted.

In most cases, fixing a credibility issue is a matter of showing why (or how) such an act is necessary, or why something is the way it is. If you have no other reason than, "Because it has to be for the plot to work," there's the problem.

Fixing a Lack of Narrative Drive

Hitting a wall is usually a plot issue. You can't move forward because you don't know what happens, so the entire book grinds to a halt.

Common feedback symptoms include: "Where is the story going?" "The plot seems to be wandering." "Are we ever going to get to a point?" "I have no idea what happens next."

Look at your overall structure and ask:

Does the protagonist have a goal in every scene? If your protagonist has no goal, she has nothing to do. Look at your last scene and think about what the protagonist would do to get out of that. If she's not in any trouble, look back at what she's been doing and see where you can muck her plans up. Every place she succeeded, find a way to make her fail instead, and pick the best option to keep the story moving forward.

Is the protagonist motivated to act in every scene? Determine why she's doing this. What's driving her to act? You might need to develop some backstory to explain her motivations.

Does the protagonist have stakes in every scene? She may have a goal and a reason to act, but if there's nothing to lose, why bother reading what happens? What will happen if she fails, not only in the one scene, but in the story overall? Is this a problem that needs to be solved? Why? And don't stop with one surface answer. Remember, "Because people will die" isn't enough to drive a novel. Ask why they will die. Who benefits from it? And why will that hurt the protagonist?

Is it an ending issue? If you don't know where you're going, it can be hard to get there. Take a look at your planned ending. Do you *have* an ending yet? Maybe the problem comes from not knowing what to do, or how the novel will end, so you don't know how to get the characters there. Determine how the novel ends and work backward to where you're stuck.

Fatal flaws aren't always fatal, and you *can* salvage a half-finished manuscript you still love—even if you don't particularly *like* it at the moment.

It's Over!

Congratulations! You made it.

Revising a novel is a ton of work, but the results are usually worth it. That spark of an idea is now a full-grown novel ready to take on the world (yes, we can be emotional over our finished babies).

Take some time to celebrate your victory. Revising a novel can be harder than writing it in the first place, and it's an accomplishment that should be rewarded. Go ahead, you earned it.

I hope you've enjoyed the workshops and that they helped turn your manuscript into a solid finished draft. If you've found this book helpful, please share with friends or leave reviews on your favorite sites.

Most of all, best of luck and good writing!

Janice Hardy
August 2016

Appendix
Quick-check analysis questions for easy manuscript review.

Common Red Flag Words

▶ Common self-aware red flag words: She knew, she realized, she felt, she thought. Not every instance will be a problem, but it's a good place to start the search.

▶ Common stimulus/response red flag words: when, as, before. Revise as needed so the stimulus comes first, then the character reaction.

▶ Common telling red flag words: Look for words such as: when, as, to (verb), which, because, to be verbs. These are often found in told prose.

▶ Common stage direction red flag words: Look for words such as, while, when, and as. These often connect multiple actions in one long (and confusing) chain.

▶ Common motivational red flag words: to (action), when, as, while, causing, making, because.

▶ Common emotional red flag words: In (emotion), and with (feeling).

▶ Common descriptive red flag words and phrases: Realize, could see, the sound of, the feel of, the smell of, tried to, trying, in order to, to make.

▶ Common passive red flag words: To be verbs—is, am, are, was, were, be, have, had, has, do, does, did, has been, have been, had been, will be, will have been, being.

▶ Common mental red flag words: realized, thought, wondered, hoped, considered, prayed, etc.

Analyze the Draft

▶ Weak goal-conflict-stakes structures: This could indicate a plot or narrative drive issue.

▶ Lack of character motivation: This could indicate a character arc or credibility issue.

▶ Sparse or missing descriptions: This could indicate a clarity or world-building issue.

▶ Heavy (or missing) backstory: This could indicate a pacing or character issue.

▶ Too many infodumps: This could indicate a pacing or show-don't-tell issue.

▶ Slow or uneven pacing: This could indicate a narrative drive or pacing issue.

▶ Lack of hooks: This could indicate a tension, narrative drive, or premise issue.

▶ Faulty logic: This could indicate a plausibility or plotting issue.

▶ Weak or missing foreshadowing or clues: This could indicate a tension, tone, or description issue.

▶ Areas that need more emotion: This could indicate an internalization issue.

▶ Weak characters and character arcs: This could indicate a character or internal conflict issue.

▶ Weak scene structure: This could indicate a plot or structure issue.

▶ Lack of narrative drive: This could indicate a pacing or goals issue.

▶ Inconsistent point of view: This could indicate a narrative, character, or show-don't-tell issue.

▶ Weak dialogue: This could indicate an infodump, dialogue, or character issue.

▶ Is the point-of-view character(s) likable or interesting enough to read about?

▶ Are their goals clear so there's narrative drive in the story?

▶ Do the characters seem real?

▶ Are there strong and interesting stakes?

▶ Is there too much back story, exposition, or description?

▶ Is the overall structure holding together?

▶ Does the opening scene have something to entice readers to keep reading?

▶ Do the scene and chapter endings entice readers to turn the page?

▶ Is the pacing strong?

▶ Are the plots, stakes, and goals believable?

▶ Does it read well overall?

▶ Do the sentences flow seamlessly or do any stick out and read awkwardly?

▶ Are the dialogue tags clear?

▶ Does the world seem fleshed out?

Analyze the Characters

▶ Do you have the right protagonist for this story?

▶ Do you have the right antagonist for this story?

▶ Do you have the right number of characters?

▶ Do you like the point-of-view character(s) or find them interesting?

▶ Do you care about these characters enough to read their story?

▶ Do the characters seem real?

▶ Are the characters believable in their roles?

▶ Are the characters flawed in ways that affect their decisions in the story?

▶ Do they have virtues that affect their decisions in the story?

▶ Do they have contradicting beliefs, both with themselves, and the other characters?

▶ How much physical description do you want?

▶ Are the main characters adequately described?

▶ Is there too much focus on physical details?

▶ Are the secondary characters described?

▶ How many details do you use to describe the various characters?

▶ Do the descriptions all fit the same format?

Analyze the Character Arcs

▶ What does the protagonist learn over the course of the novel?

▶ How does the internal conflict affect that growth? .

▶ What lie is she telling herself or does she believe at the start of the novel?

▶ When does she realize it is or isn't true?

▶ What does she want most of all as a person?

▶ Does the external plot facilitate her achieving this personal desire?

▶ What is she most afraid of?

▶ When does she face this fear?

▶ Where do the turning points of the growth occur? .

Analyze the Backstory

▶ Is the backstory relevant to the scene?

▶ Does this information help readers understand what's going on in this scene?

▶ Will knowing this information hurt the tension or mystery of the scene (or story)?

▶ What would be lost in this scene if you took the backstory out?

▶ Why do you want it in the scene?

Analyze the Theme

▶ What is the theme (or themes) of this story?

▶ Where examples of this theme are found in the novel?

▶ Where and how does the theme deepen the character arcs?

▶ How does the theme tie into the resolution of the novel?

Analyze the Story Structure

▶ Are all the pieces in the right places?

▶ Does the opening scene present an intriguing problem or mystery to draw readers in?

▶ Is there an inciting event within the first thirty pages (or fifty pages for longer manuscripts) that puts the protagonist on the path to the rest of the novel?

▶ Is there a moment in the beginning where the protagonist makes the choice to pursue the story problem?

▶ Do the stakes escalate at this time?

▶ Does something happen in the middle of the book that changes how the story problem is viewed or approached?

▶ Are the stakes raised again around this time?

▶ Is there a dark moment or setback right before the ending starts that raises the stakes again?

▶ Are the stakes raised yet again?

▶ Does the protagonist make the decision to continue the fight despite the risks or sacrifices?

▶ Is there a clear win for the protagonist at the climax?

▶ Does the ending resolve itself in a way that satisfies the story questions posed in the beginning of the novel?

▶ Is the ending satisfying?

Analyze the Plot and Subplots

▶ Does the plot make sense?

▶ Is there a clear core conflict driving the plot?

▶ Are the characters' actions believable?

▶ Was the plot predictable?

▶ Do events turn out exactly how anyone would expect them to?

▶ Are there enough twists and turns to keep readers guessing?

▶ How often does the protagonist have to make a choice?

▶ Are those choices difficult?

▶ Does the protagonist have approaches different from the other characters' toward solving problems or looking at situations?

▶ Are any leaps in logic or the decision-making process plausible?

▶ Do coincidences work to aid the protagonist instead of hindering her?

▶ Are the protagonist's motivations plausible?

▶ Is someone or something opposing the protagonist?

▶ Does the antagonist have a plan, or does he cause random trouble when the plot needs it?

▶ Is the antagonist trying to win, or does he sometimes act stupidly so the protagonist can win?

▶ Do the choices create conflict between the protagonist's internal and external goals?

▶ Is the protagonist asked or forced to do something that goes against her beliefs?

▶ Are there strong stakes?

▶ Do the stakes escalate as the novel unfolds?

▶ Will the protagonist's life change if she fails to achieve her goal?

▶ Do the stakes affect the protagonist personally?

▶ Is it impossible for the protagonist to walk away from this problem?

▶ Are the stakes clear from the beginning of the novel?

▶ Are the stakes big enough to be worth the reader's time?

▶ What's your goal (as the author) for the subplot?

▶ Are the subplots contributing to the core conflict or character arc?

▶ Will this subplot make the story better, or just longer?

▶ If you took the subplot out, what's lost?

▶ Does it explore a new problem (and likely raise the stakes) or repeat a similar scene or idea you've already done?

▶ Does it require more attention (and words) than the main plot?

▶ Is your protagonist trying to do too much in too many subplots?

▶ Is the subplot compelling enough that readers won't mind the delay in getting back to the main goal, or will they think you're dragging your feet to keep making the problem worse?

Analyze the Scenes

▶ How does this scene serve the story?

▶ How does this scene serve the protagonist's character arc?

▶ How does this scene serve the other characters' arcs? It's not all about the protagonist.

▶ Where does this scene take place?

▶ What is the point-of-view character trying to do?

▶ What goes wrong? What's the problem or challenge?

▶ Why is this important and how does it potentially hurt the point-of-view character?

▶ Who else is in the scene?

▶ What happens right before this scene?

▶ What does the point-of-view character do next?

▶ If you took any scenes out, would the plot change?

Analyze the Narrative Drive

▶ Are the character and story goals clear so there's narrative drive in the story?

▶ Is the protagonist doing something in every scene?

▶ Is there a story point (author's perspective) to every scene?

▶ Is there a story question (reader's perspective) in every scene?

▶ Are these points and questions clear from the start of the scene?

▶ Is the protagonist moving toward something?

▶ Do the scenes and chapters build on one another or are events happening one after another? Does it have a point?

▶ Where is the critical information revealed?

▶ Where do your surprises and twists fall?

▶ Is the protagonist feeling too much?

▶ Is the protagonist debating too much?

Analyze the Tension and Hooks

▶ Is there a sense of something about to happen in every scene?

▶ Are there unanswered questions in every scene?

▶ Is there tension on every page?

▶ Is there tension between characters?

▶ Is there tension in the setting?

▶ Are there moments when the protagonist is relaxed?

▶ Are there big reveals and discoveries throughout the novel?

▶ How many reveals are plot-related?

▶ How many reveals are character-related?

▶ How many reveals are backstory or world-building related?

Analyze the Point of View

▶ Is it clear who the narrator is?

▶ Is the narrator's voice consistent with the novel's tone?

▶ Is the narrator getting in the way of the story?

▶ Is the narrator revealing too much? Not enough?

▶ Are there any point-of-view shifts?

▶ Is the point of view consistent?

▶ Are there any scenes in a point-of-view style that differs from the rest of the manuscript?

▶ Is there too much filtering?

▶ Do characters know details they couldn't possibly know?

▶ Are any point-of-view characters oddly self-aware?

▶ Are there any inconsistent or out-of-the-blue emotional responses?

▶ Are any point-of-view characters stating the obvious?

▶ Are any point-of-view characters reacting before something happens?

▶ Are there any point-of-view scenes that are there only to show information the main characters can't witness?

▶ Do you use one point of view per scene (if it's not an omniscient point of view)?

▶ Is it clear when you've switched points of view?

Analyze the Internalization

▶ Is there too much internalization?

▶ Is there too little internalization?

▶ Does the internal thought clarify the dialogue or action?

▶ Does the internal thought show the point-of-view character's opinion on the situation?

▶ Does the internal thought provide necessary information without infodumping?

▶ Does the internal thought convey background information without telling?

▶ Are there internal thoughts in every line of dialogue?

▶ Are the internal thoughts often paragraphs long, and do they happen every time the point-of-view character thinks?

▶ Does the internal thought summarize a scene or idea at the end (or describe it at the start before you show that scene or idea)?

▶ Are you repeating the same idea in multiple ways?

Analyze the Descriptions

▶ Is there too much description?

▶ Is there too little description?

▶ Are the descriptions vague?

▶ Do the descriptive details tell readers what they already know?

▶ Do the descriptive details show judgment on the point-of-view character's part?

▶ Could you describe something better through action?

▶ How do the descriptive details affect the rhythm of the prose?

▶ Is the point-of-view character describing details the same way no matter what she's feeling or doing, or is she seeing it based on how she feels at that point in time?

▶ Is the point-of-view character noticing the same types of details all the time, or does she see what she feels is important in that scene?

▶ Does the point-of-view character have a reason to look around, or is she doing it so you can tell readers what she sees?

▶ Are there any detached or distant-feeling scenes?

▶ Is there an abundance of common telling red flag words?

▶ Are there any scenes with a lot of explanations?

▶ Are there passages of information that seem more like notes than story?

▶ Are characters telling each other information they already know?

▶ Is there a history lesson any time the protagonist enters a room or meets another person?

▶ Are there extra action tags in the dialogue?

▶ Are there a lot of common stage direction red flag words?

▶ Are any characters trying to do too much?

▶ Are characters "trying" a lot?

▶ Is it clear how each character feels at the start of the scene?

▶ Do emotions change in the scene?

▶ Do you know what you want your readers to feel in the scene?

▶ Is it clear why the character is having any emotional reactions?

▶ Does the opening scene convey the tone of the novel?

▶ Does the tone of each scene match its emotional core?

▶ Do the imagery and word choice of the descriptions reflect this tone?

▶ Does the tone enhance individual scenes to bring about the desired emotional impact on the reader?

▶ Does the tone change over the course of the novel?

▶ What mood do you want the characters to convey?

▶ What mood do you want the scene itself to convey?

▶ Would conflicting tone and mood enhance the scene? .

▶ Does the mood of the scene change?

▶ What do you want readers to feel in this scene?

Analyze the Setting

▶ Are details introduced right away to ground readers in the scene?

▶ Is it clear who's in the scene?

▶ Have the characters changed location since the last scene?

▶ Have the characters changed times?

▶ Does the point-of-view character spend more time talking about what the location looks like than doing anything in it?

▶ Are there a lot of sweeping word paintings that focus on the landscape or weather?

▶ Do interior scenes read like articles from an interior design magazine?

Analyze the World Building

▶ Are there enough specific details to show the special rules of this world?

▶ Are people interacting with the world or is it just a backdrop?

▶ Does the point-of-view character share her thoughts and views on the world around her?

▶ Does the world offer inherent conflicts that make the protagonist's goals harder?

▶ Does the world allow you to make a point you couldn't otherwise make?

▶ Does the world provide challenges you couldn't otherwise have for the characters?

▶ Does the world pull its own weight as far as the story is concerned, or does it just sit there looking pretty?

▶ Does the world building continue to the end of the novel, or does it fade out after it's established?

▶ Are there areas that read more like a textbook than a story?

▶ Do the details help readers understand the conflicts or problems in this world?

▶ Are the rules of this world clear?

▶ Do the rules make sense in the context of the story?

▶ Are there contradictions in the world?

▶ Is the world complicated and layered?

▶ Does the world feel like it exists when the main characters aren't there?

▶ Does this world have a history that logically influences the story events?

▶ Is the infrastructure sound?

▶ Are the people varied?

Analyze the Dialogue

▶ Do the characters sound like real people?

▶ Is the dialogue an actual conversation or two people stating information at one another for the reader's benefit?

▶ Are characters telling each other what they already know?

▶ Are there empty dialogue phrases?

▶ Is the dialogue advancing the plot or story?

▶ Are the dialogue tags clear?

▶ Are there too many dialogue tags?

▶ Are there any over-written or impossible dialogue tags?

▶ Are characters giving away too much information for no reason?

▶ Are you summarizing any conversations instead of dramatizing them?

▶ Is there subtext? Is it clear what's not being said?

▶ Is the language appropriate for the intended market?

Analyze the Voice

▶ Does each point-of-view character have his or her own voice and style of speaking?

▶ Can you tell who's speaking even without identifying the character by name?

▶ Can you get a sense of who the character is by the voice?

▶ Does the point-of-view character's outer voice sound like her internal one?

▶ Do characters use language suitable to their status, age, or cultural situation?

▶ Does the voice change depending on the situation?

▶ Do the non-point-of-view characters all sound the same?

▶ Are any of the character voices annoying?

▶ Are any of the character voices stereotyped or clichéd?

▶ Is there an overabundance of dialect?

▶ Does every character use the same vocabulary or is it varied? .

▶ Does every character speak with the same rhythm or pattern?

Analyze the Pacing

▶ What's the common pace for your genre?

▶ Is it well paced overall?

▶ Does it grab you, does it hold your attention, do you want to read on?

▶ Does something change in every scene?

▶ Does the pace speed up during major plot moments?

▶ Are there waves of fast and slow pacing throughout the novel?

▶ Are there any spots that read too fast and readers might have trouble absorbing the information?

▶ Are there any slow spots that might lose readers?

▶ Are there any spots that encourage readers to skim?

▶ Does every scene have an emotional hook?

▶ Does every scene have a mental hook?

Analyze the Transitions

▶ Does each scene end make you want to turn the page?

▶ Is there a sense of anticipation about what will happen next?

▶ Is there a sense of where the plot or story is going?

▶ Does the next chapter's opening scene satisfy reader curiosity, or does it jump ahead in time or location and flash back to deal with the previous chapter's end?

▶ In multiple points-of-view novels, did the next point-of-view character's scene start off with something equally interesting or did the pacing drop and the tension start over?

▶ Does the scene end with something to draw readers forward, or does it let the protagonist sleep, travel, or do something else that drops the tension and pacing?

▶ Does the next scene start with the plot in motion or does it set up the scene to come?

Analyze the Hook Lines

▶ Does every page have an emotional hook line?

▶ Does every page have a mental hook line?

▶ Are there funny or poignant one-liners scattered throughout every scene?

▶ Are there lines that make you smile as a writer on every page?

Analyze the Foreshadowing

▶ Are you foreshadowing the major events or reveals in the story?

▶ Are there any slow or weak scenes that could benefit from adding some foreshadowing?

▶ What emotional scenes might benefit from a little foreshadowing a few scenes earlier?

▶ What "out of the blue shocker information" would seem inevitable with a little foreshadowing to lay the groundwork?

▶ Are there any setup scenes that could do double duty as foreshadowing scenes?

▶ If you had no idea what a clue meant, would it still fit the scene?

▶ Is the clue there specifically to be noticed by readers?

▶ If the reader picked up on this clue and figured it out right then, would it ruin the suspense?

Analyze the Narrative Focus

▶ Is the goal clear?

▶ Does the goal move the scene forward?

▶ Is the bulk of the scene's information supporting this goal?

▶ Does the goal lead to the next scene?

Glossary

Antagonist: The person or thing in the protagonist's path of success.

Backstory: The history and past of a character that affects his or her actions in a novel.

Conflict: Two sides in opposition, either externally or internally.

Core Conflict: The major problem or issue at the center of a novel.

Exposition: Narrative intended solely to convey information to the reader.

Filter Words: The specific words used to create narrative distance in the point-of-view character.

Genre: A category or novel type, such as mystery, fantasy, or romance.

Goal: What a character wants.

Hook: An element that grabs readers and makes them want to read on.

Inciting Event: The moment that triggers the core conflict of the novel and draws the protagonist into the plot.

Market: The demographic traits of the target audience for the novel, such as adult or young adult.

Narrative Distance: The distance between the reader and the point-of-view character.

Narrative Drive: The sense that the plot is moving forward.

Outline: The structured overview of how a novel will unfold, typically written as a guide before the novel is written.

Outliners: Writers who write with a predetermined outline or guide. They know how the book will end and how the plot will unfold before they start writing it.

Pacing: The speed of the novel, or how quickly the story moves.

Pantsers: Writers who write "by the seat of their pants," without outlines. They often don't know how the book will end or what will happen before they start writing it.

Plot: The series of scenes that illustrate a novel. What happens in the novel.

Point of View: The perspective used to tell the story.

Premise: The general description of the story.

Protagonist: The character driving the novel.

Query Letter: A one-page letter used to describe a novel when submitting a manuscript to an agent or editor.

Scene: An individual moment in a novel that dramatizes a goal or situation.

Series: Multiple books using the same characters and/or world.

Set Pieces: The key moments or events in a novel.

Setting: Where the novel takes place.

Sequel (1): A second book that continues where the first book leaves off.

Sequel (2): The period after a scene goal is resolved where the character reflects on events and makes a decision to act.

Stakes: What consequence will befall the protagonist if she fails to get her goal.

Stand-Alone Novel: A novel that contains one complete story in one book.

Structure: The framework a novel is written in, typically based on established turning points at specific moments in the novel.

Tension: The sense of something about to happen that keeps readers reading.

Theme: A recurring idea or concept explored in the novel.

Trilogy: A story that is told over the course of three books.

Trope: An idea or literary device commonly employed in a particular novel type.

Word Count: The number of words contained in a novel.

Thanks!

Thank you for reading the *Revising Your Novel: First Draft to Finished Draft*. I hope you found it useful!

- Reviews help other readers find books. I appreciate all reviews, whether positive or negative.

- Would you like more writing tips and advice? Visit my writing site, Fiction University at Fiction-University.com, or follow me on Twitter at @Janice_Hardy.

- Other books in my foundations of Fiction series include *Planning Your Novel: Ideas and Structure* and the *Planning Your Novel Workbook*. Books in my Skill Builders Series include *Understanding Show, Don't Tell (And Really Getting It)*.

- I also write fantasy adventures for teens and 'tweens. My novels include The Healing Wars trilogy: *The Shifter, Blue Fire* and *Darkfall* from Balzer+Bray/HarperCollins, available in paperback, e-book, and audio book formats.

Acknowledgements

As always, this book would not be here without the help and support of some amazing people.

I couldn't do this without my husband Tom. He's always there with the right words of encouragement—or the right amount of nagging—to keep me going when I need it.

Ann—a gal couldn't ask for a better crit partner. I'd be lost without your sharp eyes and insightful comments. You make me a better writer and I'm honored to call you friend.

And a big hug to all my beta readers on this book: TK Read, Chris Bailey, Lisa Bates, Trisha Slay, Beth Letters, and Dario Ciriello. You guys rock, and I appreciate all the help you gave me.

My Fiction University readers. You guys are the best, and your dedication to your craft, curiosity about the writing process, and your eagerness to learn are a constant source of inspiration for me. Hearing from you always makes my day.

Thank you all.

About the Author

Janice Hardy is the founder of Fiction University, a site dedicated to helping writers improve their craft. The first book in her Foundations of Fiction series is *Planning Your Novel: Ideas and Structure*, a self-guided workshop for planning or revising a novel.

She's also the author of the teen fantasy trilogy *The Healing Wars*, including *The Shifter*, *Blue Fire*, and *Darkfall*, from Balzer+Bray/Harper Collins. *The Shifter* was chosen for the 2014 list of "Ten Books All Young Georgians Should Read" from the Georgia Center for the Book. It was also shortlisted for the Waterstones Children's Book Prize (2011), and The Truman Award (2011).

She lives in Central Florida with her husband, one yard zombie, two cats, and a very nervous freshwater eel.

Visit her author's site at janicehardy.com or learn about writing at fiction-university.com.

She also tweets writing links and book reviews from @Janice_Hardy.

Made in the USA
Middletown, DE
07 October 2016